THE REUNION

Joanne Fedler

Lusaris
A Serenity Press Literary Imprint

Copyright 2019 by Joanne Fedler
First published by Allen & Unwin, 2012.
Second edition by Joanne Fedler Media, 2019.

www.joannefedler.com (publisher's website)
www.marketingmentor.live (design by Nailia Minnebaeva)

All rights reserved. No part of this publication may be reproduced, stored in a retrieval system or transmitted in any form or by any means, electronic, mechanical photocopying, recording or otherwise without the prior written permission of the author.

Printed in Australia, UK and USA.
National Library of Australia Cataloguing-in-Publication data:

ISBN 978-1-925842-15-9 (Paperback)
ISBN 978-1-925842-16-6 (E-book)

This book is dedicated to all mothers and daughters but especially to Lisa and Kaitlyn

Contents

Author's Note		ix
What You Need to Know About Us		xi
1	The Kind of House You'll Never Own	1
2	The Long-lost Outdoors	17
3	Porno Tits	33
4	Kids Are Not Goldfish	49
5	A Box of Darkness	67
6	The Jaw that Never Sleeps	79
7	Virginia's Favourite	95
8	No Wonder My Daughter Hates Me	109
9	Perverts and Creeps	121
10	A Man's Look	137
11	Everyone is Unfaithful	149
12	Not a Trick of the Light	167
13	What Was Never Cherished	179
14	Only the Weak Forgive	193
15	The Botox Bitch	209

16	The Lies in Our Eyes	219
17	The Chosen Ones	229
18	Skin to Skin	243
19	The Wall Between Them Fallen	253
20	Leaving Our Mothers	267
21	The Spoiler	279
22	On the Market	293
	The Menu	305
	Acknowledgements	307

Author's Note

Writing *The Reunion* gave me a chance to go away with a bunch of girlfriends to Kangaroo Valley in the New South Wales Southern Highlands for a weekend, during which we drank, cooked, walked, talked and even planked—responsibly and in the name of research. This book is poised on that fuzzy line between fiction and non-fiction. Many of the conversations in this book are adaptations of real conversations I've had with my girlfriends or ones I've overheard women having with each other in parks and the school playground. However, this is mostly a work of fiction. Whatever resemblance the characters bear to me, my husband, my children, or any of my actual girlfriends is more or less coincidental, even though the most bizarre stories and conversations probably did take place.

It's easy to imagine there is no magic, drama or excitement in a day that starts with school drop-off and ends with a family meal around a table. And yet, motherhood keeps giving me plenty of material to work with. After the unexpected success of *Secret Mothers' Business*, I've learned that women love to read about the truth of our lives, as unglamorous as they sometimes are.

Celebrity mothers like Posh and Angelina may travel, walk red carpets and have the paparazzi trailing their every move, but for the rest of us motherhood is largely filled with minutiae and small labours. Most of what we do goes unnoticed and unapplauded. But it's not only in the wide world of political posturing and big business that large change happens. In the quiet conversations women have among themselves, small shifts of autonomy, personal choice and growth can occur, miracles hatch and women are reborn into themselves. This book is about the ordinary struggle to be a few unexceptional things—a good person, a good mother and a good friend. It records the belittled victories and unmourned tragedies of self-denial that happen to women as they navigate the transitions motherhood and friendship necessitate.

Gandhi said his life was his message. As women and mothers, our lives are our stories.

Joanne Fedler
Sydney
September 2011

What You Need to Know About Us

Jo
Age: 44
Been with Frank, my BFF, for sixteen years; married for eight.
Kids: Jamie (13) and Aaron (11)
Behind the scenes: Three am insomnia; fibroids recently removed; invasive puckering setting in.

Helen
Age: 49
Coming up for sixteen years with David.
Kids: Nathan (13), Sarah (12), Cameron (10) and Levi (6)
Behind the scenes: Going to need a hysterectomy one of these days, it's all just collapsed in there; chronic tinnitus, middle-age spread, libidinal death.

Ereka
Age: 46
Still with Jake. Such a good man.
Kids: Olivia (13), Kylie (11)
Behind the scenes: Suspected diabetes; still need to lose thirty kilos. At least.

CJ
Age: 48
Divorced. Living with Kito for past two months.
Kids: Liam (15), Jorja (13) and Scarlett (11)
Behind the scenes: Going for a tummy tuck soon, doing regular Botox *(can't you tell?)*.

Maeve
Age: 48
Unmarried—actually, divorced, but that was a lifetime ago. In a casual relationship with Stan for five years.
Kids: Jonah (23)
Behind the scenes: *Why on earth would anyone want to know the personal details of my health? Like most women my age, I'm perimenopausal and my teeth creak, but are you going to write that?*

Summer
Age: 41
Married to Craig (hubbie number three) for almost a year. *We're, like, so going to Fiji for our one-year anniversary.*
Kids: Jai (16), Airlee (15) and Jemima (9)
Behind the scenes: Everything works just fine—maybe a teensy bit of cellulite.

Virginia
Age: 49
Unmarried and childless.
Behind the scenes: Early menopause (womb death); early stages of rheumatoid arthritis.

1

The Kind of House You'll Never Own

'You are no bloody fun anymore,' Helen mutters.

I teeter along the cobblestone pathway behind her like a groupie in stilettos after too many martinis, dragging my suitcase on wheels. The full-blooming lavender flanks us as we make our way towards the front door of this—take my word for it—mansion. You know: the kind of house you'll never own. Not in this lifetime. Though this is hardly a 'house', a term usually associated with the modest four walls people live in. *This* is boasting. Its shoulders are caped in poison-green ivy, and it winks its windowed eyes at us. I wonder what sort of a millionaire owns this place and where they are now. Probably on their island in the Caribbean.

This is also, you might be jealous to know, our rented home for the weekend. Helen thought a girls' weekend would snap me out of my depression. But I keep telling her I'm not depressed. There are tons of reasons for the insomnia.

'*I wish I had a mother who actually cared.*' Those were Jamie's last words before she slammed the phone down on me while I was parking in the driveway not three minutes ago. And I'm not calling back. I won't take that crap. She's thirteen and three-quarters. You get used to the hatred around this age.

That said, last week, when she ripped the head off that little bobbing-headed squirrel—the one attached to my dashboard with the *World's Greatest Mum* sash—well, that hurt. 'The whole art class had to make them. We had no choice,' she'd yelled as if, given the option, she might have chosen something like *The World's Most Controlling Mum*. I was fond of that squirrel. Beheaded, it's a reminder of all I've done wrong as a mother.

'Just turn off your phone,' Helen says. As if the phone is the one who loathes me. She wrestles with the keys we'd picked up from the estate agent in Bowral. I'd waited in my car, flicking through *Deadly Peril and How to Avoid it*, which Aaron left on the back seat this morning and for which, no doubt, there'll be another school library fine. I could take it out of his pocket money again. But then I'll get a call from the school saying this time, he's selling his Pokemon cards or DS games in the playground. In the ten minutes that Helen was gone, I learned how easy it is to die from botulism, puffer fish and frozen toilet waste—the sort of freakish things it's apparently crucial for an eleven-year-old boy to know.

'They'll survive without you for a weekend. Just be unavailable.'

Helen and I have different parenting styles. Hers is the 'let them get on with it' kind. Mine is the type where I'm always graduating from one worry (like SIDS, choking on small objects and drowning in shallow water) to another (crossing roads, going unaccompanied into public toilets and getting rides with friends' boyfriends who've only just got their licences). Which, if you think about it, says more about the society we live in—that rapists and appalling drivers coexist with my children—than it does about me. Safe passage. That's all I ask for my kids. From here to adulthood. But wherever I turn, danger seems to lurk. You can't open the newspaper these days without taking a Valium. Shark attacks. Car accidents. Skiing mishaps. Terrorists. And let's not forget the paedophiles. I adore Alice Sebold, but I have to say *The Lovely Bones* didn't help. So if Jamie thinks I'm going to let her go off to Borneo for three weeks to climb some godforsaken mountain and trek through rainforests teeming with savage wildlife, she's grievously mistaken. And she says I don't care.

Helen unlocks the door and we find ourselves standing in a dimly lit entrance hall which opens out into a vault of light ahead.

'Phew,' I say. By 'phew' I mean a lot of things. Like 'Crikey, chandeliers!' and 'What's that smell?'

'Mildew,' says Helen.

Whatever it is, it's on the wrong side of neutral.

'Despite the smell it's not a bad place for a reunion,' she says.

'Well, it's not exactly a reunion, since half of us are missing,' I remind her.

We had, you must believe me, big plans after our last get-together, that infamous night at Helen's mother's house—could that have really been *six* years ago? We all made extravagant promises about meeting up several times a year, and avowed the importance of bonding with girlfriends, getting away from husbands, and putting ourselves first once in a while. But after

Levi was born, Helen disappeared. Like a bona fide missing person. The fourth child finally tipped the scales and down she went. But she's back, as wonderfully vibrant and larger than life as ever. She organised this weekend. As if her life depended on it. 'If I don't get away from my family, I'm going to murder someone,' she'd declared cheerfully.

I have half the number of children Helen has, and there are days when I barely manage to stuff that last dish in the dishwasher and swipe the floor with the wet towels from the bathroom, before collapsing onto my bed with a 'don't-even-think-about-it' look in Frank's direction. Who knows how she found time to source this *large Victorian mansion, sleeps eight, on three acres of undulating countryside with immaculate gardens including a fountain, pergola and its very own dam?* She's the busiest person I know but somehow she always finds time to do the fun things. It's a mystery, really.

Helen's remark about me not being any fun anymore is—let me state for the record—a dramatic overstatement. I haven't found Jesus or become a Seventh-day Adventist, Scientologist or an organic vegan. I haven't given up alcohol or had another baby (which, by the way, *she* did—and then who was no fucking fun?). This grotesque exaggeration is all because I didn't order the deep-fried soft-shell crab from the Thai takeaway as we drove through Bowral, and she's taken it a little personally. She appears to have forgotten that I let her shave my pubic hair the day before my wedding. As a group activity where cameras were involved. And about that time she got me so wasted on cocktails on a harbour cruise that I threw up in my own lap. I *do* know how to have fun. These days I just do it with a calorie-counting book and a pedometer.

I follow Helen into a living room from whose ceiling you could suspend a trapeze if the circus came to town. Light pours in through the high windows. In the corner, like an ageing film star who still commands the room's attention, on ink-black tiptoes stands a grand piano.

'Good space for a party, don't you reckon?' she says.

The room wants you to slide across its floors on your knees like that girl in *Flashdance*. But I can't because I might put my back out and then I really won't be any fun.

In front of us looms a grandiose staircase with stained-glass windows illuminating the landing. The stairwell then splits into two and curves up both to the right and left, so you have options going up or down. As a kid I always dreamed of living in a house like this. A house like in *Gone with the Wind*.

'What time are the others arriving?' I ask.

'Whenever. Who cares? Relax. We'll have first choice of the bedrooms.'

Not that it matters. I barely sleep these days.

'And who's the friend CJ's bringing?'

'Dunno. Don't care. Chill out. It'll be fine.'

I'd love to be this casual. Who wouldn't? But with CJ, you never know. She's a lawyer. And she's got poor emotional boundaries. For all we know, she could be bringing one of her clients along with her, a gambler, a prostitute or a drug addict—you know, the type of person I'm devoting my life to preventing my kids from becoming. Although, come to think of it, such people are fabulous entertainment value at a dinner party. At the very least, they take your mind off your own problems.

But untested dynamics are always a gamble. And this is such a rare weekend away. Then again, how bad can it get? Our last get-together was different. We were all friends, or mostly.

Our kids were at the same preschool so at least we could bitch about the same vile mothers. But that's changed. For starters, Fiona doesn't live in Sydney anymore. After her battle with breast cancer, she and Ben bought some land near Byron Bay, sold up, moved and built an eco-shack out there where she runs her massage practice and grows her own vegetables. She had so much chemo she lost her eyebrows. But she's living the life she's always wanted to live. When I last spoke to her, she had just harvested her first basket of home-grown strawberries and she sounded happier than I've ever heard her.

We all saw it coming: Liz and Carl divorced after her affair. Liz is now even more of a big-shot in the advertising world and spends half the year in Europe. When you Google her you get over a hundred thousand hits. Liz and I tried to keep in touch at first but our emails eventually dwindled. It's understandable that when you start over you'd want to shed the life you had when you were married. Losing a few friends is just part of the fallout. I'm glad Carl remarried. I once bumped into him and his new wife down at Bronte Beach with his and Liz's kids, Chloe and Brandon. They looked the picture of the 'happy family', so maybe there really is life after divorce.

We invited Dooly to our weekend trip but it was just 'impossible' for her to get away. Last time I saw her was after her mother's funeral, when I popped in with a large pot of chicken soup. She said something like, 'Just knowing she'll never call me up to make me feel bad about myself makes me feel even worse.' In those words she summed up what is totally fucked up about mother–daughter relationships.

We agreed not to invite Tam. Last contact I had with her was a post I put on her Facebook wall to say 'Congratulations'

The Reunion

from me and Frank after her new baby was born. She never responded. I think she always hated my guts.

I'd have been happy to have a weekend away with just Helen in a fancy hotel with twenty-four-hour room service, but she said that if we got a few more takers, we could get a beautiful place, somewhere 'out in the country'.

We asked Ereka and CJ for old time's sake, though we haven't seen either of them in years. Ereka can only come for one night—it's never been easy for her, because her daughter, Olivia, has brain damage. And CJ, who's apparently in a new relationship, texted back asking, *Can I bring a friend?* Helen was all for it, having worked out what Blind Rise Ridge was going to cost, and said the more the merrier—and having some new blood might be fun.

I invited a couple of friends, including Maeve, who I met at a talk at the local library by a Buddhist nun who'd been on a solo retreat in a cave for the past eight *years*, which I guess is the meditation equivalent of extreme sports: no TV, no conversation, no laundry. Maeve, can I just say, could be Susan Boyle's younger, more attractive sister. The observation is irresistible. At first I was distracted by her black leather boots and the trench coat it turned out she'd sewn herself, covered entirely in buttons she'd collected from countries she's travelled to. And that was before I noticed up close she has one green eye and one brown eye, as if God couldn't make up his mind.

'You know who you remind me of?' I began.

'Susan Boyle?' she answered wryly.

I guess she'd heard that before.

Things picked up when we agreed that the nun was terrifically serene but a terrible public speaker. By the end of the evening we'd swapped cards, and when I looked at hers the next morning I discovered she's actually a professor of social anthropology. I emailed her the next day and we met up for lunch at a little café near the university. After I wondered aloud why our food was taking so long, she told me how the San Bushmen make venom using larvae of small beetles, poison from plants, snake venom and poisonous caterpillars and that they sometimes wait up to three *days* for their large prey to die. I guess forty-five minutes for a caesar salad wasn't the end of the world.

Maeve was married once ('a long time ago') and now has an on-off relationship with Stan, a divorced professor of modern history. Her adult son, Jonah, is travelling through South America with his guitar and his girlfriend. Her biggest worry is her next academic article; her biggest headache is marking two hundred exams twice a year. She gardens, sews, goes to wine tastings and museum exhibitions, and does tai chi at five thirty pm twice a week just when I'm working out what to feed everyone for dinner. Someday my life will be just like that. Except probably with Frank.

Maeve smiled helplessly when I asked if she carries a photo of Jonah in her wallet. I guess not all mothers feel the need to show off their offspring at the slightest provocation. I on the other hand even wear a necklace with Jamie and Aaron's names and birthdates on little silver circles, which I never take off.

Maeve tells the most fascinating stories about the cultures and customs of the tribes she's studied, some of which you'd rather not hear while you're eating. If I hadn't met Frank and had kids when I did, I'd have also done something grand and humanitarian involving world travel. I'd also probably know how to say 'Where's the station?' in Zhuang and Igbo. I'd be able to tell you how the Tongans bury their dead and the

Amish celebrate marriages. Instead I can cover A4 books with adhesive plastic without getting bubbles and make board games to illustrate the effects of global warming—skills the Tongans would no doubt find fascinating. And anyway, Frank renewed my subscription to *Getaway* magazine for our anniversary.

I haven't had to hang out with Maeve while our kids did swimming or karate lessons. I don't have to feign interest in her brilliant child's achievements or listen to stories of his behavioural problems. We talk about Jonathan Franzen's books and Julian Assange's Wikileaks. Over unhurried lattes. Motherhood barely rates a mention. Like menstruation or menopause: we're all going through it, one way or the other, but why bring it up?

'I've never been away on a girls' weekend before,' she said when I invited her. So everything's got to be perfect.

I also invited Alison, from my Saturday morning Pilates class. She's a paediatrician with two kids and lives with her girlfriend Polly. Helen got all atwitter thinking we'd have a real lesbian with us on our weekend. I wondered about inviting Polly too, but figured that since this is a getaway from our partners, Alison also needed to get away from hers and the vagina was neither here nor there. And besides, someone's got to stay with the kids. But then Alison texted to say she was on call for the weekend and couldn't come after all. I'm going to have to make it up to Helen somehow.

When it came to Virginia, Helen and I had to have a long chat. Virginia and Helen go back to the first grade together. Which is lovely for them. But here's the thing: Virginia is single. And has no kids. Not even adopted or steps. In fact there's absolutely no-one she's answerable to, enslaved by or encumbered with. Not that these disqualify her from fitting in per se.

She's also a location scout for a television network and travels all over the world. So I guess we're in for a whole weekend of some child-free glamour girl filling us up with stories about this fabulous shoot and that glorious destination. I'm already crippled with anticipatory envy. 'Great,' I told Helen. 'Some new conversation. And it'll stop us from spending all our time talking about our kids.'

This house is big enough for twenty of us is what I'm thinking as we walk through the living space, which gives you the reverse feeling of 'intimate', whatever that may be. On the left wall is a monstrous mirror in an ornate gilt-edged frame with leaves, bunches of grapes and little dust-encrusted angels. It genuinely doubles the size of the room. Someone liked things big around here.

'Look at us,' I say.

'Yes, look at us,' Helen says, not looking.

'We look good,' I say.

'Speak for yourself.'

What I love about Helen is that she's still wearing the daggy tracksuit pants I've known her to wear for the past ten years we've been friends, with a trace of what I hope is breakfast porridge on her right knee. She sleeps in her clothes and walks around in her pyjamas. Everything is a shade of navy blue or black to hide dirt, and loose with elasticised waists. The only makeup or facial product I've ever known her to apply is the nappy rash cream she carries in her bag and uses as a lip moisturiser. If she were on the market, she'd be described as *a warm and welcoming substantial family home, oozing character, low maintenance and great value for money.* Vanity isn't one of her vices.

The Reunion

Suddenly, three huge creatures come into focus behind me and I swivel. It's not a happy sight. The ad said nothing about this. Jutting out from the opposite wall are three decapitated creatures. One looks like a wild boar, the second a deer with sculpted antlers and the third a buffalo.

'That fella looks like Fritzy—a guy I went out with before I met David,' Helen says.

'You dated a guy who looked like a water buffalo?'

'Without the tusks.'

Their dark eyes gleam at me in varnished suspicion.

'Why would anyone shoot a living thing?' I say under my breath.

'Adrenalin. Testosterone. Sport. The thrill of the hunt.'

'How am I going to relax this weekend with them staring at us?'

'They're not staring. They're dead,' she says, waving her hands in front of them. 'See? No blinking.'

I'm not a vegetarian, you understand. It's not that. I turn away from their cold eyes to take in the old gramophone, burgundy suede sofa and old grandfather clock, its face blankly frozen on quarter to ten even though it's past noon. Nothing here belongs to us, but we've paid good money to 'make ourselves at home' for the weekend. But it's odd to do that in a stranger's house. It feels a little voyeuristic—the way second-hand stuff always makes me feel. Blind Rise Ridge, despite its splendour, is a place that's been left behind. I can almost smell its sadness.

'A fireplace . . .' I sigh.

'Only thing that's off limits is the piano. It's being auctioned next weekend.'

Not that I can play. But why put temptation in people's way? After Helen's heavy-handed cocktails, you never know who might come down with an irresistible case of the 'Chopsticks'. I've seen things get out of hand before.

Helen plonks herself down noisily in one of the cosy armchairs studded with cushions and puts her feet up on a pouf. 'I'll have a champagne and cranberry juice, thanks.'

'You mean this place doesn't come with a butler?'

'The butler was extra,' she says with a sigh.

'Bummer.'

'C'mon, let's check out the upstairs.'

My first boyfriend, Travis, once said to me that when you pick a bedroom, you pick your dreams. His words have stuck. But it turns out that only four of the eight rooms have beds in them. I don't mean to complain, but the ad did say eight.

One of the rooms is a study with a stinkwood desk and chair, the other a mini-library with books lining the walls, including a full set of *Encyclopaedia Britannica* and a series called *Australia in the War* bound in red leather. The third room looks like it was once a child's nursery, with blue ducks on yellow wallpaper, a wooden rocking horse in one corner, and a little pianola with a stool tucked between its legs in another. Along the top of the keyboard runs a hand-painted fresco of horses and children running and playing flutes and lutes. There was once magic here. I'm not being sentimental; it's just that my kids' playroom is all electric screens and Made in China plastic junk. As I leave, I see how the height of growing children has been marked in steady succession on the doorframe and suddenly feel wistful, thinking about how fast Jamie and Aaron have grown up.

The last room at the end of the corridor is locked. Helen checks all the keys in her bunch. None of them opens it.

'What do you think's in there?'

'A couple of corpses, maybe some bottled body parts in formaldehyde,' says Helen, with what I hope is a twinkle in her eye.

I laugh and say, 'You're a cruel person.'

The four available rooms all have bay windows, which push up against the outside like breasts in a wonderbra. Two have double beds and two have two singles. Aha . . . *sleeps eight*. Helen dumps her bag in the master bedroom with an ensuite, saying she'll happily share the double bed with anyone who can stand her snoring and farting.

That's lovely for her, but can I just say, at this stage of my life sharing is not my idea of caring. I've shared way too much of myself over the years. And it's not over. I still share a bed, a bathroom and my vagina with Frank. Even after fifteen years together, I find the tireless presence of another person in my bedroom—even good old Frank, whose body noises and smells I could pick out of a line-up even if blindfolded, and which I'd probably miss if he ran off with his secretary—a challenge. He says I snore. I'd rather choke on my own vomit than verbalise this, but really, if I do, that's when I actually sleep. You understand just how much I was counting on having my own room? Now it looks like I'm going to have to endure the humiliation of keeping someone else up.

I pick a room with two single beds that looks out over a little secret garden tucked around the west side of the house. The garden has a stone birdbath choked with leaves, a fountainhead, a pond and angel statues enclosed by a semicircle of fruit trees with withered lemons. Not so long ago Jamie would have skipped into it gleefully, in search of fairies. These days the only *Glee* she gives a toss about is at seven thirty on Fridays on Channel Ten.

I open the antique cupboard with butterflies hand-painted on its doors. It's empty except for a few hangers, lined with handmade embroidered hanger covers. Whoever lived here had time on her hands.

The bathroom no longer conjures up the strawberries and cream it was once hoping to. The pink tub squats on its brass claw-footed heels, the enamel worn down the centre. The sink wears a skirt of chintzy roses, matched by the curtains at the window, like a fat girl at a disco, badly advised. At the far end stand a toilet and a bidet hunched over like an old married couple. I can see what someone once had in mind, but it's the elderly bathrooms and kitchens which ruin the charm of old places, like the skin on a woman's hands and neck that give away her age despite any renovations she may have had to the rest of herself.

I call for Helen as I walk down the staircase. You can get lost in a place this size.

'In the kitchen,' Helen yells. I follow her voice into the outsized kitchen where battered copper pots and pans hang watchful as helicopter parents above the hob.

Helen is packing away the triple-cream brie and gorgonzola in the fridge. In the fridge door is a bottle of Baileys and on the top shelf a store-bought tiramisu. Not a thing there I can touch, really.

'Dunno what you're going to do when it comes to my meal,' says Helen, laughing.

She's doing dinner tonight, I'm on tomorrow night. Lunch and breakfasts have been divided up among the others.

But I'm not a complete schmuck. I've brought all my own food for this weekend, because when it comes to food, you cannot trust Helen. She will as easily slip vodka in my diet

Coke as she would cream into my soup. And that's the thing about friendship. You've got to know what lies your best friend will tell to your face to get you drunk, stoned or simply keep you on her team.

I unpack my healthy offerings from my esky. 'There's more to life than vegetables, you know,' Helen says.

I ignore her. I suggest we divide the fridge into two sections: the guilt-free side and the indulgence side. 'As if anyone will even notice,' Helen huffs. 'You're the only one who cares.'

I wish Jamie could hear that.

Helen grabs the takeaway we'd bought in town and leads the way back into the lounge room, where we open the doors onto a wrap-around veranda which looks out over an overgrown medley of lavender, rosebushes and other flowering plants. There is an empty birdcage on the dusty glass-topped table, a hammock slung over the railing, two suspended cocoon-like chairs and—I am charmed by this—a row of coloured but very dusty bottles hanging from string from the rafters. A stone pathway cuts its way down a slope that leads to a pergola next to a small body of water.

'God, what a view,' Helen sighs.

A forest hems the horizon and the undulating hills are ribboned in shades of pistachio and cinnamon.

I put my arm around Helen and squeeze her.

'This was a good idea.'

She nods.

'No-one was murdered here or anything?'

'Why d'you think we got such a great deal? Just mind the bloodstains on the carpet.'

I can tell she's joking. She is joking, right?

'Just be happy and enjoy the moment.'

I remove my arm from her shoulder. She knows how to get to me. Okay, so I never have to regift her birthday presents. When she brought me back a leaf from the Bodhi tree from India last year—smuggling it through customs—I cried. She told me how she'd dived for it, along with thousands of other tourists, as it wafted to the ground. But she got there first. And you wouldn't want to get into a fight with Helen, trust me. Frank looked at the leaf and said, 'She probably picked it up off the streets of Delhi.' But Helen wouldn't lie to me about something that important. She's held my hand as I shivered in terror before a routine colonoscopy, stuck by me when Frank and I went through that rough patch, and distracted me from grief, homesickness and several miniature crises in both Aaron and Jamie's lives by dragging me to the movies and stuffing me full of Maltesers. She's propped me up through some hellish times. Maybe now that the kids are getting older we'll get to see more of each other.

'So where are the owners?' I ask. 'What's this place's story?'

Helen just waves her hand dismissively.

'No idea. Who cares? For the next forty-eight hours, Blind Rise Ridge belongs to us. Our rules—piano excluded. And right now, this afternoon has got soft-shell crab written all over it.'

2
The Long-lost Outdoors

There are no missed calls or new messages on my iPhone. I slip it into the pocket of my jeans. Helen opens her container, eyeing me as I open my prawn and papaya salad, *without* the peanuts. It is a nest of bean sprouts and shaved carrot. Über-healthy.

She takes a deep-fried crab leg and bites into it, then moans with pleasure. 'You have to taste the crab.'

'It's a hundred per cent fat. You might as well drink a bowl of whale blubber.'

'D'you reckon all this denial has made you any happier?'

She takes another bite of the crab which is sprinkled with chilli and coriander.

'It's made me thinner. Hey, you hate coriander.'

'Not anymore. I love it now.'

'Since when?'

'For about a year.'

'You can't just start loving coriander and forget to tell me. You're supposed to confide in me.' The hell she used to put me through when I wanted to add a few sprigs of coriander to a salad or a stir-fry.

'When do I get to see you? I have to organise a girls' weekend away to spend any time with you.'

The last time we caught up, Helen invited me to meet her at a free lecture on 'Surviving your Adolescent Daughter' at the public hospital where I certainly learned a few things about what girls of twelve are getting up to these days and embarrassed myself by not being able to answer at least three of the ten questions on sexual health. Since Frank has made it clear that sex education is my department when it comes to the kids, I figured I'd better brush up on my skills so I can answer the questions Jamie and Aaron have started posing, like, 'How do people get gay?' and 'Should a boy wash his hands before he touches a girl "down there"?' The answers to which, I confess, I don't have at my fingertips. Helen didn't even have time to grab a coffee after all the jibber-jabber about condoms and menstrual moods. All we managed was a handful of whispered chuckles while the lecturer glared at us like we were feral schoolgirls. Still, seeing her always makes me feel better.

Helen waves a piece of crab under my nose.

'Stop it.'

'You know, since you went to that food fascist, you've lost your . . . *joie de vivre*. I don't even see the point in a get-together like this if you're not eating.' She is cross, not just teasing.

'What does this look like?' I say, holding up my salad bowl. 'I *am* eating. Just not fatty things.'

Since I began my new eating plan just before my fortieth birthday and lost a heap of weight, there has been a latent hostility between me and Helen; because she's lost her partner in gastronomic crime. While I was having salad for breakfast, lunch and dinner, Helen was having a new baby—a boy, just as my pendulum predicted. While she was changing nappies, I was changing eating habits. While she was losing her mind in sleep deprivation, I was losing half a kilo a week.

These days I interrogate everything I eat as if it were a teenager on a Saturday night: *Just how much transfats are you hiding? Don't even bother trying to bullshit me. If I find out you've been lying to me, I'll remove you from my shopping list.* I now fit into the jeans I wore before both my pregnancies—a minor achievement as far as life goals go, I concede, but nonetheless. Frank said my dietician's motto—'Nothing tastes as good as thin feels'—was probably plagiarised from anorexia.com. But it's true, in a sickening sort of way. Believe me, I'm the first to mock gaunt models on magazine covers or decry media messages that encourage Jamie to fret about her weight. But I'm allowed to. Fuck it, I've earned my hang-ups.

And that goes for my extravagances. My latest is women's 'athletic gear'. It's a fashion statement that announces *I am equipped at any moment to go out for a jog or climb a mountain*—not that I've actually done either, but the point is that I am ready to. Right now I'm wearing my favourite sports shoes with cushioned soles, streaked in silver-blue and bright neon-green with mesh over the toes *so they can breathe* even though I'm not convinced toes actually need to inhale. This neon-pink zippered number I'm wearing has four pockets. Two are *concealed*. You've got to love a jumper in which you can carry keys, money, iPhone and the occasional tampon without the encumbrance of a handbag. My days of low cleavages and miniskirts are not so much numbered as, I guess, gone. In athletic gear, I don't feel so—as Jamie puts it—'tragically ancient'. As if I needed her to point out that unless I took control at that critical junction of the big Four O, it gets ugly very quickly. Funny, I don't remember ever being this rude to my mother.

'You know, you've become as bad as Tam,' Helen says.

'I beg your pardon?'

'You heard me.'

'There is no need to be a complete cow.'

Years ago, when we were all part of the same mothers' group, Tam used to drive us all mental with her no-gluten this, no-lactose that, no pesticides, no hormones, no nitrites and no-taste diet. Being with her was as fun as a honeymoon with your tax accountant.

'I bumped into her with her new baby the other day,' Helen says.

'I'll bet she's glad it's a girl. Was it a planned pregnancy? I never felt I could ask.'

'I reckon it was payback for the one Kevin made her terminate.'

'How do you know about that?' I gasp.

'You told me, you tart. Have you forgotten?'

I have. I have completely forgotten that the very day after Tam confessed to me that she'd been forced by Kevin, her plastic-surgeon husband, to have a termination of a perfectly healthy pregnancy because the time 'wasn't right' for him, and I promised her I'd tell no-one, I promptly told Helen.

'Please tell me you didn't tell anyone.'

'Of course I did. I wasn't the one asked to keep the secret.'

Helen squints into the distance and sighs. 'I should've brought Bones with me, she'd have loved it here.' Bones, Helen's new love, is a ratty cairn terrier she acquired the week

Levi started school, after what can only be described as a three-month ordeal involving application forms, an 'interview' on site where 'the dog chooses you, not the other way around', and a protracted adoption process which makes adopting a child from a Third World country look easy-peasy. This was followed by six weeks of the puppy leaving droppings all over her newly steam-cleaned carpets, crying all night and having to be walked twice a day. All my friends seem to have moved on to dogs as if something small and cuddly to vaccinate, potty-train and prepare special meals for tricks you into believing someone still needs you. After my mother's mongrel Snowy finally died at the incontinent, dribbly age of eighteen, she said, 'Freedom is when all your kids leave home and the pets die.' So that's something to look forward to, I suppose.

'I'm quite sure there are no dogs allowed here,' I say.

'Who would've known?'

'Didn't the estate agent say there's a groundsman here? He'd know dog turd if he saw it.'

'Ooh, and what do you think he'd do? Tie me up and lock me away?'

Sometimes she reminds me of Aaron. Like her, he too has zero respect for authority. Maybe Helen also spent all her school lunch breaks in detention. She's the only person I know who can get out of paying a traffic fine. The trick, she says, is to lie with a straight face, so I don't even try. I bungle all attempts at deceit, even when there's a financial benefit involved. Which is kind of annoying when a lie is a marital necessity—as in *I have my period tonight, maybe next week?*—or maternally indicated—as in *No, it looks exactly like Coke, but it's actually my tummy medicine . . . Oh my god this tastes disgusting.*

Helen stretches her arms and rolls her neck from side to side, her head a tangled mess of curls that haven't felt the gentle scrape of a hairbrush in at least a week. She pulls something from her pocket. 'Oh yeah, I picked this up on the counter at the estate agent,' she says, throwing a business card at me. 'Gary's full-body massage, sixty bucks. Do you think Gary does home visits?'

I examine the card. It's a home job. Not professional. Still, it's only a massage, not brain surgery. You can't get an hour's massage these days for less than a hundred bucks. Last year Frank bought me a massage for Mother's Day. It was at an upmarket health spa conveniently right outside his workplace, but an hour's commute from where we live—a dead giveaway that it was a lunch-break panic-purchase. That voucher sat in my bag all year until it expired. I just couldn't find the time to sandwich a relaxing hour of massage between two gruelling hours in Sydney traffic.

Like a full-body massage, this weekend away is way overdue. We've all been so busy leading frenetic lives. Not that they're *our* lives. There isn't time to have anything resembling a life squeezed in between our kids' lives.

I yawn. I am so behind on my sleep. I've been waking at three am for a couple of years now. I always hope Frank might be awake, but only in emergencies do I accidentally kick him awake. The lonely ache of darkness always draws me into cataclysmic introspection. Like why something still feels like it's missing. And whether my cousin Shireen will get over her lymphoma. And whether I have any real friends. You know, I thought we'd be friends for life, that group from our last getaway. But those friendships were, like childhood, just for a season. As our kids developed their own quirks and talents and we all carefully weighed up who might flourish in an all-boys or all-girls school, who might do best with a religious- or arts-and-drama-based education, it's as if we've scattered like shooed seagulls in the directions our children's personalities have taken us. I had no idea just how fickle I could become, and how easy it would be for me to befriend the parents of my child's latest best friend. I wonder, sometimes, what happened to the integrity of my own preferences.

'Keep them for retirement,' Frank once suggested.

So that's one reason I took myself off to the dietician. I guess I was trying to make myself count somehow. As I keep telling the kids, 'It's not all about you.' But they know that's a lie.

Then, two years ago, I started secretly saving money. Frank and I have been talking about a holiday in Tuscany, just the two of us, for the past five years. But the time is never right, it's always too expensive, and who will help us with the kids with our parents and sisters all overseas? And then the interest rates went up and Jamie needed orthodontics and Aaron extra maths tutorials. I suppose there's no rush. Tuscany isn't going anywhere.

Helen, I've started to think, also has a secret nest egg she raids. Or else David's business is booming quietly. Three months ago she took off with her physiotherapist (no David, no kids) to Bali for ten days and, before that, to India with her girlfriends from school days. And I thought we had something special. When I asked her why she's never invited me to go away with her overseas, she laughed and said, 'You'll never leave your kids for ten days.' Which is not the point. A person likes to be asked.

Helen has some soft-shell crab oil on her chin. I lean forward and wipe it off with my serviette. She nods appreciatively. She gives me appetite, this big-hearted cheerleader, for having a good time. 'It's good to spend time with you,' I say adoringly.

She gets a funny look on her face. She's not big on gushing displays of affection.

'I'm not dying,' she says, giving me a wide-eyed stare. And then, crinkling into her toothy smile, 'Come on, I'll get some champagne and we can lie in the sun.'

She scrambles off indoors and returns with two glasses of champagne topped up with cranberry juice. Over her shoulder is a hand-knitted patchwork blanket she hands to me. Together we walk down the stone stairwell to the pathway that leads to the large verge of grass beside the dam to make the most of what is left of this autumn afternoon.

Behind us, under the Morton Bay fig tree, is a wooden pergola, its curvatures forming the skeleton of an umbrella laced with jasmine that has come to an end, all withered and dried like a forgotten bridal bouquet. The small wooden bench beneath it doesn't seem very inviting, so we walk a little further down to the cushioning grass, find a rock to place our champagne glasses on, shake open the blanket and sink onto it.

The countryside is easy to love, is what I'm thinking. It's lush and certain of its worth and indifferent to judgement, the sky wide and uninhibited. I've missed the long-lost outdoors. When Jamie and Aaron were little, and I'd pushed the boundaries of how much I could use television as a babysitter, I'd hustle them into the car knowing we'd reached *that* point—where kids need to taste grass and muddy their clothes and get pinched by ants and breathe dirt. Tallied up, I've probably spent months of my life pushing swings or lifting little bodies onto the flying fox. I used to hate parks. Because contrary to the feeling you get when you say the word 'park' (which is wistful, bucolic and terrifically unfrenzied), they are, in truth, extremely stressful epicentres of preschool injury-about-to-happen. It's impossible to relax when you're anxiously anticipating your child getting clobbered on the back of the head with a swing, falling off the slippery dip, being flung from the merry-go-round or getting into an ugly brawl with other tired children over whose turn it was next on the slide. But the other day, it struck me: we don't go to parks anymore. I now beg my kids to spend time outside. A walk. A swim. *Come look at the moon. Take the garbage out, check the letterbox, help me with the groceries.* Anything. Jamie is probably suffering from a vitamin D deficiency. The only light she gets is the radiation off her computer screen.

Sometimes I feel like I've become like a park my kids don't visit anymore. Once the centre of their worlds, I'm now peripheral—I provide meals, rides to places they'd rather be, and the occasional hug when they forget themselves. Worst of all, I'm a titanic embarrassment to them. Just the other day I was charmed by a little girl pushing her dolly in a pram. 'Are you taking your baby for a walk?' I cooed, and Aaron mockingly retorted, 'Are you being creepy to little kids?'

I sometimes just want to shake him and say, 'Do you know who I was?' Believe it or not, there was a time when I could flirt the decency out of any man—married or single, sober or drunk. I knew how to use a blowtorch, wear suspenders and dance the salsa. These days I can't even sing the words to a pop song, shimmy or—God forbid—dance in front of my kids without them pouncing, squashing and reducing me to something absurd, as if my spontaneous ecstasies for music, rugged men with tattoos and long goodbyes were contrived for no other reason than to humiliate them. I have become something to be endured, apparently. They own 'cool' now.

I want to tell them, 'I *invented* cool.' But saying it is, like, so uncool.

Across the water I see dragonflies. Somewhere further out are some waterlilies.

'How's the tinnitus?' I ask Helen.

'It's like having a fax machine inside my head all the time. It never goes away.'

Helen never complains, and she wouldn't raise it, but since Levi was born she's developed this strange whining in her ears. The tests and scans have come back and it's not a brain tumour. It's *stress-related*. And it never goes away. Except for those ten days when she was travelling with school friends in India without kids or husbands. It started again on the flight back from Calcutta to Sydney.

When I first heard about Helen's tinnitus, I did some research and discovered we all have it to some degree. When we pay attention to it, it becomes louder. The only way to live with it is to pay no attention to it and drown it out with other irritating noises. You can develop a tolerance—for pain, for stretching what is 'normal' to accommodate it. I've heard people who live with chronic conditions talk like this.

'Do you mind holding this?' Helen hands me her glass momentarily to strip off her T-shirt and bra, and lies back on the blanket. Her breasts slide over her chest like two fried eggs in a pan. She sunbakes as if skin cancer were science fiction, a figment of some neurotic dermatologist's overactive imagination. She never sits in the shade, wears a hat or applies sunblock—to herself, that is. Her kids she slathers in sunblock like battered fish. 'I'll happily die of a melanoma,' she once told me. 'At least it'll mean I spent a lot of time lazing in the sun.' After Fiona's diagnosis, her irreverence seems crazy.

I, on the other hand, am hideously resentful of how years of outdoor activity have sucked the juice out of my skin, like breastfeeding did to my bosom. I do not need a rash of freckles on my arms. I could also do without the leathery bits. At times it seems as if everyone and everything wants a piece of me, even the weather. The ozone layer, by all accounts, is as thin as a sheet of filo pastry and I take this information very seriously even though I don't really know what the ozone layer is. But apparently we need it. I don't want to die of a melanoma, or of anything else, actually. And I most certainly don't want to look any older than I am. Why would I?

But if Helen's putting her bosoms in the sun, so am I. I balance my glass in the grass and whip off my shirt.

We lie there for a bit. Helen puts her hands in her undies and scratches her pubic hair. I examine an ingrown toenail.

'Well, this is fun,' I say.

'Just listen,' she says.

'What?'

'Silence.'

I listen.

No bickering, no sounds of electronics or television . . . just the peace of a Friday afternoon. Two friends, almost people, doing very little about the laundry or the dishes.

'And how's Levi?' I ask cautiously. It's a loaded question. What I really want to ask her is: 'Is Levi still wearing dresses?' But I approach tactfully.

If Helen has a raw nerve, this is it. We all thought it was 'cute' when her blond-curled Levi raided friends' daughters' dress-up boxes and pranced around in scarves and fairy wings—at age two or three. But he's six now and Helen's quietly uneasy about this 'thing' he has for girls' clothes. Is he gay? Is he a girl trapped in a boy's body? Will he want a sex change for his eighteenth birthday? Not your average parental anxiety. When we're pregnant and praying for the health of our unborn babies, most of us are thinking: intact limbs, no brain damage. No-one thinks to ask for unequivocal gender identity. It seems Levi would have come screeching out of Helen's vagina wearing a tutu and wielding a fairy wand if he'd had any choice in the matter.

'Light of my life,' she sighs. 'But he's still in dresses.' She props herself up and takes another swig of her champagne.

Since Levi's personality began to emerge beyond the undifferentiating cuteness that is toddlerhood in all children, and he started staking his claim to his preferences for what to wear and what to play with (dolls and prams, not trucks and dinosaurs), I noticed a weariness creep into Helen which I'd never seen before. The light uncomplicated happiness that spoke of her wild teenage years, and propensity to be the first to dance on the table or pass the tequila bottle, shifted. I'd have to say she's aged. Not so much physically, but in the way she speaks. She used to tease me for worrying about my kids. Now I see it in her eyes—she worries about Levi.

Not that any of us is homophobic. We all have gay friends. An uncle who wears cravats. A cousin who 'never married'. But no matter what we believe, or what we say we believe, the truth is we all just want our kids to be 'normal'—not to stand out from the crowd. We'd all rather our kids were heterosexual (my friend Jerome, who's been with the same guy for fifteen years, is convinced of this) because 'it's much harder to be gay in a heterosexual world'. But our kids force us up against all our hidden prejudices and push our noses into our double standards.

Helen and David's rule is that Levi is allowed to wear whatever he wants in the house, but when he goes out in public, he must dress like a boy. I've seen him sprint inside after an outing in his blue shorts and T-shirt, strip bare at the bottom of the stairs and make a dash for his stash of dresses. Best of all, he likes dresses that twirl when you turn around. It both melts and breaks your heart at once. It's still cute at six, but at eight? Fourteen?

Helen's been pelted with a litany of well-meaning idiocy from people who have seemingly endless counsel to offer.

'Maybe he'll grow out of it.'

'Wanting to dress up in girls' clothes doesn't mean he's gay, just a cross-dresser.'

'Maybe he'll be a fashion designer, straight as an arrow.'

None of this unsolicited advice has helped Helen at all. It's so easy to have the answers when it's not your child. I try to shut up most of the time.

I can't really imagine Aaron wanting to wear frilly pink dresses instead of rugby shorts. I know Frank would say, 'No son of mine . . .' but certainty is the privilege of the untouched, I've come to think. We never know how we'll react until we're in it ourselves. Aaron and I are currently waging the *Call of Duty* battle. Apparently I'm the Only Mother in the World who has said no to buying a game in which my son can virtually blast people into bits and get covered in blood and gore. I'm either the only sane mother on the planet or a freak, as Aaron suggests.

At our last big get-together all those years ago, my girlfriends challenged me about what I'd do if Aaron, who at four had been identified as a 'bully' by his preschool teacher, grew into a bigger and meaner version of himself. I wasn't just being pig-headed when I refused to contemplate that he'd grow into someone so estranged from the love and values I'd parented into him that he'd be unrecognisable to me. I really believed if I brought him up without guns, he'd never want them. And now that he does, something of my essence feels frayed, betrayed. I remember saying, 'At a certain point, we're entitled to walk away from our children.' That was probably a little glib. Our children, we find, are encoded into us, stitched into the DNA of our souls. We have no choice but to love them even as they cause our integrity to malfunction.

But look at Susan Klebold, mother of Dylan, one of the boys responsible for the Columbine killings in the United States. In an article she wrote in O *Magazine* last month, I read that she had absolutely no idea he was suicidal or had such violence inside him. And I thought, *As a mother, how could you not have picked up on the signs? That would never be me, never be my child. I would know. I would know.*

When I look at Helen now, though her anxiety about Levi's unknowable future is obvious, I also sense a tenderness that isn't there when she speaks of her other kids—her love for him is stretched and enlarged by his 'otherness'. Maybe our children expand our capacity to hold pain close to our hearts—we can love children who are 'ugly', 'unwell', 'incontinent', 'rude', even 'violent'. We can love what is most unlovable in them, and what we could never love in ourselves. That's what I think.

'Does it bother you?' I ask Helen, not knowing how to put my thoughts into words.

Helen takes another swig of her champagne and sighs. 'Levi's different. Looks like he's going to have a tough road ahead of him. And he needs to know that in his family, he's safe. That we love him for who he is.'

The Reunion

And with that, she sits up, and says in a low tone, 'Don't freak out . . . don't yell and don't scream . . . but there's a snake about ten feet away . . .'

3

Porno Tits

Okay, so I freak out. I yell and shriek and spill my champagne all down my front. A snake! It disappears into the brush in a flash. I don't actually get to see it.

I grab my bra and T-shirt, and run all the way back to the house, my boobs flapping in the breeze. Now I remember why I never go camping. Or hiking. The countryside is heaving with deadly perils. And so far from any hospital. Can you imagine what Borneo is like? Is there even a first-aid kit in the house? My legs are covered in mozzie bites from half an hour at the water's edge. I didn't think to pack mosquito repellent. My breasts, it seems, have survived unbitten. Even mosquitoes have standards, apparently.

When I get to the veranda, I pull my T-shirt back on and look for Helen. Down at the dam, she's managed to slip on her T-shirt—and is talking to a young man in a wide-brimmed straw hat and khaki shorts and shirt, open to the waist, whose sudden appearance suggests he must have been *spying* on us sunbathing topless. Helen is laughing and pointing at me. The two of them start walking back up towards the house.

He must be around twenty-five with sandy hair and day-old growth. He is blown up in the biceps and large in the lats. He has soft brown stag eyes and large hands and arms with prominent veins. I can smell his sweat mixed in with his deodorant from where I'm standing and I've no doubt he could push you up against a hard surface and have his way with you if he wanted.

'This is Callum—the groundsman,' Helen warbles.

'Hi, Callum.' I beam.

'Heard Matilda scared the bejesus out of you,' he says, and smiles. Oh dear. Dimples.

'Matilda?'

'She's our diamond python.'

'Snakes are just a teensy bit outside my comfort zone.'

'Matilda won't kill ya. Unless you're a rat or a frog.'

'Well, that's a relief.'

'It's the red-bellies you've got to look out for. And the king browns. If they bite you, you've got half an hour max.'

'Is that so?' I twitter.

Generally I would not find talk of venomous snakes a turn-on. Not in the slightest. But I find I'm coaxing him. God I can be annoying, descending into silliness around a couple of pecs and some manly stubble. If I aroused any sexual thoughts in him, it'd probably qualify as 'kinky' in porno circles. This thought could, in fact, make one suicidal on a bad day.

'I'm not moving off the veranda.'

He gives a hearty laugh. 'Nah, you're okay to take a wander. Just keep your eyes open. We got a couple of the deadlies.

The Reunion

But they're not friendly like Matilda. They'll stay out of your way.'

'How do you know?'

He shrugs nonchalantly. 'Just don't go poking around with sticks and wear hiking boots if you're going to go for a walk through the forest.' He gestures beyond the dam.

I should be irritated by his casual certainty. He has, you'll agree, no right to guarantee our safety. Just like we have no assurance that the universe isn't going to strike our kids down with lightning, or wipe them out in a car accident—these things happen. Sometimes, no matter how first rate your training, nor how much you think you know, you just can't see things coming. Like my friend Leonie, who assured me that Persephone would 'Never hurt—' just as her wouldn't-hurt-a-fly labrador sank her teeth into Aaron's head, causing a gush of blood you never want to see coming from your toddler's body. He needed thirteen stitches. Really, no-one was more shocked than Leonie.

What, is Callum going to rush out and give me mouth-to-mouth if I go into anaphylactic shock?

'Well, I'll leave you ladies to it,' he says. 'But let me know if you're after a tour of the property. I'm in the cottage on the other side of Silver Pond—that's what we call the dam around here—and past the copper beech.' And with that he strolls off to pull out weeds or do some other groundsmanly duties.

As soon as he's out of sight, Helen looks at me and sighs, 'He could tie me up any day.'

Helen is lying in the hammock with her eyes shut, T-shirt pulled up and breasts out to the sun again.

The momentum of my thoughts leads me to consider what a spunky twenty-five-year-old is doing as a groundsman on such an isolated property. At twenty-five, as I recall, boys are fuck-machines. I didn't see any nightclubs or places to hang out in Bowral as we drove through. He probably has a long-time girlfriend. A cute waitress with a navel ring and perfectly plucked eyebrows who visits in between her shifts in a café, Brazilianed monthly. Showering at the gym last week, I saw how it is. As I scuttled into my shower cubicle the only giveaway of my age was the fact that I was the only woman *with* pubic hair. A young man like Callum has probably never even *seen* female pubic hair. Of course, he could be gay . . . it's hard to tell these days. I can, you'll notice, expend an inordinate amount of time worrying about other people and their lives. It's not like I don't have my own problems.

I check my mobile phone again. Nothing. That's fine, it's a daughter's prerogative to emotionally torture her mother. There'll be consequences. I just hope that little tramp who's been bullying Jamie on Facebook hasn't struck again. Savannah Basingthwaite.

I've worked it out. Jamie's black moods invariably coincide with an episode of cyber-cruelty. Hey, I was a teenage girl once. And not even a particularly bitchy one. But, reluctantly, I remember the girl we nicknamed 'Trunk' (it was her legs, you see) and how no-one (including me) ever chose her as a partner for sport or made a single overture of kindness in her direction. I'll never forget the steel in her eyes, which I now recognise as courage, as she navigated the hostility of the school corridors. I marvel at the guts it took simply to show up every day in the school playground in her oversized uniform and the strawberry lip gloss she wore with reckless defiance. But Trunk, whose name was really Anthea, was huge. A walking target. No chance she'd ever have invisibility immunity from the squealing horrors teenage girls are so uniquely accomplished at inflicting on each other. What is it about Jamie that has marked her? It's an anxiety that churns in me.

Helen is spread out. With her sunglasses on she could be asleep, blessedly free of the drone of tinnitus, so I don't disturb the silence. It's three thirty-six pm according to my iPhone. Aaron will be going home with Samson, who can do card tricks and who never tells how. I know for a fact he got *Call of Duty* for Christmas, so Aaron'll be spending his afternoon in a war zone, up to his eyeballs in screen guts. Fine. I can't control his conscience. Today will be the first time I'll be missing one of Jamie's school debates. Not that she cares. And I left Frank a schedule—Aaron has to be picked up at five thirty and Jamie at quarter to six. All he has to do is warm up the bolognaise sauce I left for dinner and boil up the fusilli. But they'll nag and he'll relent. And it will be Hungry Jack's burgers all round. It's not my problem. For the next forty-eight hours I don't have to think about anyone but myself. I can just lie here and do nothing, read a magazine, watch afternoon television or go for a walk to explore the garden—if I can find Callum to ward off the wildlife. I fidget with the laces on my new trainers.

I should be celebrating. Instead, I'm lying here with my friend Helen half-asleep and half-baked, doing something that feels a lot like missing my kids. I am ridiculous. I've spent fourteen years putting everyone else's needs first. Spare time feels wrong, stolen. Without my kids' parasitic, claustrophobic, all-consuming demands, I'm raw against the world. Useless, just about. Maybe having kids is just an elaborate way of relieving boredom. Or, worse, disowning the call of your own destiny.

'I used to have great tits,' Helen says suddenly, startling me. 'Modesty aside. Porno tits, David used to call them.'

'That good, huh?' I say.

'A set of perfect uppity thirty-six double-Ds.'

'Lucky you!'

'They got me free rides across Europe in the summer of '92. I never paid a single bus fare, just stuck my thumb out. And I don't think I ever paid for a drink at a bar.'

'Handy.'

'Not much to look at now. I miss them.'

'At least you had them once upon a time.'

'Yeah . . .' She stretches like a cat, and then caresses her breasts with her hands.

'How long did you breastfeed all up?'

'Eight years,' Helen says, holding her breasts tenderly, like one might stroke the hand of the dying.

'I used to have an ironing-board stomach, with a four-pack,' I say. I'm not boasting, just remembering. It all ended when my obstetrician sliced through a decade of abdominal crunches to deliver Jamie. I rub my hand over my scarred and stretched belly. I really will have to forgive my mother one of these days for not taking me aside and telling me this pertness was just on loan. That someday it would be reclaimed. For one thing, you've got gravity against you. Firm breasts, smooth stomach—they're an unsustainable economy. And the yearning for them, a quiet personal death. 'At least I've still got a tight pussy. Thank heavens for caesareans.'

'Lucky you,' she sighs. 'After four natural births, mine's like the Grand Canyon.'

'Kegel exercises?'

'Spare me . . . I don't even know where my pelvic floor is. Probably the same place I left my libido.'

'You just squeeze like you're holding in a wee.'

'Puhleez. I hardly use mine anyway.'

'Never?'

'Once every six months.'

'And David's okay with that?'

'I wouldn't know.'

'Is he wanking?'

'Probably.'

We lie there thinking about this for a while, though I really could do without the image of David jerking off. Not that there's anything wrong with jerking off per se. Or imagining a stranger like Callum jerking off, for example. But the sexual lives of our friends—like that of our parents—are secret and taboo. I love a good old chat about sex with my friends, but imagining my friends doing the whole blowjob/cunnilingus/penetration palaver disturbs me. For this reason alone, I assume I would be a terrible swinger. I hope David is whacking off, for the state of his sexual health, but goddammit, why do I need to make this my problem?

'Hey, did I tell you the good news? I'm going to need a hysterectomy one of these days. Six weeks where I don't have to get out of bed, drive or cook. Can't wait,' Helen says.

Times are desperate when invasive surgery is hailed like a well-earned vacation. But I confess, I too silently relished my recent abdominal surgery for the chance to be released from all mothering chores. Something had been growing inside me. Unfortunately it wasn't metaphorical. I thought I looked three months pregnant, despite all the weight I'd shed. My Oxford-qualified surgeon informed me my uterus was 'riddled' with fibroids. But he couldn't tell me why fibroids pop up, what their intentions are and whether they're simply harmless vagrants or like the pigs in *Animal Farm* who appeared innocent at first but actually intend to take over. My options were to have them cut out, wait for menopause (when lowered oestrogen shrinks them naturally, like your favourite cotton T-shirt in the tumble-dryer), or have a hysterectomy.

I'd discussed it with Helen over the phone.

'What do you want to keep your uterus for? It's done its job, it's just giving you hassles now. If it were an employee, you'd have fired it ages ago.'

Frank disagreed. 'You shouldn't just get rid of it. It's part of your body,' he said, as if my womb, like one of his marathon medals, had sentimental value to him.

'Spoken like someone who's never bled a day in his life,' I replied.

In the end, I decided to keep it. I felt I owed my uterus a duty of care into its old age, dementia and decrepitude, like one would owe the family pet that drools and has become incontinent.

'You're fine about a hysterectomy then?' I ask Helen.

'You've got to know when to let go and pass the baton. Sarah's just had her first period. One menstruating woman in the house is more than enough.'

It's hard to believe we're at this end of the uterus conversation when our daughters are just beginning it.

These days, my 'baby' Jamie is getting breasts of her own, and I watch them bloom like something yeasty rising, alive. I am struck with an ambivalence so alien to myself that it shocks me. Watching her inhabit and embody the womanliness that allowed me to give life to her is almost like looking in a mirror. I want her to love what is hers unfurling in the secrets of her adolescence and not to force her to memorise the neuroses, accepted norms and screwed-up rules of how to be a woman like her times tables. When she started getting hair on her legs, I didn't want to make an issue of it when she was impervious to the imperative of hairless calves. It was never my intention to pop her childhood bubble of Everyone's-beautiful-and-special. I was going to wait for her to ask, 'Mum, can I shave under my arms?' I ended up leaving a razor on her bed with instructions, terrified of the names she'd be called if I didn't intervene.

When she was a baby, a little girl, swaddled in innocence, her origination from me was still sweet in my heart, like her morning breath. My sagging breasts, the massacre of my stomach, the distortions of my flesh were a small price to pay for the beauty she brought to me. We were extensions of one living thing, human fractals. These days, as she grows to my height, wears the same size shoe as me, borrows my makeup and throws my own words back in my face—*Don't manipulate me . . . Don't give yourself a hernia . . . I'll get to it in a minute*—the syrup of our oneness, the way she swam in me like a tadpole in its pond, has thinned to water, worked its way through us, until it has become not flesh, not bone, but a story, a poem, a philosophy of how she came to be. I remember a baby moving inside me. I remember holding a tiny creature in my arms for the first time and the way my milk surged through me, a tributary to the ocean of her mouth. But the large, strident, sullen-at-times glorious woman-in-making—I do not recognise her as the being I remember. I know it to be her. I have watched her grow from wriggly worm-infant to fairy-wand-wielding tree-climbing nymph, from gap-toothed imp to awkward bookish girl, and now this strange, quiet, funny, thoughtful teenager who quotes

The Goons. But there is a cognitive dissonance between what I know to be true, and what I am able to remember as I mother her—terribly, at times. I miss the uncomplicated codependence, when my love for her was not negotiated, compromised or invaded by moods, misplaced anger or hormones, but ever-present, as fresh as breast milk.

'It's all happening so quickly,' I say. 'Can you imagine what our lives would be like without them?' I give a sort of hysterical laugh.

Helen is quiet for a while.

'I don't know . . . I mean, this is my life, right? It's what I do. And yeah, it's great, the house is noisy, it's busy, it's full of balls and musical instruments and *Happy Feet* and Cheezels—but, fuck, my life is *only* this. And I mean only. I spend my entire day in my car. If it's not this one needing to go to the doctor, that one needs new school shoes, or it's this one's music ensemble, or that one's parent–teacher evening, or another birthday party. I sometimes wonder what it would be like to have made different choices.'

'Midlife crisis,' I diagnose.

'I'm not saying I'd change my life. But . . . I could *picture* something else. You know, I used to love riding motorbikes. Me and Virg rode across Europe when we were in our early twenties. She was on a Ducati and I had a Suzuki.'

'Get out of here! I never knew that about you.' I look at Helen. Leather jacket, helmet, spurs? How do I not know this about her?

She sighs. 'Yeah, why would you? We never talk about anything but kids.'

'Don't we?'

She shakes her head. 'Sometimes I feel like I've lost the ability to be excited about life in general. I need a change . . .'

'Like a job?'

'Something bigger.'

'A divorce?'

She snorts. 'Maybe a new country . . .'

'Like Tuscany?'

'Yeah . . . or California.'

'Earthquakes,' I point out.

'Earthquakes are exciting.'

'Excitement is for single people,' I say. When it comes to kids, you want somewhere boring, secure, where people drive at the designated speed limit and obesity is the biggest teenage issue.

'What's she like—Virginia?' I ask, wondering if I really want to know.

'Big and smart. At school she cleaned up with all the academic prizes. Huge reader. You can ask her anything—there's nothing she doesn't know. Been to over eighty countries. She can say "Do you want to sleep with me?" in a hundred different languages. And she's looked a charging hippopotamus in the eye. She's totally the coolest person I know.'

'I thought I was the coolest person you know.'

'You're the coolest *mother* I know.'

'I don't think you can survive a charging hippopotamus,' I mutter.

'Ask her about it. We did some pretty wild things together.'

'Like what?'

'Oh, there was that small orgy we had with three waiters we picked up in Spain . . . and drugs. Lots of drugs.'

As she talks, I sense something in her close to regret. But I can't tell with Helen. I can't remember when last I did something that would qualify as *wild*. Being grateful that these days my kids can get dressed on their own, make their own breakfasts, catch a bus, stay home alone while I dash out to the shops or to the gym or even go out for dinner with Frank is hardly cause for throwing a party. The wildest thing I've done recently was a visit to the Tool Shed in Oxford Street. I came out with a brown paper bag full of possibilities. Frank and I haven't had the chance to use any of the equipment and outfits yet. We're just waiting for the right moment.

Me and Frank. We have to grind harder these days to figure out what keeps us together outside of the kids, but that's normal, I guess. The space between me and Frank (a negotiated compromise between an uncharacteristically messy Virgo and a neat-freak with mild OCD) has become more squashed as the dynamics between us shift to accommodate the invasions of our kids' personalities: an extrovert with low impulse control and an artistic introvert in the grip of a hormonal tsunami. Every family decision, from where we'll dine to where we'll spend our holidays to what TV shows we'll watch, is now a four-way negotiation, instead of a two-way one in which I could often get my own way just by offering a blowjob. We've moved from the duo to the group dynamic—and it's exhausting. The gap between me and my own exquisite desires (which often don't extend dramatically beyond 'no radio in the car' or an hour's walk in the early evening) increases as our kids stake their own desires more and more vociferously. And if I should so much as dare to suggest that my needs are on a par with theirs, they've now hooked onto the unassailable retort for which I have no rejoinder: 'I didn't ask to be born.' Apparently, since I brought them here,

I am responsible for their happiness and my urgent wee can just wait while they finish brushing their teeth.

While Frank and I hardly ever fight, the antagonism between the Montagues and Capulets had nothing on the simmering venomous hostility between my offspring. I spend hours of my life negotiating ceasefires as if I'm living in a war zone where the contested territory is no more than a remote control or the last hard-shell tortilla. By the end of the day I'm wrung out; I've no idea how Ban Ki-moon does it without vodka in the bottom drawer. Poor bugger.

Come early evening in our home, the witching hour has become the bitching hour.

'You little brat.' (Jamie screeching)

'Stupid moron.' (Aaron)

'Think of all those poor only children who have no-one to talk to, no-one to play with. They are all *alone*,' I say, trying to pack as much heartache into that word as I possibly can.

'I like being alone. He ruined everything.' (Jamie)

'Can't we swap her on eBay for a baby brother?' (Aaron)

'If I hear another word about basketball, I'll throttle him.' (Jamie)

'If I hear another word about boys, I'll throw up.' (Aaron)

I imagine this is how Isaac must have felt when he saw how things went to shit between Jacob and Esau. It's endless circles of petty bickering. Until *The Simpsons* comes on. Then he calls her to come watch and there they sit on the couch. Together. Laughing at Bart. It's either very normal or very psychotic.

The other day, during one of their usual slinging matches, I burst into tears. 'Why? Why? I can't take it another moment.'

I wasn't being intentionally dramatic. I just hadn't had much sleep.

They stopped mid-insult and came and sat on either side of me. Jamie patted me on the back and Aaron held my hand. They told me that they didn't hate each other. Really. That much. Only sometimes. When he/she was annoying/awake/on the toilet when the other needed it/hogging the remote. They made promises; they would try to get on. The day went much better after my outburst. So you see, it's a waste of time for me to act like an adult. I get better results when I descend to their level. It brings out the adult in them. So now, whenever I'm desperate, I sob hysterically. That usually buys me a few days of peace.

And that's all I ask, really. A little bit of tranquillity as payback for everything I sacrifice for them. And let's face it, I've been on a sacrifice roll for a while now. In the days of early motherhood, it was my sleep, my sanity, my unblemished body. Not that anyone's counting, or keeping a ledger, but at some point—we're all just human—we hope that as we give up for the sake of others, so we shall reap at some stage in the future. Or that perhaps the sacrifice will end and it will be someone else's turn to sacrifice. But what I'm finding out as the kids grow older is the many other ways in which it is possible to live as a human sacrifice—ones you'd never imagined until you had to cancel your personal trainer for a parent-teacher evening; swap the outlandish hope of a relaxing holiday for standing in line at Ocean World to see killer sharks you couldn't care less about; and switch channels on TV because *Sex and the City* is not appropriate for underage people who think they know everything but in fact know nothing. As they get older, sacrifice is losing its allure and I'm definitely leaning more in the direction of quid pro quo.

At some point in the future, our children will become independent of us, and only then can we become independent of them. Is that what it's all about: working towards a freedom we had before the kids came along?

'Do you sometimes feel as if life—real life—is passing us by?' I ask Helen.

She purses her lips. 'What do you mean?'

'I'm tired of being a crap mother. I want to do something really well.'

'Take up flower arranging. If my sister-in-law can do it, anyone can.'

'Maybe . . . I'd like to write a book.'

'About what?'

'Tuscany'

She laughs. 'You've got to get there first.'

I know that.

'Write about vampires. People love to read about vampires.'

'I don't know anything about vampires,' I mumble.

'Make it up,' she says, clambering out of the hammock. 'Time for a refill and snack, what do you say?'

She returns to the veranda a few minutes later with a tray. On it is the bottle of champagne, the bottle of cranberry juice, a tin of smoked oysters, the brie and slices of a baguette.

She refills my glass.

'What'll we drink to?' she asks.

'Tuscany,' I say.

'And motorbikes,' she adds.

4

Kids Are Not Goldfish

Champagne starts all flirty but means business quickly. My brain is cheeping with bubbles when we hear Ereka's voice calling us from the front.

'Coming,' I yelp, jumping to my feet and hurrying through the lounge room, past the mirror—*Is that me? Yes it is*—towards the front door. There's that smell again. I hope it's not coming from the locked room upstairs. Because you hear about these things.

I haven't seen Ereka in ages and to say she's filled out would be a kind observation. In her sea-green kaftan with sequins on the bodice, she'd be on the market as *oversized, wide frontage, cosy Bohemian interiors, exquisite features, with lots of room for a growing family; fantastic opportunity to subdivide*. Wearing an armoury of jangly silver bracelets from her wrists to her elbows, she is Liberaced in rings popping with enormous gemstones, trussed up with the strap of a bright bag and a wicker basket. Her ginger hair, which I always envied, has thinned. Of all things, I senselessly hope she isn't losing her glorious red hair. For that, just by itself, would be cruel.

'Wow, Jo, you've lost heaps of weight. You look fantastic!'

I almost twirl around to show her the new me, but that would be rubbing her own weight gain in her face, so I smile and say a very meek, 'Thanks, doll.'

'Oh, this place is gorgeous,' she murmurs, stepping inside. 'Look at the mirror . . . and are those crystal chandeliers?' She stops and sniffs.

'What do you reckon that is?' I ask.

'Neglect. Ingrained sadness.' Being an artist, she smells in emotions. But she doesn't seem overly concerned.

Leaving her basket in the entrance hall and jingling as she moves, she twirls in wonderment, her fingers on her lips. Something delicious—gingery—is in that basket and it's freshly baked.

'You didn't bake, did you?' I ask.

'Pffft . . .' She laughs. 'French deli in the city—ginger honey cake with lemon myrtle crème fraîche. Someone's work of art.'

'It sounds fattening,' I say.

'Only about seventeen tubs of butter in it. I shouldn't buy this stuff, but life's so short . . .'

Life is shorter with high cholesterol, surely? I'm coming up for five *years* on my diet. You get used to saying no to things you want to taste. It's no different from monogamy. When something makes you dizzy with desire, like the smell from Ereka's basket, it's a simple case of remembering: you made a commitment and you can't have it—whether it's a slice of cake, the personal trainer at your gym, the fireman who lines up behind you every morning at your local coffee shop or the plumber with the snake tattoo down his forearm who comes to fix the leak in the kitchen. Extra-marital affairs, much as some of us may want them, are domestic tidal waves. Ask Sandra Bullock. Wanting something is really not enough of a reason to have it.

It's not as if the desire goes away; no-one says it does. It's what you do with it that counts. So you take control. You remember what you vowed and why you're doing this in the first place. *Nothing tastes as good as thin feels.* You reinvoke the long-term benefits of monogamy like a mantra: the joys of uninhibited flatulence and the comforting knowledge that someone else is monitoring your menstrual cycle even more vigilantly than you are . . . and you just say no. What you do with your vibrator in private is no-one's business. That's not cheating. That's fantasy. It's what makes the fidelity festival of substitution, repression and denial bearable.

Only later, when the maths teacher looks at the pair of your shining faces on parent–teacher evening and relays how fabulous your daughter is at long division, that's when you'll know why you said no. You'll consider that hot sex with a stranger is not even in the same ballpark of terrific as this moment. You'll be abashed that you contemplated sacrificing your marriage for *that* little indulgence. But that's lust for you—it is blinding and beguiling and a little tacky and doesn't stay the distance. Like two quick glasses of champagne, it gives you momentary wings before you come crashing down. In relationships you want the slow release of low GI. If marriage had a super power, it would be stamina, not flight.

I help Ereka carry her bags to the kitchen where she unpacks the tart onto the counter. I open the box and inhale the ginger which is doing naughty things with the cinnamon and . . . maybe cardamom or cloves? Something illicit and sticky has caramelised along the side of the tart. Saliva pools in my mouth.

'This thing is evil,' I tell Ereka.

She opens the fridge, giggling, and offloads her bottle of tequila, some orange juice, a tub of mascarpone and punnets of berries. 'And some snacks,' she says, placing a packet of Cheezels and two bars of Lindt on the counter.

'How much have you lost?' she asks, opening the Cheezels and offering them to me.

'About sixteen kilos.' I close the lid on the tart, remembering that I am a new me in fancy athletic gear.

'What's your secret?'

'Well, for starters, I don't eat that anymore,' I say, gesturing to the Cheezels. 'It's not really a secret. It's more like a lot of willpower. I still want to eat that stuff . . .'

'But you just say no.'

'That's about it.'

'And do you ever binge?'

'Not really,' I say, almost apologetically, like I'm letting the fat-girl side down.

'Where do you get your self-discipline from?' she asks. 'I've gone gargantuan in the past few years. Can't get rid of it, and it just seems to keep piling on.'

Since I cannot refute that she has in fact become very big since I last saw her, and I don't want to patronise her by telling her she hasn't, I smile and say, 'Helen will be very glad you're here, because I've been officially fired as her eating partner.'

I grab a champagne glass for her, link my arm through hers and lead her to the veranda.

*

Ereka raises her glass to her lips, bracelets clinking. She's already onto her second glass of cranberry champagne, drinking it down like the diet starts tomorrow.

'How is that divine hubbie of yours?' Helen launches into a speed-date type catch-up.

Erika pauses. 'Fine.'

'Uh-oh, when did Jake get downgraded from amazing to fine?'

Ereka forces a chuckle. 'He's good . . . he's great.' She looks like she's exhausted her list of adjectives. And she's only on the Gs.

She takes a long sip of her champagne and dips back into the Cheezels. She looks up at our expectant faces. 'What? He's okay . . . we just don't get a heck of a lot of time to spend together. It's time. Not him. Not us.'

'Oh right, we're supposed to spend *time* with our husbands, I almost forgot,' says Helen, grinning. 'I've got to schedule an appointment with David to talk about our weekend arrangements. He's never off call. That business is his baby. What's Jake's excuse?'

'You know, with the financial crisis and everything . . .' Ereka's voice tapers off. 'We've had a lot of expenses. There's always something extra Olivia needs. More tests. Jake worries about money all the time. It's become a substitute anxiety.'

Ereka must get tired of explaining her life. Of offering the rest of us perspective because she's got a child with brain damage.

'Yeah, everything's gotten expensive, hasn't it?' Helen agrees. 'Every other day you read about a guy in debt who pops himself off. Such a cop-out. But what really gets to me is when they take their family with them.'

I glare at Helen. Is this meant to be helping Ereka?

'That pressure to be the breadwinner is hell,' I say.

'Aw, please—men get the better end of the deal,' Helen says. 'David could never stay home and do the kids full time. They'd have drowned, been lost or died of starvation. If they don't bring home the bread, what the fuck are men for?'

Ereka muses, 'The vows are "for richer, for poorer"...'

'Oh, was that meant to be taken literally?' Helen laughs. 'Anyway, how's the sex? Don't they say stress kills libido? You read about that in every health magazine.'

'It sure does.'

'Jeez, you guys were my sex-life heroes,' Helen says. 'Don't tell me it's all gone to hell.'

'That was a long time ago, that conversation.'

'Once a fortnight?'

Ereka's right—it *has* been a long time since that drunken conversation. But Helen, like a child who hasn't checked the water temperature first, dives straight back in. Small histories tack us together, but I don't know that they entitle us to lifelong intimacy.

Ereka looks trapped. 'Once a month—if we're lucky.'

'Me and David have become like brother and sister. I love him but can't be bothered to fuck him.'

'It's a flaw in monogamy,' I say.

'What is?' Helen asks.

'The more you love someone, the less they turn you on.'

'That doesn't sound right,' Helen says, wrinkling her nose.

'You've got to get down and dirty. You need a bit of edge. A bit of stranger. Some outfits and equipment. Otherwise it's all too nice. You don't want to fuck nice.'

'I don't mind fucking nice,' Ereka says. 'I just don't want to fuck irritable.'

'We're just tired,' Helen says to Ereka.

'Don't you think tiredness becomes an excuse?' Ereka asks.

Helen leans her head back. 'There are about a gazillion things I'd rather do than have sex, and eating and sleeping are right at the top of my list.'

Maybe that's my problem. A good sleep and a good feed.

Ereka turns to me. 'How are you and Frank?'

How *are* me and Frank? I wonder. We still talk. The other night I told him I want to be buried in a coffin in the shape of a hot chilli pepper like they do in Ghana. And he actually switched off the cricket and said, 'Jo, maybe you should see someone.'

Insomnia makes you tired. It sometimes makes you say stupid things. But still, those fantasy coffins in Ghana take the edge off the gloominess of funerals. I smile at Ereka. *Keep it light*, I remind myself.

'Actually, after his vasectomy, we had a bit of a renaissance. I'd forgotten how good sex smells. After eight years of condoms, I thought it smelled of rubber.'

'When did he have a vasectomy?'

I think Ereka is looking horrified.

'Two years ago.'

'That's very brave of you guys.'

'What do you mean?'

'To make it so permanent. What if you want more kids?'

I take a gulp of my champagne. The bubbles launch themselves up my nose. I surrendered the fantasy of a household full of rowdy teenagers and their friends a while back. I felt it fall through my fingers, a mixture of heartbreak and relief.

There are things about yourself you'd rather not recognise. Like how, after Helen had Levi, my tolerance for small people had shrunk. I'd forgotten about child-proofing the living room and holding hands in the shallow end. And the way toddlers dribble their spit and snot all over you. You certainly can't wear fancy athletic gear when someone treats you as their Kleenex. I found I'd wound all the lenience of my boundaries back into myself. These days, there's no way I'm going to use the toilet brush after someone else has used the loo, clean other people's bath rings or wipe up urine splashes. If Frank gets to the point where infirmity or frailty requires bottom-cleaning assistance, I'm outsourcing that to paid help.

'But, Ereka, we're done having kids. Frank was done at Jamie, so he's already in the red with Aaron.'

'But what if . . .' Ereka doesn't finish, but I know what she's asking. She's asking, 'What if one of your children D-I-E-S and you want to have another one?'

'We thought about it, we talked about it, and we decided that we weren't making decisions about our lives based on fear,' I say, thinking about coffins and Janet Price. It's amazing what you can find out on Facebook. We were at school together. Last month she lost her middle daughter in a car accident. I'm getting to it. But these things take time. You can't just rush a condolence message. Suddenly I feel a bit hot in the chest.

'Besides, if you lose a child, you can't just replace it,' Helen adds helpfully. 'Kids aren't goldfish.'

'Exactly,' I say. I will send Janet a message. An email. No, a card. With a stamp and all.

We agreed that Frank would 'save some semen'. But in case you think it's like shoving leftover soup into the deep freeze for an unexpected dinner party, it's not. It costs a bloody fortune to store a little vial of viable spunk just in case of a tragedy, I finally decided I was almost 'too old' for another pregnancy and I couldn't keep having babies just so I could feel unconditionally loved by small people because I'd become a hideous humiliation to my pre-teen kids. Besides, it would have pushed Tuscany out by at least another decade.

'You and Jake were talking about having more at one stage, weren't you?' Helen asks.

Ereka holds her hands over her belly, the way pregnant women do, a gesture of shielding comfort. 'Yeah. I always imagined I'd have a big brood, like you, Helen—but we have our hands full with Olivia. Maybe next lifetime,' she says wistfully.

'How *is* Olivia?' I ask. She must be as big as Jamie now.

Ereka puts on her Olivia-is-fine face. 'We've got her in a lovely school, the teachers are wonderful, so committed and caring. They grow their own vegetables and have their own tortoise. And she's best friends with the most divine boy, Todd. He's got Down's. He's her guardian angel.'

The way she talks about Olivia reminds me of something. There is a push in her voice. A discipline. The restraint of someone who is walking the tightrope between straits of self-pity and despair. As if she is trying to convince herself of something.

'They've taught me a lot about love,' she says softly.

'Are they boyfriend and girlfriend?' I ask, wondering if Olivia has pipped Jamie to that post.

'Heavens, no. He looks after her like she's his little sister.'

I am not comparing our kids.

'Has she got her period yet?' Helen asks.

She nods. 'Two years ago almost.'

'She managing okay?'

Ereka shrugs. She doesn't talk for a few moments. I sense how much she's been through since we last saw her. She's traversed emotional Everests. Where the hell have we all been in all that time? Getting on with our normal lives. And complaining about them too.

'In some ways it's harder, but in others it's easier.'

She speaks slowly.

'She doesn't get embarrassed when she has accidents, so she's spared that. She can't keep track of changing pads or remembering to put one in. So at that time of the month, I have to mother her like when she was in nappies.'

Being with Ereka makes me small and superficial. I fretted about Jamie coping, about her bleeding through her skirt at school and managing her periods. It never crossed my mind to wonder how Olivia would struggle and the unfairnesses one could rage against as the mother of a menstruating brain-damaged teenager. I live in the shallows. So why do I feel like I'm drowning sometimes?

'And Jake's parents haven't helped,' Ereka says, almost under her breath.

'What do you mean?' Helen asks, leaning over to grab the packet of Cheezels on the table and helping herself to a handful.

'They put pressure on us to get Olivia sterilised. Can you believe it? To have her tubes tied at thirteen. So she'd never menstruate or give birth.'

Ereka shovels a handful of Cheezels into her mouth.

I catch Helen's eye. Maybe we're both thinking it. Wouldn't it be easier—*kinder?*—to relieve Olivia and Ereka of the saddle of menstruation? Realistically, will she ever fall pregnant or give birth? Ereka would end up having to take care of any child Olivia has. Olivia can't even take proper care of herself.

'It sickens me,' Ereka continues. 'And you wouldn't believe how common it is in girls with mental disabilities. It becomes a question of what's *convenient* for the family. Not what's best for the woman or the girl.' Her cheeks are flushed.

I shift in my seat. *Convenient for the family.* Not my favourite phrase. It's not a secret; if she ever asked me about it, I'd tell her. Besides, it was long before I ever met Ereka. I was working at the Women's Alliance for Gender Equality (WAGE) when Angela's parents contacted me. They seemed like such nice people. Angela was their oldest daughter, severely mentally disabled and living in an institution. She was also six months pregnant, raped, probably by one of the staff, but since we had no way of knowing or proving it, it didn't matter. Her parents wanted a termination, though at such a late stage, it was only legal if the woman's life is at risk if the pregnancy continues—but Angela was perfectly healthy. I didn't ask the questions I wanted to: why it had taken everyone so long to notice or why no-one had visited her in six months. But no matter where you stand on the abortion question, 'termination' at six months is not the right word for what you're doing. I knew people in the right places. We got a 'legal termination' and Angela Delaney was sterilised. It was what her parents wanted. I know Angela could never have taken care of a child, but she could have birthed that baby. And maybe, with a bit of assistance, even breastfed. The baby could have been given up for adoption. But none of this was *convenient for the family*. Still, I don't judge. I just did my job.

'It's hard enough making decisions about which school to send your kid to, or consenting to operations on their behalf,' Helen says.

'Jake and I have never fought about anything when it comes to Olivia—until this.'

'So who won?' I ask.

'I won,' Ereka says, without any hint of victory. 'We're not sterilising Olivia. It's her body. We can't take away her right to menstruate.'

I've never thought of menstruation as a right, really, more of a biological affliction. The longer I do it, the more I'm convinced that no-one needs to start menstruating at twelve when most of us these days dodder on into our seventies and eighties. By now, you'd have thought technology would have given us a way of having fifteen years of periods between twenty-eight and forty-three so we could get our careers out of the way and have it all, like feminism promised. I'm thrilled, truly, that Jamie has her period (she's 'normal', can hopefully have her own kids if she ever wants to), but I'm over mine. It's been a week-long flow every twenty-three days for the past thirty-two years. If you do the maths—that's 105 days of annual haemorrhaging, 3332 days of my life so far. We're talking nearly nine *years* of intermittent gratuitous cruelty, soiling thousand-thread-count Egyptian cotton sheets, destroying favourite undies, forgoing hikes through rainforests, swims in waterfalls and oceans, and diverting lovemaking with strangers I'll never come across again. So call me selfish for wanting to be free of the headaches, bloating and bitchiness that comes on top of the endless plugging. The monthly toilet paper, tampons and pads required to stem the flow is an environmental strain. Sterilising any one of us would be a major contribution to the greening of the planet. Think about it.

Of course, I would *never* say this to Jamie, who has only just started menstruating. I don't want her to think of it as a curse or a burden or even a sort of biological injustice. Even though it is clearly all of those. Personally, I wouldn't wish the sort of periods I have on that little viper Savannah Basingthwaite.

Right now, I have a sort of fatigue about my post-fertile body. All I want is for it to give me less trouble. That's it. I'm grateful to my womb. It did a great job. But it's time to move on. When I contemplated putting it out to pasture given how riddled it was with fibroids, I was stalled by the option of saving my ovaries. What, like spectacular leftovers in a doggy bag? They're not whales. Who cares? I mean, what are ovaries *for* once you've had your kids? To be fair, it was only then that their true quiet warrior-like nature was revealed: they're hormonal ninja bouncers, keeping early menopause from gate-crashing our bodies with its entourage of unfriendly symptoms, such as dried-up vaginas, sweats and hair in odd places. We need oestrogen for supple skin and other juicy bits. An excess causes fibroids. A shortfall and we become the Sahara desert. When does the fun of being a woman actually start? Probably in Tuscany.

Why, I asked my surgeon, shouldn't we yank out the ovaries while doing a spring-clean to prevent ovarian cancer? Because, he pointed out, then I'd need hormone replacement therapy, which can cause breast cancer. So basically, if I understand it, what it boils down to is that we have to pick our cancer. I suppose we can at least palpate our bosoms ten times a day if we like, in the name of medical vigilance—unlike the ovaries, which, given their geography, aren't accessible to a squeeze.

And that lump could be your gallbladder for all you know. And then there's the annual pap smear, mammogram, ultrasound and colonoscopy. Each birthday these days seems like it takes more medical aid and discomfort to reach.

'So do you think Olivia might have kids someday?' I ask.

'I don't know, Jo. I don't know what life holds in store for her. But I can't make that decision on her behalf now. She's only thirteen. Mentally disabled women do get married, you know. They do have kids.'

I don't ask it, but I think: 'Yes, but should they?' Should kids be raised by a mother who can't even change her own sanitary pad? Jamie complains that I don't change her sheets.

'All this stress has made me enormous. I just can't stop eating.'

'You have every right to eat,' Helen says, passing Ereka the plate of cheese and smoked oysters. 'And whatever else gets you through the day.'

'Food and Facebook seem to be my two favourite—my only—hobbies.'

'Facebook?' Helen asks. The past ten years of technology have passed her by. Admittedly, she has been neck-deep in motherhood. She's only just learned how to SMS. I keep telling her email and Facebook will make her life easier. But she says she doesn't have the time to learn how to use them.

'I only use it to spy on my kids,' I say.

'I've hooked up with people from my past, old friends, old boyfriends . . . you *spy* on your kids?' Ereka asks.

'Jamie's being bullied, so I keep an eye on her.'

What I'm doing probably qualifies as cyber-stalking, if you want to get all ethical about it. It started with my curiosity to find out about this little teen terror who is causing my daughter anguish. It's astonishing what you can learn about a person from Facebook, I'm telling you. Savannah Basingthwaite updates her profile picture once a week. Coy pout, hands through hair, lips pursed. And beneath it a flurry of eager comments from her extensive fan club (at age thirteen, how do you even know eight hundred and forty-seven people?), which goes something like this:

> Fan A (female): babe that's just stunning!! How beyootiful can u get???
> Fan B (male): Mad hot pic
> Fan C (male): hmmm yummness
> Savannah Basingthwaite: funnyness weirdness u guys crack me up
> Fan D (female): ha ha ha stunner u gawjuz thingness
> Fan E (female): OMG u r amazing and soooo fuckin prettyyyyy xxxx luv u
> Savannah Basingthwaite: ha ha thanxness was at a party and seriously never knew what to wear
> Fan F (female): YOUU ARE SOOO AMAZINGG!!! I'm so jealous
> Fan G (male): hot xxx
> Fan H (female): best body, go die
> Savannah Basingthwaite: look whos talkingg u have the best body we can die together
> Fan I (female): you are hot azz ;)
> Fan B (again): nnice photo fukin sexxy
> Fan E (again): why can't I be as hot as u????
> Savannah Basingthwaite: ummmm looks whhoss talking u r sooo amazing its not funny hahahaha

> Fan E (again): iloveyousomuchyouareamazingstunnersexybitch
> Savannah Basingthwaite: urhotsexybodygorjuzzincredloveyou

There's only so much of this I can take before I have to step away from the computer for fear of throwing up on my keyboard. And it's not just the grammar and the spelling. I 'get' the whole teenage 'rebel against convention by butchering language and creating a new lingo'. I admire anyone who makes their own world, and their own rules. I caused my own brand of trouble when I was a teenager. But I'm on the other side of rebellion now, trying to hold the world steady, not up-end it. And the fact that Jamie has to participate in this bizarre, abbreviated, oversexualised cult of communication is only one of the anxieties gnawing at me.

At least with my FB spyglass, I can watch from the sidelines. There may be nothing I can do to stop the nasty comments on Jamie's profile: *You spaz. You fat pig.* But without Facebook I'd never know just what she's going through.

I should SMS her and make peace. I am the adult.

Ereka wriggles her toes. I notice her toenails are painted bright blue and her big toenails have what look like diamantes on them.

She sees me looking at them.

'Toenail art,' she says.

'Do you do it yourself?' I ask.

'I can't reach my own toes over this huge belly. I go to a nail salon in the city. It's my secret indulgence.'

'Very pretty,' I say, wondering why I don't have a secret indulgence. And then I remember my athletic gear. But somehow it feels shallow and materialistic, unlike Ereka's toenails, which seem like a sacred adornment.

'Very impractical,' Helen chimes in. But she doesn't have an artistic synapse in her brain.

'Sometimes pretty can make the difference between wanting to live another day and stepping off the kerb as that bus comes past,' Ereka says.

I look at her with wide eyes.

'Only kidding,' she says, slapping my arm.

I turn away and squint into the sun. Jokes are how we speak the truth without shattering. And I don't want Ereka to witness just how much those twinkling toes both break my heart and give me sudden courage.

5

A Box of Darkness

Maeve traipses through the French doors onto the veranda in a sapphire-blue chiffon shirt and a Japanese print skirt with birds and blossoms.

'Who let you in?' Helen asks.

'The front door was wide open,' she says, beaming. 'I take it I've come to the right place?'

Her feet are clad in mary jane shoes of cherry red, and around her neck is a necklace strung with unevenly shaped and coloured wooden blocks. I'm struck anew at how fabulous she is.

'Maeve!' I stand to give her a lively hug. Perhaps short people don't enjoy the hug as much as tall people, given how their heads tuck neatly under one's chin, reminding them of the enforced hug-your-Aunt-Florence intimacies of childhood.

I introduce her to Helen and Ereka, who looks like she wishes she'd come in a chiffony-number with a skirt in Japanese print and red mary jane shoes.

'Champagne?' Helen offers, handing Maeve a glass, which she receives with a bemused look. She covers it with her hand as Helen tries to top it up with cranberry juice.

'Don't you drink?' There is alarm in Helen's voice.

'Why spoil a good champagne with fruit juice?'

'Hard-core,' says Helen, nodding approvingly. 'Hey, you know who you remind me of?'

'Susan Boyle?'

'Yeah!'

Ereka cocks her head. 'But much prettier,' she adds.

Maeve smiles at Ereka. 'Well, before I decline into drunken torpor, I'd better use the ladies' room. And where should I put the food and drinks I've brought?'

'Follow me,' Helen says, threading her arm through Maeve's and leading her to the kitchen. 'So, have you ever tried singing?'

When Maeve and Helen re-emerge, laughing, Maeve hands me a small square gift tied with an orange ribbon.

'What's this?'

'A belated birthday present.'

'My birthday was five months ago. I'm not accepting gifts at this point.'

'I had a small fixation on this precise DVD and it took a while to find it.'

It is wrapped in origami paper. I pull the ribbon slowly. Real silk ribbon, that can be reused. I vaguely hope it isn't Susan Boyle.

'Oh, lucky fish,' says Ereka when the gift is revealed. 'I *adore* Leonard Cohen.'

'Excuse me, but Leonard and *I* have a special relationship,' I say, clutching the DVD to my chest.

'"Dance Me to the End of Love" was mine and Jake's wedding dance,' Ereka says with so much ownership I feel as if I've snatched the handbag of her happiest memories.

'And I had the dubious pleasure of handing over my virginity to Percy Holmesford while "Hallelujah" was playing on an old LP,' Maeve says. 'It rather enhanced Percy's poor performance.'

I have no such Leonard Cohen story. I feel remotely cheated on. But I'm not sure whether it's by Leonard or Maeve.

Maeve takes a wedge of cheese from the platter, but instead of eating it, she holds it between her fingers. She is a *freestanding federation cottage, classically inspired, quietly located and beautifully maintained.*

'Tell me how we got to end up staying in this exquisite old home,' Maeve says. 'It's a grandmother of a house, wouldn't you agree? It stokes one's curiosity. Anyone know its history?'

I shrug. 'Helen, tell us. You found this place.'

'I don't know much about it, except that it's a deceased estate.'

Maeve glances around searchingly as if with proper investigation the answer will reveal itself. *It's got to be here somewhere.* I give up too easily. She's my social pacemaker: *Have you read that article on banning smoking in public? Listen to that TED talk by Malcolm Gladwell. What do you think of Michael Moore's new documentary?* My kids used to do that when they were little—*Is that a whale? Do flies have souls? Why's that old man limping?* And despite how tiring it is to answer endless questions, it kept me alive to what I'd otherwise fail to notice. The other day, I overheard a little boy squeal, 'Look, Mum! A snail!' I can't remember when my kids last shrieked with enthusiasm. Nothing excites them these days. Not sunrise. Not hail. Not a spider's web. Possibly the new iPad.

'Maybe it was an orphanage,' Ereka suggests.

'I reckon it was an upmarket brothel. I'll bet that pink bathroom has seen its share of Victorian blowjobs,' says Helen, and laughs.

'Not with a nursery,' I say.

'I'd trade my sex life for this kind of space,' Helen sighs.

'You don't have a sex life,' I say.

'Not technically. But there's heaps of potential . . .'

'Contemplate the housework.' Maeve shudders and finally puts that piece of cheese in her mouth.

'Servants,' I say. 'As far as I can tell, the lady of the manor spent her days crocheting blankets and embroidering platitudes. There's one hanging above my bed.'

Ereka reaches for the plate of cheese and oysters. 'In some circles crocheting and embroidering are considered *art*,' she says. Almost crossly.

'You're absolutely right—in days gone by, when women were mostly uneducated, what else could they do with their creativity once they were shackled to marriage and motherhood except numb their depression with needle and thread?' Maeve says.

Ereka stands and stretches, then approaches the empty birdcage, caressing it with her hands.

'She'd have had lovebirds to keep her hopeful,' she says, not speaking to anyone in particular. 'I used to have lovebirds when I was a little girl.' Ereka's observations are wistful. There is a loneliness to them, as if she's marking all the ways in which only she sees the world. 'And we had chickens too,' she continues. 'Stuffed in cages on our front porch. God, they made a racket. And they smelled terrible.'

'Wouldn't want Cameron to hear that,' Helen says. 'Ever since his school got a wildlife expert to come and give a talk last year, he's gone all anti-zoo and anti-animals-in-captivity on me. Like I need a lecture seven times a day about free-range eggs and how cattle are farmed. Worst part—he's become a fucking vegetarian. Do you reckon I could sue the school for brainwashing him? Get them to pay for his iron supplements? I keep telling him a growing boy needs red meat.'

'I think you should be proud of him,' I say. 'It shows a sophisticated thinker.'

'He can be a vegan soy-drinking Hare Krishna when he moves out of my home. I don't have time for special requests, consciences or allergies. Unlike Jo, who's been making Aaron special meals ever since he was a baby.'

'Yeah, well, I am getting tired of that,' I mutter. 'And he's expanded his repertoire . . . a bit.' She's embarrassing me in front of Maeve.

'It's only taken you—what? Eleven years?' Helen slaps her knee and laughs uproariously. Have you ever noticed how easy it is to raise other people's children?

'How's Nathan? Has he lost weight?' I ask, steering the conversation back to Helen's children and their problems.

'You've got to love testosterone. It's chewed that puppy fat and turned it into muscle. But now it's the hair under his arms and on his legs and chest and willy that bends my brain.'

'I challenge you to retain your equanimity when he's bringing girls home. And skulking around emptying bins with used condoms.' Maeve grins. 'I suppose I should be grateful that it's not boys he's bringing home . . .'

I know Maeve is as pro-queer as you can get without actually being a lesbian herself. So this is a strangely diminishing comment. I glance at Helen, but she's stuck her fingers in her ears and is singing, 'La la la la la,' like a child who won't be told the broccoli is delicious.

It's bad enough that they're catching up to us in stature, eroding our power over them with every inch they grow. In our house it's only the bra cup that separates the girls from the women. While folding laundry the other day Frank broke out in a sweat. 'Yours or Jamie's?' he asked, holding up a pair of knickers. And then, 'I'm not folding undies anymore. I don't like the ambiguity.'

'I fancy a stroll down there,' Maeve says, pointing towards the dam. 'I could be wrong, but the rosebushes seem to have been landscaped. Would you say that looks like an S?'

We all look at the rosebushes.

'There are snakes,' I say.

'Funny that—in the countryside,' says Maeve, laughing.

'Just an hour ago I was nearly bitten.'

'The way you carried on, I thought you'd had your arm ripped off by a crocodile. That poor snake's going to need therapy for post-traumatic stress,' Helen says.

'It was a nasty vicious creature with silver eyes and a purple tongue,' I say, shuddering.

'You didn't even see it! It was a perfectly harmless diamond python. This is its home and we're the intruders,' Helen reminds me.

'My son went through a charming phase where his choice of household pet was a diamond python,' Maeve says. 'Contrary to all appearances, they really are harmless.'

'I nearly twisted my ankle running back from the dam,' I say.

'And in your fancy new trainers too,' Helen jibes.

'You let your son have a python as a pet?' Ereka asks.

'Seemed the shrewdest way to let him get over it. My parenting philosophy was to only use "no" in an emergency. I'm sure if I'd denied him his python, he'd be a snake-charmer today.'

There is much about Maeve to admire. And I'm sure she'd agree, saying no to Borneo is exactly the kind of emergency she means.

'How many kids have you got?' Helen asks.

'Just one—though Jonah's hardly a child. He's twenty-three,' Maeve answers.

'Started young?'

'I was twenty-five.'

'Husband?'

Maeve gives a deep throaty laugh. 'I do believe I had one once.'

'What happened to him?'

'We became an unfortunate divorce statistic. Perfectly amicable.' She doesn't say more.

'You've been a single mum your whole life?' Ereka asks.

Maeve nods.

'That's rough.'

Maeve smiles mildly. 'It wasn't the calamity one imagines. You get to make all the decisions autonomously with no need for negotiation. Private schools are way out of your league so that choice is made simple. And, quite delightfully, travelling with one child is affordable—Jonah and I travelled quite extensively, mostly for my work. I can't say I've found motherhood particularly gruelling. But then again, I only have the one.'

'Still, you don't often hear single mums talk like that,' Ereka says. 'Just wait till CJ gets here—you'll get an earful about the horrors of single motherhood.'

'Speaking for myself, I've always thought there's no point in dwelling on the negatives.'

'Oh, I can't wait for you to meet CJ,' says Helen, cackling.

'Living on your own . . . what's it like?' Ereka asks wistfully.

'Astonishingly blissful. But it happens like this,' she says, clicking her fingers. 'Jonah was six. I blinked and he was eighteen with a packed suitcase and a round-the-world ticket, bucking for his independence. And then he was gone.'

'Levi is six. It feels like forever . . .' Helen muses.

'You've been at it for too long, fourth lap,' I say.

'It happens to all of us, sooner or later,' Maeve says. 'Goodbye is one of parenthood's inevitabilities.'

There's a pause. Ereka sniffs.

'Probably not in my case.'

Maeve looks at her questioningly.

'My daughter Olivia has brain damage. She's not going anywhere.'

'How dependent is she?' asks Maeve, her voice sympathetic.

'Olivia's always going to need someone for the basics. If it's not me, I don't know who . . .'

Older mothers talk with dread about the empty nest. But what is worse is the nest that can never be left. The cradle that becomes the coffin. Parturition happens in stages. We're always birthing our children into wider circles of separation. None of us wants to mother indefinitely. Not the way Ereka has to.

'So what will happen to her when you pass away?' Maeve asks. Which, you've got to admit, is quite a forward question so early on in the weekend. But then again, she is an anthropologist. They study this shit—life, death and everything in between.

Ereka shrugs. 'I can't die.'

Maeve looks at her oddly. 'But, seriously, when you do?'

So much for keeping it light.

I fidget with the plate in front of me, not intending to eat anything. Maeve is ploughing into uncharted territory. I pick up a smoked oyster and eat it abstractedly.

'I don't go there. I just take it day by day.' She squeaks the gate of the birdcage open and closed.

Maeve nods, unconvinced.

'I don't think about the future. It's too scary.'

Of course, why would anyone think of the future? Being out of our control and all that. Having a child is a bizarre existential manoeuvre for anyone with control issues.

'It's sobering to contemplate just how fickle the future can be,' Maeve says.

Ereka is still preoccupied with the birdcage. 'You know, when I was pregnant with Olivia, I had it all mapped out. The school she'd go to, the ballet, piano and archery lessons, the horses she'd ride. I didn't have a clue that dreaming like that is a dangerous way of tempting fate. I gave up making plans after she was born. As far as I can see, the future betrayed me.'

'But plans are different from insurance, aren't they?' Maeve asks.

'I don't think in terms of "what's next" anymore,' Ereka says, and as she does the little gate comes off in her hand, and she squeals, 'Oh, I've broken it!'

'Relax, it's old and rusted,' Helen says. 'It was probably going to get thrown out anyway.'

Ereka cradles the broken gate in her hands. She looks like she is about to cry.

'Ever heard of Mary Oliver?' Maeve asks. 'She's a contemporary American poet.'

'Are people really poets these days?' Helen asks. 'Is that like a real job? A *poet?*'

'No, I haven't,' Ereka says, not with any enthusiasm trying to reattach the gate.

'Even to those with an antipathy to poetry, her poems are remarkably accessible. There's one I'm particularly fond of in which she's given a box of darkness. And only many years later did she understand that it, too, was a gift.'

There is a discomfited silence. Ereka sets the broken gate on the ledge of the veranda and lifts her glass of champagne.

She smiles at Maeve. Perhaps wondering why people insist on using that word 'gift' so blithely. Or thinking that though she might feel blessed in the odd moment, on a day-to-day basis, when she's wiping her thirteen-year-old daughter's dribble and helping her with her sanitary pads, she'd like to exchange that gift for one less unrelenting.

A box of darkness. I am cringing inwardly. I imagined Ereka and Maeve might hit it off. Did she just suggest that suffering is ennobling to someone who is suffering? I hope not. For the luxury of never having stumbled a day in Ereka's shoes, we are banned from doling out platitudes and romanticising her life. Observations unwelcome. Whether critical or compassionate. But if Ereka is irritated, she's gracious enough not to show it. It's a double whammy. Not only does she have to deal with her life, but with everyone else having an opinion about how she should be handling it.

'What happened to her daughter?' Maeve asks when Ereka heads inside to the bathroom.

'Oxygen deprivation at birth—terrible outcome of a botched home birth.'

I suddenly feel very defensive of Ereka, for hers are not ordinary sorrows. When Ereka chose a home birth it was after months of careful research. I also toyed with the idea of a home birth with Jamie. But after my mother got hold of me with a cheery, 'Women die in childbirth,' I panicked myself into a hospital birth. Ereka and Jake are not people who make decisions based on fear. If she had an ounce of my neuroses, Ereka would probably be the mother of a normal thirteen-year-old girl who called her a 'tragic bitch', SMS-ed her friends every five minutes and hung out in malls. Ereka has to live with that rogue decision, born of faith and trust, every day of her life.

From her recliner, Helen muses, 'I've always wondered why they never sued.'

'Who should they have sued? God?' I ask, standing up and examining the broken birdcage gate. It's completely rusted through. No chance of reattaching it.

'The midwife . . . I dunno. Someone must be to blame.' Helen makes a little tower out of a cracker, a wedge of cheese and smoked oysters, and pops the whole thing into her mouth, chewing gracelessly.

'She'd never have sued. Even if it was an obvious case of negligence. Besides, the midwife is a really good friend of hers.'

'They need the money for Olivia. Why do you think they're struggling financially? She needs carers and teacher's aides and who knows what else in the future,' Helen says. 'I'm just being practical.'

Maeve ferrets in her bag and brings out a pair of paperclips. I watch as she straightens them out. She gets up, takes the broken birdcage gate from my hand, then kneels down and fixes the gate, using the paperclips to fasten it.

'When you sue in our legal system, the plaintiff has to adopt the role of victim,' says Maeve, testing that the gate opens and closes, 'which is not terribly empowering. And what you often find is that pinning one's pain onto a third party doesn't relieve one's own.'

She speaks with a tone that I recognise as authority. As someone who has walked not in red mary jane shoes or black leather boots, but in some pretty uncomfortable moccasins.

'I still think they should've sued,' Helen says.

6

The Jaw that Never Sleeps

I'd forgotten how loud she is. And this is *before* alcohol. CJ's raucous cackle perforates the afternoon. I remember now with a sinking feeling how legalistic and obnoxious she can be. I always suspected she silently hated anyone who was happily married. But maybe her new relationship has rounded some of her spikes. Despite her ostensible self-confidence and success as a family lawyer, she's one of those women who believes she's not a real woman unless she's with a man. Besides, her anti-Tom invective was getting a little tedious.

She bounds onto the veranda and screeches, 'Jeeeeesus, it's been ages.' She pounces from me to Helen with hugs and kisses. She stops in front of Maeve. 'Hey, I don't know you, do I?'

'Jo's friend, Maeve,' says Helen.

'Jo's got friends?' jokes CJ.

'The odd one or two,' I say perkily.

'She looks odd,' CJ says, winking.

'Oh, I am,' Maeve smiles drolly. 'Don't be fooled by the trappings of decorum.'

CJ's friend is a colt-like woman with a skinny neck wearing a white jumper sequinned with *New York Yankees*, torn denim jeans and a leather strap around her neck with a silver heart. Her haircut is expensive, dyed blonde with not a single root showing. A weekly commitment. Her breasts are perched on her chest the way the surgeon left them. While the rest of us are puckering, wrinkling, creasing and crumpling, she is taut and tight.

She is carrying a plate covered in cling wrap.

'Everyone, meet Summer. Summer, this is everyone,' CJ says.

'Hi Summer,' we all chorus. I am certain in this moment that I too would have had a much fairer chance of looking like the better half of a mermaid if I'd been named after everyone's favourite season.

'Well, hello.' She smiles and puts the plate down on the table. Then, pointing to each of us in turn, she recites our names: 'Helen . . . Jo . . . and Ereka?' I suppose she did have two hours in the car to prepare.

'And this is my friend Maeve,' I say.

Maeve waves ceremoniously at Summer.

'I've just been, like, beyond excited about this weekend, to hang out with a bunch of girls. I haven't had a weekend off in, like, eighteen months—and what a house. OMG,' Summer squeals.

Until this moment I had no idea just how badly I would like to slap people who use the term 'OMG' in speech. As a word.

She could be described as *ultra-modern, well-appointed, superbly landscaped, lock up and go*. There is a skilful assurance to her adorable twinkly blue eyes. She's had her admirers, and never—not a day in her life—been short of male attention. When I was a teenager, I'd have given anything to hang out with a girl like her, sparkling as if life were an audition for a Coke commercial.

I examine the dish on the table. Deep-fried zucchini blossoms.

'Who brought the zucchini blossoms?' I ask.

'Me, me and me,' says CJ, tossing her hair in mock glory.

'I had to hold them all the way here on my lap,' Summer adds. 'It was torture . . .' Clearly she's using torture in the pinching-stilettos sense, not the way Amnesty International intends.

'Did you make them? Have they been tested on humans?' I ask.

Summer giggles.

'Actually, Kito made them. They are stuffed with *Persian* feta,' CJ says grandly as if she could tell the difference between silky feta from Persia and the nastiest cheapest home-brand kind. But everyone knows you have to eat them straight out of the pan otherwise they are sad and limp. Like cold French fries.

'Kito's your new man?' Ercka asks.

'Very much so,' she oohs.

'If David brought me burned toast he'd made all by himself, I'd need CPR to resuscitate me from shock,' Helen says.

Summer whoops at this, like it's the funniest thing anyone's ever said.

'You only get in a relationship what you negotiate,' I say.

'Men are like dogs: they need to be trained,' says Summer, gesturing extravagantly, distracting me with her French-manicured hands. You know, it's not that I don't understand the price of vanity. I spend money on costly wrinkle creams and Dead Sea facial mud to look more *naturally* attractive. But don't these bits of obviously false plastic seem also to advertise *I bite my nails*? Personally I prefer my beauty products to conceal my emotional problems.

'Kito needed no training,' CJ croons, reaching for the plate and lifting the cling wrap. Those zucchini blossoms are definitely soggy and disgusting by now.

'Is he a chef?' Ereka asks.

'A garden landscaper,' she drawls as if she was promoting the length and width of his man-tackle.

'He's an environmental SNAG,' Summer adds helpfully.

It must be splendid to have one's man straddle the gender divides. I'm not thinking so much *Rocky Horror*'s Dr Frank-N-Furter in suspenders, more Jamie Oliver in an apron. Frank is so wonderful in every way a husband could be wonderful. I don't think it makes me a princess if every now and then I wish the man knew what to do with a side of beef.

Ereka offers the plate around. Everyone takes one. I decline.

'What's wrong with the zucchini blossoms?' CJ asks crossly.

'Nothing, I just . . .'

'She's on a diet,' Helen says. 'Can't you see?'

'I thought you looked . . . leaner,' CJ says, as if it's a slur.

'She looks great,' Ereka says.

I'd definitely prefer less scrutiny.

The Reunion

Summer cradles her glass of champagne and twirls her finger in it as if she's popping bubbles.

'So, Summer, what's your story?' I ask, to change the subject.

'Well, where should I start? Let's see, I'm a Scorpio but only just. I'm on the cusp of Libra and Scorpio, but I'm much more a Scorpio. We're, like, totally unpredictable and completely obsessed with sex. LOL. I'm Chinese Year of the Rat, which is kinda weird, 'cos I'm more a Dragon. And I looooove music. Especially . . . can you guess who's my favourite?'

I must look bewildered. Perhaps I manage to shake my head.

'P!nk,' Helen shouts.

'No, not P!nk. Lady Gaga. When she was here, I was in the front row at her concert, shouting, *I love you, Lady Gaga!* The woman is a god to me.'

What are we, like, in fifth grade? Is she intentionally misunderstanding me? Even Savannah Basingthwaite could do better than this. And LOL? Is that an acceptable word to use in adult discourse? The other day I banned Aaron from electronics for saying *WTF*, because swearing is punishable in our home whether in full or in acronyms.

'So do you work?'

'Do I work? CJ, do I work?' She laughs. 'I'm in real estate—commercial and residential. Love it, love selling houses. I usually work every weekend, but I just had an awesome sale and thought—what the hell, girlfriend? Give yourself a break. You deserve it.' Right now she's not so much *lock up and go* as *rambling*.

'And because Craig's away,' CJ interjects.

'Oh, yes, and my hubbie is overseas on business. But wanna know what my real passion is?' Summer smiles broadly, leaning in towards me conspiratorially.

Plastic surgery? Anal bleaching? I'm afraid that even venturing a guess might insult her.

'Travel?' Maeve offers.

'Oh, I love to travel—who doesn't love to travel? But no . . . You know, you remind me so much of someone,' she says, wagging her finger at Maeve.

Maeve smiles weakly.

'Give us a clue,' Ereka suggests.

'Give it up, Summer,' CJ says. 'No-one's going to guess Zumba. No-one but you gives a fuck about Zumba.'

'Oh, you're such a spoilsport, CJ,' Summer says mock-crossly. 'I was going to give the girls a demonstration.'

'Please,' I say. 'I'd love to see it.'

'Too late now.' Summer does a mini-huff. 'But yes, my real passion is Zumba. I go to six classes a week. It's the best fun you can have without drugs.' She giggles. 'The music gets in your blood, it just, like, hijacks your brain and all you can do is dance.'

I've seen some of those moves and they look like a prelude to a back injury.

'I brought all my music with me on my iPod. I'll play some if we can find a sound system here.'

'That sounds . . . jolly delightful,' I manage.

Summer is the jaw that never sleeps. She's a funfair, her wisps of platinum hair stray across her face like finely spun fairy-floss. She doesn't understand how questions work, the give and take of social etiquette. You get her started and she'll continue until forcibly stalled. And best of all, she's oblivious to my judgements of her.

'I've seen Zumba advertised on TV,' Ereka says. 'It looks like fun.'

And that just sets Summer off again. I switch off and turn my attention to CJ.

CJ's hair is longer than I've ever seen it, and has been recently coloured. She has that plump, relaxed quality to her face that a woman who is being well loved has, as if love has regifted her with youth—I don't see any lines around her eyes and mouth. She has lost the emaciation of her divorce. The mole above her lip still invites kisses. She got—and good on her—a second wind mid-life, falling in love all over again as if she'd never been run down, had her heart splintered and been left for dead. She's *as good as new, recently renovated and restored, well maintained with old-style features.*

When Summer pauses for breath, Ereka plunges into the gap. 'CJ, will you tell us about the new man already?' She bites into a zucchini blossom. The feta oozes out the sides and she licks it before it drops. It actually doesn't look terribly disgusting. 'How did you meet him, what's he like? Tell us *everything*. Sweet Jesus, these are beyond divine . . .' She licks her fingers. 'Show us a picture.'

'Show them that picture of Kito,' Summer says, switching between conversations. 'The one with his shirt off,' she whispers.

CJ takes out her iPhone and starts flicking through her photos. 'He is the absolute opposite of Tom, in every single way.'

'Tom's CJ's ex,' I explain to Maeve.

'Excuse me, please only use his official title: TFB.'

'That Fucking Bastard,' Summer decodes.

So she's also CJ's cheerleader.

'Here,' CJ says, holding out her phone. I grab it. There is a photo of a dark-haired semi-nude man—hairless chest and an unmistakable slant to his eyes, set in some luscious olive-looking skin, not quite as drop-dead gorgeous as Keanu Reeves but a fair imitation. Definitely the product of some Euro–Asian love affair. Not that there's anything wrong with that. It's just that CJ . . . well, for all the time I've known her she's been a complete bigot. Love has apparently conquered all that racist crap. But something about this picture makes me feel left out. Like my market profile should read *old and unfashionable*. I've taken photos like this. I've been the *subject* of photos like this, if you don't mind. Twenty years ago. If I were carrying a photo of Frank without his shirt on around on my mobile phone, it would be as some sort of tasteless joke. I can't see that this photo of Kito is even appropriate. Suddenly I feel even older.

'He looks . . . callow,' I say, passing the phone to Maeve. Maeve takes a cursory look and passes it to Ereka.

Summer looks bewildered. I suppose 'callow' is a two-syllable word. And she's probably confused it with 'shallow'.

'He's thirty-six,' CJ snaps.

'Ooh, cradle-snatching too.' Helen laughs approvingly. 'The sex must be hot.'

CJ just smiles and smiles.

'Such smooth skin,' Ereka says, passing the phone to Helen.

Helen holds it close to her face and then she laughs. 'He's a Chink!'

CJ grabs the phone back from Helen. 'He has Chinese ancestry, Helen. And "Chink" is an offensive term, I'll have you know. It's a very rich culture.'

'Eating plenty of raw fish, are you?' Helen guffaws.

'For fuck's sake, Helen, sushi is *Japanese*.'

I wish there was some way I could let Maeve know that, contrary to all appearances, this is not a Getaway for Girl-Schmucks. It's early still, things can improve. Then again, how could anyone have prepared for Summer? Inviting Maeve along was probably not the best-thought-through idea.

'How did you meet?' Ereka asks.

'Actually, I met him through Summer.'

Summer nods, delighted to have been summonsed into significance.

'Summer was a client of mine and Kito was her . . . boyfriend at the time.'

'Not really boyfriend, we were just having an affair,' says Summer. 'We were really good friends—with benefits. He was my support person when I was divorcing my second husband. He came with me to my consultation with CJ. But the minute Kito and CJ met, it was, like, hey, hello, can we talk about my case? Oh my god, they were googly-eyed for each other. How could I stand in the way of true love?'

'Yeah, so that's how,' CJ says, sounding like she's wrapping up this conversation and enough with the questions already.

'Divorcing your *second* husband?' Maeve asks, launching into the least awkward or nosy of the questions Summer's confessions evoke.

Summer smiles, her big blue eyes wide—like, yes, even she is surprised to discover this.

'So are you married again?'

'I am! Craig is my third—hopefully my last—husband. But who knows?' She shrugs helplessly as if divorce is just something that springs itself on you unexpectedly, like a summer shower when you left the house without an umbrella.

'You got kids?' Ereka asks.

'Oh, boy, do I ever! Three of them! Jai is seventeen. In boarding school. But he is so much trouble, isn't he, CJ? We've banished him to a place where they can handle teenage boys without actually murdering them. And then Airlee, who's fifteen going on thirty-five, and my baby Jemima is nine. They're both with their dads this weekend. Best kept secret of divorcees—you get so much time to yourself! I don't know how you full-time mothers do it.'

The way she talks makes me feel left out again. Married is the norm, right? And she's making it sound like it's a pathology. Like we all got caught up in some big silly mistake and she—Summer with the boob implants and false nails—has figured it all out. I'm not trying to be mean, but doesn't she have a collection of what the books unkindly call 'kids from broken homes'? This is just my small-minded observation, you understand, which I'd never in a million years be so bitchy as to share.

'Don't you miss them when they're with their dad?' Ereka asks.

CJ grunts.

Summer chuckles. 'The truth is, I don't. I'm not a very good mother.'

A nervous titter escapes my lips. We've all mouthed those words, but not the way Summer does—without a trace of guilt, the way one might confess, 'I'm not very good at tennis.' With Summer, you get a massive return on your conversational investment. The teeniest prod and she lets it all spill out. I hang around with too many psychologists and therapists who weigh each comment and guard their personal borders like US homeland security. But my weekend entertainment, it seems, has just arrived. One really doesn't need reality TV.

'Do you have to get divorced to get free time from your kids?' Helen asks. 'I could really do with a piece of that action.'

'You're so funny,' Summer says, pushing Helen.

'No kids with your current husband?' I ask.

'Forget it, not a chance. Craig and me, we just want to keep things pure and simple between us. Clear as vodka. Besides, he'd, like, so freak out if I loved anyone more than him, wouldn't he, CJ? Which would be pretty difficult, because he's my soul mate.'

Lucky Summer. Married—for the third time—to a guy who insists on being the centre of attention. And yet there is something cheerfully upfront about their commitment, which, come to think of it, might cure the flaw in romance: kids. Over the years I've watched divorces pop up around me like bulbs in bloom. Ah, another one over there. And look, several just here. And I can't help wondering if people ever actually thought it through—you know, that love displaces? Babies dislodge our lovers and become the new beloved. Romance, like a one-way ticket, gets us in, but abandons us to figure out: the family way or the highway? Just as a new world is established, it begins to crumble. And it doesn't stop there. Things shift again as our kids move on from us. As they're doing right now.

My adorable mother-in-law once proudly announced that she 'always put her husband before her children', as she watched me run around after my kids like they were the next Dalai Lama. (And who knows? They're still young.) Back then I thought she was criticising my mothering. Now I realise she was protecting her son. And she was watching me fall. She was actually warning me that kids will take what they can get as long as you're giving and then they will leave you, because that is what kids must do. And only then will the care and attention you invested in your spouse be tallied. We never think of the generosity we're going to need to sustain us in our geriatric years. Or what love will mean after the children have gone.

'And do you love Craig more than your kids?' I ask Summer, almost jokingly.

'Duh! My kids drive me crazy. Jai is so rude, I can't even talk to him. I'm just the cunt that gave birth to him, excuse my French. He fights with Airlee, makes her cry, till I think I'm going to poison myself if it goes on another minute. My kids are so vile, they only think about themselves. *What are we doing this weekend? Can I borrow fifty dollars? Why can't I have a sleepover with twenty of my BFFs?* Not Jemima—she's my darlingest girl—but the older two, the bloody teenagers.' She holds her hands out in front of her to mimic strangling someone. 'Craig never shouts at me. He buys me whatever I want—and I mean *whatever*,' she says, gesturing to her breasts. 'He tells me he loves me about a thousand times a day, doesn't he, CJ? Kids can't compete with that.'

If she's being controversial, it's unintentional. I feel certain about this. But I wonder, why verbalise it? The frontal cortex is designed for these very occasions when censorship is called for. Toddlers may be 'so cute' for blurting out 'Why's that man got boobs?' and 'That old lady smells funny', but at a certain point there's no excuse for speaking your mind. Social etiquette demands a low level of dishonesty at all times. I'm sure we all know this.

And really, why make it a competition? It's bad enough trying to manage favouritism for particular children. Why complicate matters further by dragging the spouse into it?

All I know is that if Frank died on me, I'd dissolve into a heap of grief, live in the dark with blown-out light bulbs and leave Aaron to watch the footy on his own for a couple of years. But I might return to life. Accept a date now and then from an older version of someone like Callum. I'd survive, somehow. Wretchedly. I can't say the same about losing a child. Shit, I do need to get a letter to Janet Price.

'Does he have kids of his own?' Maeve asks.

Summer shakes her head. 'He's not really into kids.'

Yes, I've sat next to those types on aeroplanes. Single men with manicures and Moleskin diaries. Who wear product in their hair and go for facials. Often gay. Worse when they're straight. Whose sidelong glances make it clear that being seated next to a portaloo would be preferable to being seated next to someone with a small child.

'How does he feel about your kids?' I ask.

'My garbage? I sometimes call them that. Because it sounds like baggage. Just kidding! Craig puts up with them. Jai behaves around Craig. Not that he's home. And we have rules about when the girls are allowed out of their rooms, how loud their music can be. Craig is, like, so awesome with rules. It's not like our bestest time when the kids are there, but we just hang out for when they go to stay with their dads. And then the party starts!' She wriggles her butt on the seat.

'Wow,' Ereka says.

Summer smiles, not getting what that *wow* means. But it's not veneration.

'It's kids that break marriages up,' Summer continues. 'I mean, CJ, the kids totally ruined it for you, didn't they? It just gets all too hard to be in love and to breastfeed and to keep everyone happy.'

'The kids didn't ruin anything,' Ereka says with prickles in her voice. '*Tom* ruined it. By having an affair.'

'Because he felt sidelined by the kids,' CJ says.

'Well, that's pretty weak. Some men need to grow up and realise they're not the centre of the universe,' I say.

Summer looks confused, unaware she's said anything contentious. She wants to make everything nice again.

'But I want Craig to be the centre of my universe. He makes me happy.'

'Here's to your happiness,' Helen says, taking a slug from her glass.

'Well, thank you, Helen,' Summer smiles, sipping from her glass.

'How does Kito get on with your kids?' I ask CJ.

'He's an only child so having kids around is novel for him. He's good with them. He'd like us to have a child, but there's no way I'm going there again. Besides, my friend Eleanor who's forty-three just had to terminate at twenty weeks. Down's.'

'She didn't *have to*,' Ereka says.

'Sorry, she *chose* to,' CJ corrects herself.

'So how long have you and Kito been together?' I ask.

'Officially? Eight months,' she sighs dreamily. 'Unofficially, about a year.'

'Really? A year?' Summer asks.

CJ frowns. 'Yeah.'

'We only broke up a year ago,' Summer says quietly.

'Well, we only started dating after you broke up.'

'Oh dear, are you still In Love?' Helen asks.

'Head over heels,' Summer says before CJ can answer. 'They are all over each other. It's, like: Get a room, you two . . .'

'You and Craig practically bonk in public. Newlyweds.'

'No we don't.' Summer blushes. 'Besides, Kito sticks his tongue down your throat at every opportunity,' she says.

'Yeah, he does,' CJ confirms, shrugging bashfully.

'How nauseating,' I say. 'Spare us the details.'

'No, do not spare a single detail,' Helen urges. 'We want to hear it all.'

7

Virginia's Favourite

It happens at my age. My memory short-circuits. I probably should've said more than just 'a bunch of my friends' when Maeve asked who else would be coming this weekend. But I swear I'd almost forgotten about Harvey. At some point during CJ's uncensored description of how she and Kito have incorporated Harvey, her large pink dildo, into their sexual repertoire—with Summer, her cheerleader, rah-rahing here and there as if she'd been there filming the whole thing—I think I see Maeve shift in her seat and look out at the view longingly.

I stand up, put both my hands on CJ's shoulders, kiss her on the top of her head and say, 'Long may it last,' before gesturing to Maeve to follow me.

'But you haven't heard the best part,' CJ chides.

'Save it for later,' I tell her, pulling Maeve towards the French doors. 'We'll be back—I just want to give Maeve a tour of the house.'

'New relationship,' I whisper as we make our way towards the staircase. Maeve is carrying her hand-woven basket, while I carry her smart red crocodile-skin suitcase.

'She's in that honeymoon phase. It's quite enviable,' Maeve says.

'You'd think, being a lawyer, she might moderate her version for her audience,' I say, realising I am trying to apologise.

'Goodness, why on earth should she? I'm the newcomer. Besides, it sounds as if she's got a first-rate thing going between Kito and Harvey.'

I suppose, as an anthropologist she's seen it all.

'Wouldn't it be fabulous to turn a place like this into a commune for single mothers?' Maeve suggests as we make our way up the stairs.

My feminist inclinations aside, there are few prospects that excite me less than the thought of having to share a big house with a group of undersexed single mothers and their fatherless children. I am definitely sliding from the kids-are-so-adorable-the-more-the-merrier stage of parenting into the grow-up-and-get-a-job phase.

'I'd turn it into a writer's colony,' I say. 'Leave the kids at home.'

'Your idea wins. Can't imagine what I was thinking.'

I hold the door to the pink bathroom open. Maeve peeks in and gives a hearty laugh.

'It has a certain bawdy appeal. I see what Helen means about a Victorian brothel.'

I show her my room with its bay window, chaise longue and antique cupboard—and I say, 'Of course it's okay for us to share.' She plants her basket on the bed next to mine. We've spent time together. It'll be fine. I know her views on the impact of HIV on Third World countries, global warming and Ian McEwan losing out on the Booker Prize to Anne Enright in 2007. But right now these hardly seem sufficient cushions of intimacy required to be roommates. With our pillows just a metre apart, I realise she's little more than a stranger. And with any luck, she also snores. Though what am I thinking? There's nothing fortunate about mutual humiliation and neither of us getting any sleep.

I leave Maeve alone to potter around. There's no excuse for hovering. It's the loiter of the desperate. Instead of going down the stairs, though, I find myself in the nursery. I sit down at the stool in front of the pianola and press a key. I wouldn't even know if it's off-key. Jamie would. She can play the piano, the saxophone, the electric guitar. She has talent, pity about the attitude. I take my iPhone out of my pocket. I press on my camera roll and scroll to the photos we took at my birthday a few months ago. There's a picture of me and Jamie, our arms around each other, our faces pressed cheek to cheek. You'd swear she loves me.

I remember when she was small enough to fit on a pillow beside me. It's not like something faint I have to work to recall, but more vivid even than our fight on the phone hours ago. It was as if I exhaled her, something warm and from me. My bed was her bed. My plate was her plate. My spit was her spit. My body was her playground. I had no emotions of my own; mine melted, bled and leaked into hers. When she cried at her first vaccinations at six weeks, I cried. Becoming a mother extended me like a fold-out table. I became two people instead of one. After Aaron, I became three. Three times as many things hurt me, scared me, excited me, drew me in. It was claustrophobic and too much for one person. But it becomes a way of life, the way you begin to understand yourself.

So when they started to turn inwards and face themselves, closing doors to shut me out, I was winded. No longer to be let in—to the bathroom, their bedrooms, their fears and anxieties. Nowadays I have to guess if they've had a bad day—I'm never confided in. I imagine how they've spent their pocket money—I'm never told. Of course I'm glad they've got their secrets. Glad in the 'I recognise and respect your privacy' sense. That special entitlement I've always felt to bear their pain for them, to be the bearer of their rejections, humiliations and heartaches, has expired. My new job is to manage my pain at not being part of their pain and 'model' how to manage the yucky bits of being a person.

But unfortunately having kids doesn't turn us into genteel, compassionate humanitarians qualified to model exemplary responses to crisis, loss and rejection. So our kids are in deep shit if we are small-minded, petty, bitchy, materialistic people to begin with.

I like this nursery. It is frozen in yesterday's childhood. I feel safe here, like I could sleep here.

I take a peek into the other rooms. CJ and Summer will probably share the room with the two single beds and I see Ereka has laid claim to the other one with the double bed. I take it Virginia will share with Helen.

From downstairs I hear Helen chime, 'Time for sundowners.' I call to Maeve, 'Sundowners on the veranda,' and make my way down the stairs past the watchful mirror and towards the cluck of conversation, where one can only hope CJ has moved on from Harvey's show-stopping talents.

Helen is squeezing limes at the table with CJ's help, concocting some lethal drink with vodka and sugar. As if I can even have a sip of that.

She pours the mixture into six small glasses. Summer slides off the hammock, gripping a Diet Coke, and removes her sweater, which momentarily reveals her tummy, navel ring and tiny swallow tattoo. Not a stretch mark in sight despite three kids. Either pregnancy didn't leave a trace of corporeal graffiti on her or there's been surgical aid. I take a seat on one of the suspended wicker chairs, wishing my tummy muscles expressed to the wide world how many hours I spend on them in private. Maeve arrives draped in a hand-knitted Mexican shawl.

'Oh, this is just so much fun,' Summer sings, picking up two of the cocktails and handing one to Ereka. CJ downs hers.

'So, Maeve, what do you do?' Summer asks.

'I'm a social anthropologist.'

Summer blinks. 'So, is that like someone who digs for those old bones and fossil things?'

Maeve swallows. 'No. Actually that's an archaeologist.'

'So what does a social anthropologist do again?' Helen asks.

'We study different cultures and ways of life—it's essentially the study of humankind.'

'Actually Maeve is a *professor* of social anthropology,' I emphasise.

'I don't think I've ever met a real professor before,' says Summer. 'Actually, I'm lying. I did once sell a house to a Nigerian professor of—what was it? Either pharmacy or forensics . . . It was something with an F, I remember that much.'

I'm going to need a stiff drink to get through the evening. 'Where is your friend Virginia?' I ask Helen.

'She'll get here when she gets here.'

'Who's doing dinner tonight?' Ereka asks.

'I am,' Helen says. 'And it's all under control. Listen, girls, before Virginia arrives I should probably just let you all know that her mother is dying of thyroid cancer. Not that she'll want to talk about it or anything, but just in case . . .'

'How awful,' Ereka says, shaking her head mournfully.

'Sorry to hear that,' CJ agrees.

'Totally sad,' Summer sighs.

Maeve is quiet.

I sidle up to Helen. 'You didn't think to mention this to me?' I whisper.

'What?' Helen says, innocent-like.

'We've organised a long-awaited fun-filled weekend away, and you've invited your friend whose mother is dying of cancer. You didn't think that might, I don't know, be a bit of a downer?'

'Nah, she'll be fine. She probably won't even mention it,' Helen says.

'Excuse me, but if your mother was dying of cancer, why would you go away for the weekend?'

'She doesn't have that sort of relationship with her mother. Her mum's a bit of a cow. It'll be cool.'

'Oh,' I say, embarrassed by how relieved I feel that we won't have to counsel some heartbroken stranger through her grief. I wonder what that's like—not to care a whole lot about a dying mother. Given that my own mum is anything but a cow, I just can't imagine it. If she was dying, the last place I'd be is cavorting with Helen and her sadistic cocktails.

'So what are you serving us for dinner?' Ereka asks.

And I swear, my friend, my best friend, says with a big smile on her face and her arms out wide, 'PIZZA!' as if this is supposed to be good news.

'Oooh, yummm,' Ereka grins.

'My best,' CJ approves.

'Gosh, I haven't had pizza in ages—I'll share one with someone,' Maeve says.

'Bring it on,' Summer cheers, waving her hands.

'I can't eat pizza,' I say.

'You can fall off the wagon for one night,' Helen says. 'Don't be a spoilsport.'

'You seriously don't eat pizza?' Summer asks, as if I've just let slip that I don't wash my hands after a number two. 'Are you allergic to cheese?'

'No, I'm not allergic. But pizza is very—' I can't think of a word that won't sound patronising '—unhealthy . . . full of nutritional poison . . . rich. I'd prefer something with fewer lipids, less carbohydrate and more protein.'

'You just don't want the calories,' Helen says.

'So maybe I don't. Crucify me for that.'

'See what I mean?' Helen nods to CJ and Ereka.

CJ snickers.

'Oh, that's nice, you've been talking about me behind my back.'

'I just asked Helen how you'd lost all that weight,' Ereka explains. 'She was saying you're very *disciplined*.'

I am annoyed by this. Disproportionately so. Discipline is not a personality disorder, a sexually transmitted disease nor an addictive substance. It is, in fact, a highly sought-after characteristic people pay exorbitant fees to personal trainers and life coaches to master. Yes, it takes a lot of discipline to lose weight. I have said no to many things I would have dearly loved to gobble up in the past three years. I've turned my nose up at crème caramels. I've chewed on lean protein while others have had burger juice running down their chins. I've been ostracised, judged and belittled for my self-control. Jibed and bullied by others who only want to drag me down into the pits of back fat and thigh wobbles with them. But I ask you: is there a crime against gastronomic discipline? Last time I checked there was no Convention on the Elimination of Personal Restraint in the Event of Pizza.

'So out of all the things you trawled through your recipe books to cook for us tonight, you chose *pizza*? The one food that is an instant fat-injection . . . I'm disappointed,' I say.

'It's really, really good pizza,' Helen says. 'Gorgonzola, salami, porcini mushrooms, artichokes and olives with truffle oil. You love artichokes. I'm adding artichokes especially for you.'

'Actually, that's more like a coronary on a plate,' I say. 'And what a tragic waste of your exceptional culinary skills. Any halfwit can make pizza.'

'Well, it's Virginia's favourite,' Helen says. 'And since her mum's dying . . .'

And just like that, Helen lets me know that despite our ten-year friendship, our holidays together with our kids, our shared mothering milestones and recipe secrets, her being my wedding planner, organising my hens' day on a boat on Sydney Harbour, and me being one of the first people to hold Levi in hospital and bless him into this world, in the end, history trumps all. She chooses Virginia. Virginia who isn't even here yet.

I reach for one of those little cocktails and I down it. It burns and stings and explodes down my gullet like a shot of sweet morphine. I slug another one. 'This is So Much Fun,' I say, heading for my third.

Night comes quickly. With autumn daylight saving, one minute twilight winks and the next everything is pitch black. Some days the transitions in motherhood feel this rushed. No sooner do I catch up with where my kids are than they're onto the next phase.

Sitting out on the veranda with the dark so close and the view taken by its shadows unnerves me. Unnecessary questions bother me at this time of day—like whether snakes can slither upstairs and whether the smell I can't put my finger on has something to do with ghosts. CJ and Summer are engrossed in a snug duet of conversation of which I only catch snippets, including 'the latest Prius' and all its features. Cars interest me as much as other people's dental work so I wander back into the lounge room, slightly tipsy, and am startled all over again by the faces of the hunted dead protruding like phantoms from the wall.

'You lot again,' I mutter.

I stop and stare, not recognising myself in the massive mirror for a moment as if the house—or, more likely, the alcohol—has made a stranger out of me. There's an incongruity about my reflection, as if I can't quite be sure it's mine. I stare at myself. This is what people see when they look at me. Familiarity blunts the eye, so age sneaks in incrementally, through the cracks, under the door. Without mirrors, ageing loses its bite and might be experienced as nothing but a thinning of vitality, like the air on a mountain peak. We'd slow down, feel the slackening of collagen, the slow ebb of libido, but without the pinch of anxiety these loosenings foreshadow. I run my fingers through my hair. From afar you can't really see all the grey bits. Distance is kind in that way, but doesn't invite intimacy, or any real truth.

When I was nineteen, *Jitterbug Perfume* was my favourite book and Tom Robbins my favourite author. King Alobar would secretly leave his castle each night to observe his reflection in the water and pluck out his grey hairs. In his kingdom the first signs of 'enfeeblement' or 'decay' indicated a king's powers were waning, and for this he would be put to death. I suppose I could be grateful that I don't have compulsory beheading to add to my list of ageing anxieties. But the sense of dread when the first white hairs pop up is inescapable. My mum once told me, 'You know you're growing old when your *pubic* hairs start going white.' So that bought me a couple of months of extended youth.

I have every intention of embracing ageing with dignity. But I'd like to go down fighting like my eighty-nine-year-old granny Sophie, who, being wheeled into theatre for what would prove to be her final surgery, took one look at her handsome young doctor and, with a gasp of horror, lamented to the nurse, 'Oh my goodness, what my hair must look like!'

I suddenly have this pained feeling in my chest that my anxiety about Callum seeing my breasts is not far off Granny Sophie's remark. I wonder where he is and what he's doing with all those biceps and triceps. Whether he might stroll by later tonight to see how we're all doing. I notice I am hoping this is the case. But if he were to find anyone sexy here, it would be Summer. And no number of Pilates roll-ups or collagen-enhancing creams can change that fact. Frank—bless him—always tells me he 'still finds me sexy'. Despite how that qualifier 'still' sticks in my guts, the truth is, he doesn't count. He's my husband. It's his *job* to find me sexy whether he likes it or not. The real indicator of my sexiness is if *other* men find me attractive. The problem is, because I'm married, even those who might find me attractive probably wouldn't think to articulate it, given how adulterously such compliments might be interpreted by, say, one's husband.

The doorbell goes.

'I got it,' Helen yells, bolting from the veranda for the front door. The others trail in following her, Maeve first.

'Zuki!' I hear.

'Cati!' Helen laughs and then there's giggling interspersed with what sounds very much like a dog barking, but I must be mistaken.

Helen introduces us to Virginia. She is tall, not far off six foot, angular in the face with high cheekbones, un-made-up, short greying hair, casual-chic in a loose fawn hemp shirt, jeans and buckled brown leather boots. When she smiles, she reveals a mouthful of metal braces which look like they've landed on the wrong face, like makeup on little girls. She waves to us with the hand encased in a wrist guard clutching a bottle of—is that Moët? But I'm too busy looking at the enormous mutt tucked under her arm to do a proper hello.

She sees me looking at the dog.

'Sorry, it's my mum's,' she says, as if this explains its presence. She lowers it to the floor and it begins sniffing and shuffling around in a frenzy of excitement. Someone has food-jammed that poor dog into canine obesity.

'Aw, I should've brought Bones, then you guys could have had a play date,' Helen says, scratching the dog's head. Virginia gives Helen the bottle of Moët.

'What's up with the mobile-phone coverage? I've not been able to get a signal since I turned off the main road,' Virginia says to Helen.

Helen shrugs. 'Could be the ridge blocking the signal. But you're off duty now, relax.'

'Can't be out of range all weekend. I've got calls and emails I've got to answer—and Celia . . .'

'Oh, right, forgot about her.'

'Where's the landline?' Virginia asks.

Helen leads her to the entrance hall.

'Not sure we're allowed to have dogs here,' I mumble to Maeve under my breath, opening my bag to check my phone.

She shrugs and says softly, 'It's a big house, don't worry . . . Besides, it'll alert you to snakes.'

I can't imagine I'm the only one who thinks it's just a little too familiar to pitch up late to join a crowd of people you don't know, with a household pet under your arm, and expect everyone to welcome you like a long-lost friend just because you've brought a bottle of champagne that costs as much as liposuction. I could be allergic to dogs for all she knows. I haven't had tests done. And not to be judgemental or anything, but seriously, *this* is the coolest person Helen knows? *Elevated views*, maybe, but that's it. I'm definitely missing something.

There are no messages on my phone even though it has a signal. I put it back in my bag quickly before Virginia takes it over for the weekend to answer all her business calls.

'That's not acceptable,' I hear Virginia say from the entrance hall. There is business in her voice.

The Reunion

When Virginia and Helen come back into the lounge room, Virginia's lips are as thin as a washing line.

'Chill, we'll sort it out,' Helen says, patting her on the back.

Virginia inhales and nods. She breathes out through her mouth, probably remembering she's just arrived and hasn't really made a marvellous first impression. Squeezing out a smile, she says, 'So what do you think of the place I found?'

'I've never stayed in anything so grand in my life,' says Ereka.

'It's totally awesome,' Summer agrees. 'Definitely worth around the five mill mark.'

Virginia found? What's going on here? I give Helen a questioning look.

'Virginia found this place—it's being considered for a local soap opera.' She looks sheepish.

'What soap opera?' Ereka asks.

'I can't talk about it yet, but I promise you it will be full of everything—love, sex, betrayal, revenge, murder, heartache . . . the works. You won't want to miss it.'

She's right. Who'd want to miss all that?

8

No Wonder My Daughter Hates Me

Helen and Virginia disappear up the grand staircase to do a walk-through of the house, Virginia with her iPhone, taking shots of everything. Summer runs after them, shouting, 'Wait for me!'

We hear cupboards opening, and the floorboards above us creaking. When they come down, Helen is saying, 'He'll probably have a key.'

'Who?' I ask.

'Callum. For the locked room.'

'I've got to have access to all the rooms—I've got to do a report on this place.' Virginia's smile has withered again.

'The bathrooms are beyond tragic,' says Summer, grimacing.

Back in the lounge room, Virginia inspects the chandeliers, rubs her shoes over a frayed bit of the Persian carpet, even lifts the lid on the grand piano and presses a few keys before she and Helen disappear into the kitchen from which loud chatter and laughter trickle out on and off. I used to be Helen's right-hand man. Especially in the kitchen.

I'm not exactly sulking when I turn my attention to the bookshelves. I like books, is all. *The Da Vinci Code* . . . *The Grim Glory of the 2/19th Battalion AIF* by R.W. Newton . . . a Penguin edition of *Wuthering Heights* . . . *Escape from Hell: The Sandakan Story* by Walter Wallace, two hardcover books on gardening covered in plastic, a bunch of *National Geographics* . . . *Behind Bamboo: An Inside Story of the Japanese Prison Camps* by Rohan Rivett . . . a dog-eared copy of *Twilight*. *Twilight?*

Maeve joins me at the bookshelf. She's wearing different earrings and her block necklace is gone. She 'changed' for dinner.

'Someone had a keen interest in the war,' Maeve comments, scanning the shelves. She starts flipping through a book called *Women's World*. 'Listen to this inscription: *To my dearest Delia, a jolly good wife and mother—but there's always room for improvement. Merry Christmas, your ever-loving husband, Harold F. Wiltshire, Blind Rise Ridge, December 1952.*'

'It's astonishing how few women of that era actually murdered their husbands,' I mutter.

Half an hour after Helen and Virginia's collaboration in the kitchen, the aroma of melting cheese has filled the house, drowning out any other smells and drawing us all in like a siren. Helen whistles to all of us from the kitchen, and we all make our way in there, Ereka leading the brigade. On the long wooden table, Helen has laid out six large pizzas dotted with enormous olives, tufts of gooey gorgonzola, half-moons of artichokes, shards of salami, outcrops of porcini mushrooms and a sprinkling of roasted pine nuts. There is a small helping of just artichokes. For me. In a different life, I'd have fallen all over that pizza like a girl without a thought of her reputation come morning. Instead I pick at my tuna salad and the occasional artichoke. Pizza-envy is no big deal. I've resisted worse. But the views from the moral high ground are not as sweeping and spectacular as you might imagine.

Maeve looks at me consolingly. 'Can't we tempt you with even a slice? Not even a morsel?'

I shake my head. 'It's a slippery slope, Maeve.'

'Your courage is admirable. You are a warrior in the fight against flab.'

'She's pig-headed. Not to mention a killjoy.' Helen doesn't even wink to soften her words.

'Restraint is so . . . middle-aged,' CJ says. 'Like those wrinkles around your mouth.'

'I'm using special creams with amino acids,' I inform her, though really—is it any of her business?

'You don't have any wrinkles,' Summer lies, sipping on her third Diet Coke since she arrived—not that I'm counting. Her slab of twenty-four cans has taken up an entire shelf in the fridge.

'That stuff is poison,' CJ says to Summer. 'I don't know why you drink it.'

'I am so addicted,' Summer says, like addiction is the cutest thing EVAH.

I chew a piece of cucumber, which, being full of fluid, is really good for the skin. I'm doing what I can to stall old age. Nonetheless, lately little lines have appeared around my mouth. Folds. I believe the official term is 'puckering', a perfectly benign expression when referring to clothing, less so when applied to one's face. I've spent plenty of money on 'skin-firming' creams and 'wrinkle-vanishers'. Nothing has firmed and not a single wrinkle has vanished, though I feel compelled to report that the puckering feels much smoother. According to Olay, I have all the seven signs of ageing, a line-up of demoralising symptoms including lines and wrinkles, dullness, dryness, blotchiness, age spots, roughness and visible pores. And that's just the skin. Let's not talk about organs south of the equator, or trying to remember where I left my keys. Suddenly, the terms 'after-party', 'recreational drugs' and 'unprotected sex' seem otherworldly, as if I'm peering through a looking-glass, receding from life-as-others-are-living-it while I don my slippers and look forward to an early night with a decent book. I've embraced the discouraging realisation that even after a year of triceps exercises I still have flabby arms. Certain dress lengths are . . . well, wrong. And I seem to be fighting a futile war against puckering. But it is rude and unfriendly for anyone—least of all one of one's peers—to point this out. I am monitoring my own puckering, thank you very much.

'You have incredible self-control,' Ereka manages through the crunch of her third slice. 'I so envy people who can exercise restraint. I really wish I could say no.'

It's not like I even see it coming. I have no time to plan or think or just take a deep breath, like I've been teaching Aaron to do when things annoy him. The ribbing, the jibing, the underhanded comments, the put-downs disguised as compliments, my deep-seated anxiety about facial puckering and that mind-altering smell of grilled cheese all just knock me off my feet like a freak wave and I'm churning up, and the words are tumbling out of me. 'Then just say it,' I snap.

I would like to look at it another way, but it's almost impossible not to read what I've just said as a verbal slap in the face. Ereka looks startled. 'I . . . I don't know how to say no,' she stammers.

And then I'm standing up, grabbing her plate with the rest of her pizza on it and swapping it with my salad, and I'm saying, 'Like this.' Everyone is staring at me in disbelief. Ereka's eyes are as big as tomatoes.

'Relax, Jo,' Helen says. 'Ereka can eat pizza if she wants to. Just put her plate down.'

'Of course she can. But what's the point in saying, *I wish I had more willpower*? You have willpower. You just choose not to use it.' As I say this, I'm aware of a sick cold sensation moving up from my stomach to my throat, the bile of my remorse for attacking Ereka. Ereka, the last one among us who deserves to be attacked. Who needs support and understanding. I am such a bad person. No wonder my daughter hates me.

'Chill out,' Helen growls.

'You need to take a couple of deep breaths,' CJ says. 'Really, you seem very stressed.'

Ereka looks crestfallen. I feel like I'm about to puke with self-disgust. I put her pizza back down in front of her and move my salad back to my place. 'Sorry, Ereka. Here, enjoy your pizza.'

Ereka breathes heavily. Shock, of course there's shock. What sort of a witch am I? She pushes her plate away.

'See what you've gone and done now,' Helen chides.

'I'm really sorry. I just . . . you know . . . there's no magic to losing weight. You just decide and then you act on it.'

'Nobody cares about losing weight and how they look except you,' Helen says. 'And what's the big deal whether you're a size ten instead of a sixteen? Does it really matter?'

I am a stupid bitch. This is clear to me as I look at Ereka's crumpled face.

'Who are you trying to impress?' CJ echoes. 'Who're you losing weight for? Frank loves you just the way you are, doesn't he?'

He does. I'm not losing it for Frank. Why am I pushing so hard?

The pizzas are getting cold. No-one has taken a bite for a while now. Summer is sipping quietly on her Diet Coke, apparently struck mute. Maeve has a mystified look on her face. Virginia has stopped constantly checking her iPhone for a signal. I have truly ruined this dinner. Possibly the entire weekend. I may as well just pack my bags and go home now.

'No, don't blame Jo,' Ereka says, looking up. 'She's absolutely right. All this talk of wanting to lose weight, and then not doing anything about it . . . Everyone pussy-foots around me. No-one ever just says, "You big fat pig. Just stop eating so much."'

'You are not a big fat pig,' I say. 'I never said you were a big fat pig.'

'Yes, but I feel like one. A warthog. A whale.' Tears well in her eyes. Oh god, she's going to cry.

I go over to her and put my arm around her. 'It's a lot easier than you think. You just decide that certain things are off the menu. Like . . . like when you're married. You don't have to think about being faithful every day, or make the commitment every time you meet a sexy guy. You just know—that's a no-go zone.'

Ereka nods and wipes her eyes on her sleeve. 'You know, I eat all the lollies and chocolates and ice-cream in the house because I don't want my kids to get fat like me . . .'

'That's very kind of you,' Summer says consolingly.

'And Kylie's even started this nonsense of asking, "Mum, am I fat?" And she's only *eleven*.'

'Oh my god, Airlee's favourite shows are *The Biggest Loser* and *Britain's Next Top Model*,' Summer says, rolling her eyes.

'It's sick,' Helen says.

'You should think about coming to a Zumba class. You can lose so much weight and it's such fun,' Summer offers.

Ereka nods. 'Thanks.'

'Perhaps it feels as if someone else's needs always trump your own,' Maeve says calmly.

'Well, they do. You don't know what it's like . . . what it's like . . . Excuse me,' Ereka says suddenly, and she gets up and leaves the table.

Should I follow her or leave her alone? I look around for a clue, but no-one is making eye contact with me.

'What's the matter with you? Why'd you lash out like that?'

I wish I knew how to answer Helen.

'I'm sorry,' I say. 'I was completely out of line.'

I stand to follow Ereka, when Virginia speaks. 'Get off her case, Zuki. Jo was just telling her the truth. I mean, if she wants to lose weight . . .'

I turn and look at Virginia. That is probably the most generous interpretation of what has just happened.

'Telling the truth is always hard,' Virginia continues, and I feel myself exhaling for the first time since I grabbed Ereka's pizza away from her. 'No-one wants to have to say the emperor's got no clothes—but deep down we all silently applaud the person who does.'

'But Ereka's been through hell,' CJ says. 'You've got to cut her some slack.'

I nod. I nod hard. Why didn't I cut her some slack? Poor Ereka.

'I told you about her daughter,' Helen reminds Virginia. 'She doesn't need the truth. That woman has had enough cold, hard truth to last a lifetime.'

'Perhaps,' Maeve says, 'and this is just an observation, she'd appreciate more honesty. If everyone avoids saying what they're thinking, it could feel patronising?'

'I agree,' Virginia says. 'Look, I don't know her exact circumstances, but if you can't be honest with her, what kind of friendship is that?'

Summer looks confused about who to support here. Her head just swivels as people offer their opinions. As she's never met Ereka before, she probably doesn't get the full impact of what's just happened.

'Hell, if I'd known my pizzas would cause such a ruckus, I'd have served bloody pasta,' Helen says.

'She's our friend. It's not our job to upset her,' CJ says. 'Life's done enough damage to her.'

I can't bear the look of confusion on Summer's face anymore, so I say it: 'Her daughter Olivia has brain damage.'

'Oh,' Summer says, nodding.

'You heard her going on earlier, Jo—how she can't die because there'd be no-one to look after Olivia. Imagine that stress . . . and you've got to carry on about how fat she is. Nice one.' Helen whacks me on the head with her palm.

I am a bulldozer in fancy athletic gear. I sink down onto the kitchen bench and put my head in my hands.

'She's fragile,' I say, almost to myself. 'You have to be gentle when people are fragile.'

Maeve comes up beside me and says, 'Maybe she's not as fragile as you assume. Hardship breeds strength, not weakness.'

I run my fingers through my hair. 'Excuse me, I just need some air,' I say.

I walk through the lounge room and out onto the veranda. Ereka is not there.

I stand and look out into the night. The moon above kindles the sky and etches everything in a silver shimmer.

I wipe my eyes and sniff. Something full in my chest bangs against my ribcage. I may have self-control when it comes to pizza, but not when it comes to the things that really matter. I sigh and sit down on the top stair of the veranda. The stone is icy against my bum.

I feel just this way after I've yelled at my kids. Jamie and Aaron each have their own unique ways of winding me up to blasting point. But it's my job, as the adult, to defuse. Our kids are not our punching bags nor our scapegoats. Lashing out may give the momentary illusion of catharsis, but it's not worth *this*. The guilt-swamp of remorse. But how am I going to make things right with Ereka? Poor, tired, worn-down Ereka. I haven't been much of a friend to her in the past few years. And after my outburst in the kitchen, who needs friends like me?

Suddenly I feel obese with guilt. I should've called Jamie straight back today. Just explained to her—again—that she's too young to go off to a Third World country without me there to protect her.

From inside I hear the bubbles of Summer's laughter. I have to consider that maybe she really is guilt free. Perhaps she simply doesn't feel responsible for every little thing that goes wrong for her kids. They've figured out guilt-free desserts, so why not guilt-free mothering? Guilt's as unhealthy for our self-worth as transfats are for the thighs. It's both the corrupting and narcissistic response to all our children's foibles, faults and personality flaws.

But, see, it's a problem of investment. Our children are not an unusual hobby we can take up only to find we don't have a particular aptitude for it and then promptly sell all our equipment on eBay. They're not a wall colour we can paint over if we find one day we've just stopped liking it. They're not even an eating habit we can change with enough pressure from our doctor or wardrobe. 'You are what you eat' has nothing on 'You are who your children turn out to be'. Our kids' physical perfections and imperfections expose the quality of our gene pool. But their behaviour is a commentary on who we are as people. They are an incomplete and incessant feedback on everything we have nailed and stuffed up.

I'm nervous in that superstitious way of fixating too much on my children's beauty. Sometimes I'll come into their rooms at night when they're asleep on the pretext of checking they have clean school uniforms, and I'll stop and catch my breath, the way I did when I first saw Uluru as the morning light struck its face, and I will be afraid. I will be terrified of the warmth in my chest, the seep of something so much greater than love and devoid of humility and almost a kind of personal hubris when I see them. I force myself not to stare. I turn away and shake myself free of the heartache my satisfaction at seeing them gives me, knowing that no-one (maybe Frank, perhaps their grandparents) sees them the way I do. This knowing is also a kind of terror at the indifference of the world around them, in which their uniqueness is registered as nothing more than a subjective sentimentality on my part. Children are inherently untranslatable. They only matter in this profound way to us, their parents.

So I feign nonchalance. I pretend I have had no part in making them perfect. I've been a conduit. They have manifested themselves. I am no more to be congratulated at their perfection and achievements than I am to blame for their stuff-ups. Motherhood is a form of resistance. We must fight against taking credit and assuming blame. Aren't these equally perversions of our input? A form of ownership? I am clear that I neither want to be that stereotypical Jewish mother who runs down the beach shouting, 'Help, help, my son the cardiologist is drowning!' nor the one who cannot forgive herself for her child's drug addiction, teenage pregnancy or gambling debts. I want kids who are neither victims of my conceit nor my ego-disabilities. But they've got to survive having me as their mother in order to get there. I didn't see 'Mothers' in Aaron's book, but we should be there somewhere between the Hippos and Snakes.

I stand up and shake the moonlight off me. I go back inside and climb the stairs. The door to Ereka's room is shut. I put my ear to the door and hear the sound of a grown woman sobbing.

I knock gently.

'Hey, Ereka? It's me. I'm so sorry.'

She is quiet for a moment, then says, 'I just need some time on my own.'

'Uh, okay. Sure. Is there anything I can get you?'

She doesn't answer. I don't blame her. It was a stupid question.

9

Perverts and Creeps

As I come down the stairs I bump into Virginia on the landing, holding her mobile phone up like the Statue of Liberty's torch. Her smile is more of a grimace as she shakes her head and follows me down to the kitchen.

Summer, in rubber gloves, is scrubbing the table. CJ is washing dishes, Maeve is drying. Helen is wrapping the pizza leftovers in cling wrap. She is the only one of us who would have the presence of mind to pack cling wrap for a weekend away. But doesn't knowing about the work that goes into fun take the fun out of it? Camping, for example. Lovely idea. Can't manage the logistics. And gynaecologists, whom I've always imagined would be terrible lovers, their passion extinguished by all those years of exposure to the female anatomy replete with Latin names. Not that I've ever had sex with a gynaecologist; this is just a thought, you understand.

My salad remains half-eaten on the table. Helen is not making any moves to cling-wrap it.

'She's shut herself in her room and wants to be left alone,' I announce.

Helen puts the leftover pizza in the fridge.

Maeve approaches me but doesn't put her arm around me or anything like that. 'Are you alright?'

I sniff. 'I don't know what came over me.'

'Hunger, probably,' Helen says, drying a dish with her T-shirt. Summer and CJ laugh. I deserve not to have my feelings considered.

'You're just jealous she's got such mad-bitch willpower,' Virginia says, punching Helen.

Virginia. She's growing on me. I smile at her.

'So, Virginia, did you really look a charging hippo in the eye?' I ask.

'Zuki!' Virginia sighs, rolling her eyes.

'Well, you kinda did . . .' Helen giggles.

'Really, that wasn't funny.' Turning to me she says, 'It was my first assignment doing a doco on black magic. We were filming in Zambia and one of the guides was on a boat ahead of us. Suddenly this hippo rears out of the water like bloody Jaws, and bites the boat in half, taking the guide's left foot too. I sat screaming in my boat, and shat my pants. And I'm not talking figuratively.'

Helen does a little chortling Rumpelstiltskin dance as she leaves the kitchen to go to the loo.

'Japanese encephalitis, nearly dying of altitude sickness—they had nothing on the hippo . . . It was the scariest moment of my life. And don't believe anything Helen tells you. She's a liar. Always has been.'

'You outdoor types,' CJ says. 'Just stay indoors, where it's safe.'

'Actually,' Summer says, 'most accidents happen indoors.'

'With hippos?' CJ quips.

Maeve offers me a biscotti. I decline. 'I don't know much about hippos,' I say. I don't mean to sound glum. I've just never even seen a real live one.

'They're the most dangerous animal in the world,' Maeve confirms. 'They can outrun humans.'

'Give me a tiger, a shark or a tarantula over a hippo any day.' There are adventures in Virginia's observations.

'Apparently George Washington's false teeth were made out of hippo tusk,' Maeve says.

'I did not know that,' Virginia says, as if anyone would.

If she ever gets tired of being a professor, Maeve could hire herself out as the Phone a Friend lifeline for *Who Wants to be a Millionaire?* Though it would be hard for me to get to see her. If she were *everyone's* friend.

'Hippo tusk doesn't yellow with age.'

'How come you know so much about hippos?' CJ asks. 'Social anthropologists don't study animals, do they?'

'I've been on a couple of safaris in Botswana and other parts of Africa. The guides are full of fascinating trivia which seem to stick to my brain like lint. Here's another one: what do you call a group of hippos?'

I shake my head. How would I know?

'I should know this,' Virginia says, tapping her forehead.

'A horde,' Summer offers, loving the guessing.

'A bloat.'

'A bloat?' Summer repeats. 'As in *I don't like cabbage, it makes me bloat?*'

Maeve nods. Summer looks bewildered.

I faintly hear my mobile phone ring in my bag in the entrance hall. At last. I'm always open to an apology.

'Have you still got that stupid Robbie Williams song on your phone?' Helen shouts from the entrance hall. Yes, okay, putting your favourite song as your mobile phone ringtone is, I can now confirm, a shortcut to detesting it. 'Angels' used to make me cry. Now it just gets on my nerves. I must get Aaron—who is a techno-whiz—to delete it for me and put on something innocuous like the sound of an actual telephone ringing.

'You want it?' Helen asks.

'Yes, grab it.'

'So there must be a signal,' Virginia exclaims, holding up her iPhone and squinting at its face. 'What are you on?'

'Optus,' I say.

'Shit, bloody Vodafone,' she curses.

Helen waltzes back into the kitchen holding my phone. 'Didn't get there in time. Missed call from Jamie.' I'll bet she purposely didn't break a sweat to get it. She hands me my phone. It beeps with an SMS. I check the message.

You've ruined my weekend. And my life.

Oh well. At least I'm having an impact.

'Why didn't you tell her you were "out of bounds" this weekend?' CJ asks. 'My kids wouldn't dare try calling me.'

'We had a bit of an "I hate your guts" exchange when I arrived here this afternoon.'

'She'll get over it,' Helen says. 'It's Frank's problem, not yours.'

'Ignore it,' CJ says. 'It's manipulation.'

Lovely—thanks, CJ, for the parenting advice. Not that she's a bad mother or anything. All I'm saying is that a mother should keep an eye on her own daughter. Jamie and Jorja are

Facebook friends. Okay, so I checked Jorja's profile. And I'm quite sure Jorja starting a Facebook page called 'Ban Briony's BO' (whoever poor Briony is) qualifies as cyber-bullying and either CJ doesn't know about it or doesn't care. That's what happens when you're happy—you get distracted. You probably sleep well, too. At least I keep the lines of communication with my daughter open.

'And besides, how will she ever be resourceful if she keeps running to you for everything?' CJ asks.

I'm not apologising for the fact that I like to 'be there' for my kids and know where they are at all times. Jamie's desire for independence outstrips her capacity to handle it under pressure. I let her do normal teenage things like catch the bus and wander the streets on Halloween without parental escort. As long as she's in a group. And has her phone. I'm not saying I don't release a lot of cortisol in the process. I'm saying I let her.

'My girls do the freak-out on me every time I say no to a sleepover,' Summer sighs.

'Why won't you let them have a sleepover?' Helen asks. 'I wouldn't survive without palming off a couple of mine each weekend.'

'It's just, like, a family rule,' Summer says casually. 'I mean they can sleep at their dads', no problemo. Just not, you know, people I don't know. Strangers. I'm, like, so not overprotective, actually, or that kind of thing, am I, CJ?'

'Except for your weird no-sleepover rule,' CJ says.

Even I let my kids sleep over. I guess everyone's got their madness.

'What did you and Jamie fight about?' CJ asks.

'This morning's argument started when I told her she couldn't get a ride with her friend Mimi's boyfriend to the Katy Perry concert next weekend.'

Summer grins. 'I just, like, *love* Katy Perry.'

'Thanks to that slag I can't use cherry chapstick anymore,' Helen laments. 'Sarah sings that stupid song all the time.'

'They all sing it,' CJ says. 'It doesn't mean they're all going to turn into lesbians.'

'And so what if they do?' I say, looking at Helen.

'How old's the boyfriend?' Virginia asks.

'Seventeen and he's just got his licence. I mean, she just doesn't get it.'

'She gets it, alright,' Helen says, putting her arm around my shoulder. 'She gets that you're a control freak.'

'Why won't you let her?' CJ asks. 'Jorja's got a group of friends and one of the older brothers has a licence. Saves me from having to take her anywhere.'

'Well, lucky Jorja. It's not safe, CJ,' I say, shaking Helen's arm off me. 'It's not safe.'

'Is it just me, or do you worry too much?' CJ asks no-one in particular.

I do not say what I think. What I think is: 'You don't worry enough. If you just got your tongue out of your lover's mouth to catch your breath and checked your daughter's Facebook page one of these days, you'd worry plenty.' And I'm not even talking about the drunken pictures.

'But that's just a distraction from the real fight about Borneo. She wants to go there for three weeks,' I say.

'Borneo's fantastic,' Virginia says.

'Why Borneo?' CJ asks.

'There's a leadership program with other kids from her school where they go into the jungle and do a community project and climb Mount Kinabalu.'

'What an incredible opportunity.' Of course Virginia would say that.

'It's six thousand kilometres away. For twenty-two days. They'll be out of contact for the entire time. They need about twenty vaccinations.'

'But she wouldn't be going off on her own, would she?' Maeve says. 'It would be an organised trip with qualified people, right?'

I nod. 'But I won't be there.'

'You can't always be there,' Helen says. 'At some point, you've got to let her go.'

Of course, she's right. It's not as if I'm trying to micromanage God. But He needs to know that I'm watching Him. Like last year, when Aaron begged us to allow him to play rugby. 'Over my dead body,' slipped out of my mouth. He was shattered. All his friends were playing. Only 'gay' kids don't play. He'd die, throw himself under a train, never forgive us and lose his passion for life if we didn't let him.

I tried to paint a picture for him of what his life would be like if he broke his neck. What *my* life would be like. The limitations it would place on his social life. I suggested soccer. Tennis. Table-tennis. Chess. But it was like telling Romeo, 'Forget Juliet—there are other fish in the sea.'

Aaron sobbed, ranted, begged. My life without him playing rugby was becoming unpleasant.

Frank commented that we might be emasculating him by refusing. I'm certain there will be ample negative feedback, accusations and pointed fingers from my children when they're old enough to report back on just how badly I fared as a mother, but one criticism I will not tolerate is that I cut my son's balls off. I let them cut his foreskin. That was for religious reasons. But I saved his balls. If my son turns out to be a wimp, spineless or have erectile dysfunction, I'm not wearing that.

So we struck a deal. Aaron could play one season of rugby on condition that there were no injuries. He agreed and was so dumbly happy I feared for his intelligence. First game—he scored most of the tries and was awarded MVP of the match. I had underestimated his ability. Where, excuse me, did he learn to play rugby in the first place? Not on my watch. The next weekend, Aaron fell off a fence playing tips. He broke his wrist and his arm was in plaster for six weeks. That was the end of his rugby career. I think I managed to keep my euphoria to myself. And only gave God the thumbs-up in private.

Allowing Jamie to go to Borneo is too far a stretch for me right now. But I'm not holding her back. I'm not.

'There are perverts and creeps everywhere,' I say.

'Oh my total god, that is so true,' Summer says. 'And in the places you're least likely to suspect.'

'They're all inside your head,' Helen guffaws.

'Oh really?' I say. 'What about that theology teacher at your kids' school?'

'Oops,' she laughs. 'Forgot about Mr Pirelli!'

'What happened?' CJ asks.

'He was head of theology studies. Recently arrested on child pornography charges, after the police busted a big ring.'

'All these bloody repressed God-botherers,' CJ mutters.

'That cliché seems to never get old,' Virginia says wearily, like a police officer who's seen it all a million times.

'But why do people never think that it will happen in, like, their actual backyard?' Summer asks. 'When you read about it all the time in the newspaper?'

'But he never touched any of the kids at the school,' Helen says.

'How do you know?' Summer asks.

'No-one's come forward.'

'Why are you defending him?' I ask.

'I'm not. I just can't stand the witch-hunt mentality. You know, he was just looking at pictures.'

'Every picture he wanked off to was of a child being sexually assaulted!' I say. I can't understand why she doesn't get this.

'Yeah, but he didn't *personally* abuse them.'

'But it's because of people like him that there's a child porn industry in the first place,' Virginia says, slapping Helen on the arm. 'Have you ever heard of supply and demand?'

Helen throws her hands up in a gesture of 'don't blame me for that'.

'People don't, like, believe children—not even their own actual mothers,' Summer says.

'That's because children lie about this stuff all the time,' CJ says. 'I've seen it so often in divorce cases—the mother gets the kid to say she's been sexually abused by the dad just to get custody or a better maintenance order.'

A bright rash of colour seeps up Summer's neck. 'But sometimes . . .'

'It's true,' CJ says to Summer. 'I've seen it too many times. Innocent men get accused and it's a really tough accusation to defend. There's always a lingering suspicion. It's a cruel way of getting back at someone. Shit, and I never even thought to try it on Tom.'

I'm sure she's joking.

Summer nods in the face of CJ's greater experience but she fingers her silver heart pendant.

'So what happened with the teacher?' Maeve asks Helen.

'Lost his job, was found guilty of possession of child porn and is serving a long jail sentence. But I'm telling you, it's a pity. He was an excellent teacher. Kids loved him.'

'What did you tell your children?' Maeve asks.

'That Mr Pirelli was very *sick* and had to go far away for *treatment* and would probably never come back. Which is kind of true.'

'Why didn't you tell them the truth?'

'You fancy explaining what pornography is to a ten-year-old?'

'They know already,' CJ says. 'They know everything these days. Liam has a stash of *Penthouse* magazines already—and it's all over the net anyway.'

'You allow that?' I am shocked.

She shrugs. 'Teenage boys are a law unto themselves. Wait till Aaron gets there. You'll fall off your high horse before I can say "beaver shot".'

'I will not allow that shit into my house.'

'You won't know,' CJ says. 'They do it behind your back.'

Summer nods. 'They, like, so do. Whatever you say, they do the opposite.'

'I've already explained to my kids what pornography is. They need to know what it is so when they come across it, it's no surprise, like smoking and drugs.'

'Too much information too early,' Helen says to me. 'Your problem is that you don't respect innocence.'

That is a lie if ever Helen's uttered one. I am a childhood conservationist, the David Attenborough of innocence. I've worked tirelessly to keep the corruptions of X-rated effluence from the ponds of my children's souls. I still carry the scars of my botched tooth-fairy-preservation attempts with Jamie. Helen's the one who blithely told her kids when they were little 'There's no such thing'.

'I bloody do respect innocence. Which is why Jamie can't get in a car with a seventeen-year-old who's just got his licence, and hang around malls and stadiums till all hours of the morning.'

'For god's sake, Jo, Jamie is fourteen,' CJ says.

'She's still thirteen.'

'Your imagination is haunted,' Helen chuckles.

'Excuse me, I didn't imagine that Jamie Bulger was abducted from a shopping centre.'

'He was two,' CJ says.

'Yeah, well, all I have to say to you is two words: Madeleine McCann. Terrible things happen out there.'

'Poor little thing,' Maeve says.

'Don't you, like, think the parents must have done it?' Summer suggests.

I know she's just trying to join the conversation, but I'm mortified by the nonchalance with which other people's unimaginable tragedies are crushed, contorted and spewed out as a throwaway comment. Gossip is so cruel. I should give it up myself one of these days.

'You've got to be kidding!' Helen gasps.

Summer looks like maybe she's changed her mind already. 'Well, it's just my opinion. The mother looks like a killer, doesn't she, CJ?'

CJ doesn't respond.

'What mother would do that?' Helen asks.

'You hear of mothers who kill their children,' Summer says. 'Sometimes, like, on purpose, and sometimes by accident. 'Cos it's always the person you least suspect, don't you think?'

'There's no proof the parents did it,' CJ says, finally reining in her friend with legal logic.

'Assumptions are tricky,' Maeve intervenes. 'It seems pointless to speculate, don't you agree? Given that they've never found her.'

'I don't understand why they left their kids alone in the first place,' Virginia says. 'I mean, is that normal? I don't know, not having kids of my own, but it did strike me as strange.'

'We've all left our kids alone when we technically shouldn't have,' Helen confesses.

'I wouldn't have left my kids alone,' I say. 'Not at that age.'

'Because you're neurotic,' Helen says.

'You don't think maybe the McCanns wish they'd been a bit neurotic now?'

'You don't seriously blame the parents?' CJ asks.

'I'm not blaming anyone. All I'm saying is that I'd never find myself in their situation, because I'd never leave a sleeping child alone in a hotel room. I just wouldn't. Not at that age—maybe I would now.'

'Weren't they just tragically unlucky?' Maeve asks. 'I mean, what about Jessica Watson? Her parents actually supported her ambition to sail around the world on her own at seventeen.'

'Oh, how cool is she?' Summer enthuses.

'I'd never let Jamie do that.'

'Even if it was her dream?' Maeve asks.

'There are other dreams. That's dangerous.'

'Do you think Jessica Watson's parents were irresponsible?' Maeve pushes.

I shift in my chair. The truth is, of course I do. They were just lucky their daughter came home safe. If that story didn't have a happy ending, her parents would have been as maligned as the McCanns. 'Why take a chance with your child's life?' I ask.

'The minute you fall pregnant, you're taking a chance with your child's life,' Helen says. 'But you can't watch over them every second. You've got to give them some independence.'

I shrug. I have to admit Helen's kids are all tough and independent. She's allowed them to cook at the hot stovetop, chop vegetables with sharp knives, ride their bikes in the street and walk the neighbourhood on their own since they were little with nothing more than a 'Be careful' to guide them.

A few years back, when Nathan was nine, he asked if he and Aaron, who was seven, could walk to the shops to get an ice-cream. 'Stay together and only cross when the little green man is flashing,' Helen said, and carried on rolling meatballs for dinner.

I'd grabbed the boys by the wrists, and urged in a low tone, 'Walk straight to the shops. Keep on the footpath. If a car pulls up, run to the nearest house, ring the doorbell and ask if you can use the phone. Do not get into anyone's car. Do not speak to anyone other than each other. Return immediately by the same route. If you are not back in fifteen minutes I will call the police. Do you understand?'

As the two boys ran off into the afternoon, I realised that there was no way for me to shake a drop of adult anxiety about real dangers into the snow dome of Aaron's innocence without shattering it completely. Our children unknowingly have one foot in the world of Jeffrey Dahmers, Josef Fritzls and Anders Breiviks and one in the magic kingdom where no-one dies, is ever tortured, raped or starved to death. To them 'stranger-danger' is nothing more than a rhyme and evil nothing more than a bad guy the hero will always defeat.

Maybe I lack a certain capacity for robustness—or perhaps faith—for the 'letting go' part of being a parent. It's a weakness, a condition. Like some people have diabetes or a slipped disc in their back.

I glance down at my phone again. Being a parent is not a popularity contest and being despised is simply part of the job.

And just for a moment I wonder, *What is Jamie's dream?* and whether she'd even bother telling me if she knew.

It's not like I'm not paying attention. I know her shoe size, her bra size, her menstrual calendar. I know she loves mangoes and sushi maki rolls with tuna and cucumber. I know her favourite cake is cheesecake.

On the counter is Ereka's cake. The one with the ginger and lemon myrtle something or other and twenty trillion calories.

I look at it.

'Hey, why don't we all take the cake and go up to Ereka's room?'

'Perhaps she needs a little more time,' Maeve says.

'Cake is probably the last thing she feels like after you called her a fat pig,' CJ says.

'I did not.'

The Reunion

'Or was it a mountainous walrus?' Helen pipes up.

'No, a humungous hippo,' says Virginia, and giggles.

'Why don't you all gang up on me?' I say.

'Leave it to me,' Summer says. 'I'll get Ereka down.' And with that she skips off. Do breast enlargements inflate your sense of omnipotence? What does she think she has that I don't?

10

A Man's Look

Who knows exactly what Summer is planning behind closed doors? While she's upstairs trying to lure Ereka down, we all gather in the lounge room to sip on the dessert wine Helen has opened. Virginia paces up and down with her iPhone, running her fingers through her hair, until I can bear it no longer and offer her mine. She declines. Instead she puts her phone away and joins the rest of us with what looks like a triple shot of whisky. Maeve is telling Helen about the Abayudaya, a tribe of Jews in Uganda, and how the husbands don't have sex with their wives while they're menstruating, while the dog falls asleep with his scruffy jaw on her knee.

So believe me when I say I am more than delighted when Summer comes down with her arm threaded through Ereka's. Ereka has a glazed look in her eyes I have no doubt is chemically induced.

'I've taught Ereka the first basic Zumba move. Let's show them.' Then the two of them raise their arms above their heads, take two steps to the right and then two to the left, and then shake their pelvises, before Ereka collapses into a self-conscious giggle, jangling like an Indian carnival.

'You are, like, such a freaking natural,' Summer whoops, high-fiving Ereka.

Maeve then suggests a game of Scrabble. She's just happened to bring her set along with her. All eyes turn to Ereka, who says, 'Great idea, I love Scrabble.' I guess Maeve is not to know that, with the exception of Cluedo, I detest all board games. I'm just grateful it isn't that pernicious, endless, opportunistic, avaricious game of them all—Monopoly. My kids, of course, adore it. Especially the *Simpsons* version with the credit cards. To get out of playing with them, I usually develop a crippling migraine, a broken back or contagious meningitis. When I'm forced into a game, I do my best to lose all my money as quickly as possible, refusing all hand-outs from my kids who will, heartbreakingly, part with their own fortunes to keep me in the game. Naturally, cheating or feigning an inability to remember the rules is the easiest way to get them to kick you out, because, as Aaron says, 'No-one likes a cheater.'

Tonight, feeling guilty as I am, I can't refuse. So I play. Pathetically. Even Summer beats me, getting lucky early with a Q and a U which she adds to an IT. At which Helen—who by this stage has had plenty to drink—shrieks, 'You took my spot!' holding up her C and L.

It is all downhill after that. CJ's TITS is followed by Virginia's SUCK, Ereka's TESTES and Maeve's remarkable addition of ATIO she manages to append to my FELL.

Helen keeps refilling our shot glasses with sweet wine, and when that's finished, Baileys. I drink down, I don't know—four, maybe five glasses, making sure Maeve keeps up. Finally, when

I'm trailing Summer by at least thirty points, I stretch and announce that I'm buggered and I'm going to bed. Maeve says she'll join me as she's starting to see double and together we make our way up the staircase.

Doonas must've been invented by some housewife sick of hospital corners. I kick at the tightly tucked sheets. I'm cross with them in a way I should not be—tightly made beds ought to have no influence over me. Lying flat now, I'm too weary to even think about how many calories I've consumed in the past few hours out of guilt, remorse and spinelessness. I take my phone out of my bag. There's no signal up here. Anyway, I've had too much to drink to come up with anything that isn't small-minded and hurtful.

Maeve opens her suitcase, which has been neatly packed with consideration for the fact that the clean clothes might like a separate compartment from the dirty. Underwear merits its very own special mesh bag. My bag in the corner is a trash heap of fresh fraternising with the filthy, knickers partying with jumpers. I feel castigated by her precision, as if it, simply by contrast, says something about me. That I am careless. When, really, I am fastidious in all the ways that count. Mistakes here and there. We all make them.

Maeve removes her chiffony shirt and lays it across her basket. She stands with her back to me as she leans forward and unclips her bra. There is a scar just under her scapula and I will not ask whether it is surgical or accidental. She would, I imagine, rather I wasn't engaged in a silent commentary to myself about her body. She whips out a white cotton sleep shirt, pulling it over her head. Neat and functional. It falls to below her knees. She likes things large. I wonder if Stan is a big man. And then I remind myself it is none of my business. From her vanity bag, she removes a handful of tablet cards, and pushes through their foil coverings before leaving the room to do her private business in the strawberry bathroom. And I will not do anything as invasive as check the boxes to see what pills she needs. They could be vitamins, supplements, that sort of thing.

But mine and Maeve's relationship will never be the same again after tonight. I've seen her in her bra. I've seen the scar on her back. I've witnessed the small tasks of self-preservation she executes when she's alone. These rituals of cleanliness and habit we perform in the sanctuary of retreat expose us. Something of the mystery of our connection has gone. I wonder if I am losing her.

She returns to the room, fiddles with her things and takes out a small velvet bag. She looks as if she wants to say something, bring me into a confidence. She puts her suitcase on the floor and then says, 'Would it disturb you, terribly if . . . it just glows a little.'

She removes a night-light from the velvet bag.

'No, not at all,' I say. *A night-light?*

'Just say the word if it does and I'll switch it off.'

She arranges it next to her bed and slips under the covers.

'It just takes the edge off the darkness.'

We lie there with our bedside lights casting half-circles on the wall for a while.

'Are you still dwelling on what happened at dinner?'

'I should've just kept my mouth shut.'

'Because she has a disabled child?'

I nod.

Maeve's silence suggests she thinks I am wrong. Or perhaps I am not thinking cleverly enough about it. But I don't know what hurdles Ereka has to cross to get to bedtime. 'My experience of being a mother is so different from hers.'

'But you're more than a mother, surely? So is she.'

Of course *I* am. 'I don't know if Ereka has a life beyond her kids. Everything revolves around Olivia. She'll probably never get to travel to Africa and learn about hippo tusks.' I don't mean to sound critical.

'But it's just a socially constructed role—motherhood. When it feels tight, it's probably squashing the life out of us. Like those wretched ugly sisters trying to squeeze their feet into the glass slipper. I've always been convinced Cinderella must have been a midget.'

That is so un-PC. Maeve herself isn't far off a midget. A sort of biggish Susan Boyle-ish one. I lie there thinking of shoes and feet.

'Is that how it felt being Jonah's mum?'

'At times, certainly. We single mothers are considered mothering low-life—the high-school drop-outs, the failed marriages, the women-left-by-husbands-for-younger-women, the out-of-wedlock pregnancies . . . So I just didn't buy into the role. Out of self-preservation. And I enlisted help, I didn't attempt to do it all on my own.'

'From your mum?'

She pauses. 'Unfortunately, she died in a car accident when I was fifteen.'

'Oh shit, I'm sorry, Maeve.'

'It was a long time ago.'

'How did you cope?'

Maeve sighs out a long breath. 'Not heroically, I'm afraid. The world fell apart.' She stretches both her arms up to the ceiling, wriggling her fingers.

'Your dad manage okay?'

Maeve yawns. 'Not really.'

I lie there, waiting. It suddenly feels like hovering.

'Sorry, we don't have to talk about it,' I say. I turn and switch off my bedside light. 'Night.'

Maeve switches her light off too. Her night-light bathes the room in tender luminosity. Somewhere in the house the dog barks. The room settles around us. Its creaks subside. Its corners soften. When Maeve speaks again, her voice sounds like it's coming from far away.

'It was a Thursday in October. The final episode of *Rich Man, Poor Man* was scheduled to show on TV. Remember how spectacularly attractive Nick Nolte was in those days? I had posters of him all over my room. My mother, my sister Solange and I would convene on the couch, Mum in the middle peeling oranges. But that afternoon, when we got home from school, our father met us at the front door and told us there'd been an accident. My first thought was: "Can we still watch *Rich Man, Poor Man*?"' Maeve laughs softly. 'Can you believe it? Children are unconscionably in the moment like that. They can only imbibe tragedy in small bits. They need some ordinariness to keep going.'

I don't say anything but, believe me, I am listening, my eyes wide open in the half-dark.

'He collapsed soon after that. He went away for a while, packed me and Solange off to stay with my mother's sister— Aunty Lily with the ghastly goitre in her neck. I always feared she'd pop from that goitre. Like someone was blowing her up like a balloon from the inside and wouldn't know when to stop.'

I imagine suitcases. Lawyers. Two young girls, holding hands. The ugly aunt with a kind heart. 'God, you must have missed your mum.'

'Solange took it worse, being two years younger. I was, frankly, livid. I couldn't believe our mother had abandoned us with such abrupt finality. I wasn't finished having a mother— she'd promised to teach me how to drive and how to sew . . .' Maeve's voice is moist with tonight's excess alcohol. Something has loosened in her. It feels like I'm eavesdropping on a private conversation.

'Beyond the age of fifteen, I haven't the foggiest notion what it's like to have a mother.'

I feel off-centre. Knowing something she doesn't. I turn to face her in the glow of the night-light. 'That's so hard. My mother . . . knowing she's there, even now . . . it holds me steady. My mother is what I understand by the word "home".'

She is quiet. Taking my word for it.

I remember when Jamie was born the surprise of opening into a renewed love, not only for my daughter but for my mother. It was an unexpected homecoming. As I embraced my baby, we were encircled in a wider arc of something bigger, as a tributary enters the ocean and is swallowed whole. Her birth was an evocation, a reverberation, the contractions resonated, looping us into a collective unconscious of origination. In birthing, I repeated a pattern, the design of my own genesis, I was affirming the mother–child bond. *I am making as I was made.*

'I think I only fully loved my mother when I had Jamie . . .' I stall. Maeve had Jonah long after her mum died. Grossly insensitive. Again. 'Sorry, I don't mean for that to sound . . .'

'Don't apologise. It's rather helpful to hear.'

Drowsiness hovers, but I push sleep away. When Maeve speaks again, her voice has deepened.

'Our father came back after a few months, but he was barely recognisable. It wasn't just the beard on a face I'd only ever known clean-shaven. It had something to do with his stride. It seemed to have shortened. People describe soldiers returning from a war as broken. But that wasn't accurate. It was an immobility. As if his senses were shutting down, one after the other. Nothing moved in him. Nothing moved him. Perhaps that accounts for my antipathy to meditation.'

'Is he still alive?'

'He passed away five years ago. After a decade of Alzheimer's.'

'How ghastly.'

'Actually, the Alzheimer's was a gift. Curiously, he seemed relieved. Not to have to remember.'

'Shit. Thank god for sisters, then.'

'Ah, yes . . .' She gives a small sputter of laughter. 'I suppose it might be amusing if it weren't so tragic . . .'

'What do you mean?'

'Well.' She clears her throat. 'Solange and I were pretty much joined at the hip after our mother's death.'

I don't like that 'were' in her sentence. It flashes like an ambulance light.

Maeve pauses. 'I do need you to give me your undertaking that you won't treat me differently . . .'

'Okay,' I say, making a promise I have no idea if I can keep.

'Massimo and I married when I was twenty-four, which makes Solange twenty-two when she fell pregnant after an impulsive and rather unglamorous one-night stand with a married man. But she was gladder than I'd ever seen her since our mother's death. It was the first birth I'd ever attended. And what sweetness her baby boy brought to our lives after all that loss. But then, when he was eighteen months old . . .'

I am holding my breath.

'Silly goose—she had a cerebral aneurism.'

The sentence crashes like a fallen chandelier.

'Caused by a weakness in the wall of the cerebral artery. Not detectable. Nothing one can predict nor take preventative measures against. Sort of a time-bomb inside the skull. We usually spoke twice a day, she'd call me before she left for work, and I'd call her at night before bed. As fate planned it, Massimo and I were trekking in Nepal for exactly ten days and we hadn't had any contact for over a week. By the time she was found, by neighbours who heard a baby crying, Jonah was starving, dehydrated, soiled with faeces and urine. Severely traumatised. Barely alive.'

I realise I've covered my mouth with my hand. Soap opera stuff, this, really.

'I wasn't intending on becoming a mother so young, perhaps even not at all, but we adopted Jonah. Well, I did . . . Massimo didn't last long after that. He wanted "his own" family. And it seemed only fair to let him go. He remarried and has three charming girls.'

My heart does an alley-oop in my chest. This is a lot of story for one person. Here is a mountain of intimacy I didn't count on summiting. 'I didn't realise Jonah wasn't yours.'

'He is mine. I just didn't carry him for nine months.'

'How come you've never told me any of this?'

'It never came up, did it? Besides, I don't define who I am by what I've lost. And pity is an emotion I cannot abide in a friendship.'

Have I not been paying attention? Have I been doing a man's look the way Frank does when he can 'never find anything in the fridge', even when what he's looking for is right in front of him? I imagined I was a good friend.

I look over at Maeve, shiny in her hydrating night creams. Pieces fall into place with a clatter. Her professionalism, her immaculate clothes, her arm's-length life where Stan 'visits' and then leaves, so she doesn't have to love anyone enough to lose them. I'm not a psychologist, I'm just painting a picture here. How can we ever really know another person? It's not like I even know everything about my own children. I used to. Every bump and blemish, every hair tangle, every word they knew to utter. But they're bending away from me as they lean into themselves. I'm not quite in the dark. But the light is dwindling.

'Is there anything else I need to know?' I am a little afraid of my own questions.

'That just about covers it. One always hopes one's exhausted one's tragedy quota for this life.'

It would be the right thing to reach out and put my hand on Maeve's arm. But, for one thing, there is too much space between our beds. And despite the exposé of the canyon of her deepest wound, there is no access there. It is not a tourist attraction.

'Don't indulge in feeling sorry for me,' she warns.

Right-o. Of course, if it were me, I'd be issuing invitations to a Big Pity Party for Poor Me. But that's me. Maeve is in the acceptance phase of her life. She's probably been through anger, denial and all the rest. But, okay, I get it. *That's* how you become whole. Self-contained. Maeve doesn't feel sorry for herself, and she doesn't feel sorry for anyone else. She's tired, just from the telling. But beyond the fatigue in her story, she's saying that even when things are not chosen, there are ways to make them alright.

I turn on my side so my back is to Maeve. I remember Nick Nolte in *Rich Man, Poor Man*. He was a man-boy—like Callum is now, like Aaron will be someday. When I saw him years later in *Prince of Tides*, he'd turned into an overweight middle-aged actor. I remember feeling cheated.

'So did you watch it? The final episode of *Rich Man, Poor Man*?'

'I did. Tom dies, remember? He gets fatally stabbed.'

'But before he dies, he reconciles with his brother Rudy. Not quite a happy ending, but, you know, better than nothing . . .'

Maeve is quiet for a long while. 'Solange lay alone in our room sobbing about our mother while I sat in the lounge room sobbing about Tom Jordache.'

I wait. I know there is more.

'It scared me. To know I was that kind of person.'

'You were just a kid, Maeve.'

She doesn't answer. I stare into the half-darkness in front of me.

A while back, Frank and I took the kids to the Jenolan Caves, underground cathedrals of crystal which might have gone undiscovered had it not been for the Whalan brothers searching for a fugitive. As we walked through the bejewelled belly of the rock, so far from sunlight, oxygen and wind, I knew, in that oddly terrifying beauty, that some places are not meant to be unearthed. Secrets have their place. They hold things together. Dislodge them, and you can collapse a dynasty.

'What do you think is in that locked room?' I whisper.

'Without a key, we'll probably never know.'

I am rolling, gliding into sleep. I hear the sound of Maeve's breathing. I imagine she is asleep, when I hear—maybe I imagine it—'Virginia should go be with her mother.'

11

Everyone is Unfaithful

Maeve's covers are pulled up neat and tidy like a first-day-of-school tie. I sweep the blankets off me slowly, my body aching as if someone has filled my elbows and knees with sand while I slept on and off. Through the night, the house kept waking me with creaks and groans, like Frank will do someday no doubt. I stared at Maeve's night-light from three am for what seemed like endless hours, but I must have dozed off again because it's disappeared, like a nocturnal animal come dawn.

At the window, there is mist as far as the eye can see, as if Blind Rise Ridge has been swallowed by a cloud. In the pink bathroom I stand in a wet patch in one of my bedsocks, making 'Fuck' the first word I utter this morning, though really, I do have to up my game today. *No insults. Be nice.* In the tub I find what look like small jewels—three blue and silver ones—which can only come from somewhere on Summer, though don't ask me to guess where. The detachable brass showerhead spits water at me. It's essentially an ablution insult but I don't want to get into an argument with the amenities. I'm about to mascara my eyelashes with Lashalicious. *Who're you doing it for?* Fuck Helen and CJ, really. I close the mascara. Frank would be proud, though really this cannot count as a major personal achievement. He doesn't understand makeup. 'It makes me want to take a facecloth and clean you up,' he says. He gets horny watching women's soccer. To him, sweat's the only enhancement to a woman's natural features.

I slide into my jeans and my snug new sporty bamboo sweatshirt with mesh over the shoulders and two side pockets, zipping my iPhone into the top one. Unlike maternity wear, which 'grows with you', this apparel is strictly designed to constrict your breathing in the event of any expansion. I can't find my new trainers but then I remember I left them downstairs at the French doors when we all took off our shoes playing Scrabble last night.

I put my ear to Ereka's door, checking on nothing in particular. Then I walk down the hall and try the doorknob of the locked room. You never know. At last I descend the stairs in my socks. Halfway, I slow down to raise my arm and give a royal wave, nodding at the adoring crowd. '*Yes, thank you, I'll be signing copies of* She Made it to Tuscany *after the photoshoot . . .*' At the bottom, through the archway into the lounge room, I catch a glimpse of myself in the mirror. My god, is that me? After my morning caffeine and, Frank's preferences aside, a dash of Revlon, I'm always hopeful some loveliness will be resuscitated. But one should never take it for granted.

I hear barking behind the closed kitchen door. That Sumo dog shuffles out towards me and jumps up against my jeans. 'Get off,' I chide, pushing it away. Its tail is a blur of wags.

'I don't know what you're so happy about,' I scold, making my way over to the kettle. 'Gatecrasher.'

There is, let me say right up front, a nasty smell in the kitchen. A new one. A dog turd on the floor. 'Just perfect.' I step around it.

With the kettle on the boil, I call, 'Come on,' leading it out of the kitchen to the living room. It stands wagging its ridiculous tail at the French doors which are ajar but not wide enough for it to squeeze through. Maeve must have gone for an early-morning fog trek. I scan the room for my trainers. Someone's moved them.

As I push the doors open, the dog runs outside into the mist like a chubby child after the school bell has rung.

I don't care, truly. But what if it runs off into the forest and can't find its way back? Or Matilda mistakes it for a hefty rat? I follow it outside and call, 'Hey, come back.' It's nowhere to be seen. Jesus.

My trainers are not on the veranda. I yank off my socks and pad down the path barefoot towards the dam, calling, 'Hey you, come back.' The mist blinds me. The dog comes plodding back through the haze with a pine cone in its mouth, which it drops at my feet.

'No thanks, I'm not playing. I've seen how these things go and you guys just don't know when enough is enough.'

The dog drops down low on its front paws—the kind of thing you might think was cute if you liked dogs.

I kick the pine cone away with my bare foot, and the dog is gulped whole by the fog. What's its name again? Tennyson. So that's what happens to poets after they die—people name their dogs after you. *The Lady of Shalott*—what a masterpiece. Poor woman, weaving her magic web from her mirror in her tower. Not much of a pick-me-up, but I suppose the Romantics weren't aiming for self-help. I wait. He trudges back with the pine cone in his mouth and drops it at my feet.

'You need to leave me alone now.'

Tennyson growls at the pine cone, nudging it towards me.

'Just do your business and then come back inside. Don't do anything stupid.'

Tennyson follows me back towards the house with the pine cone in its mouth as if I'm its best friend or something, reminding me of Jonathan Horris, whom I tried to break up with kindly and ended up crushing. But that's dogs and men for you—they think you're playing hard to get when you say no.

Back in the kitchen I circumvent the dog turd. I make a pot of coffee, find a tray, some mugs and the skim milk.

Tennyson watches me.

'Got no idea what's for breakfast. You'll have to wait for Virginia.'

I do a cursory rummage through the contents of the basket I saw Virginia carry in last night. There's a packet of flour and yeast. No dog food. I guess she must have left in a hurry.

In the fridge is leftover pizza, yoghurt, tiramisu, cream, butter and my vegetables. I'm trying to be helpful here but I'm quite sure there's nothing that the dog can eat. Helen's dog Bones recently devoured a full bar of Lindt chocolate that had been left on the kitchen counter and had to have its stomach pumped. The vet warned Helen that 'dogs can *die* from eating chocolate', which is surely a euphemism for 'feel a little nauseous', as anyone might do after a Lindt binge. I've known dogs to survive eating detergents, lizards, spiders, their own vomit, other dogs' vomit, so a little too much sugar . . . I mean, really.

An artichoke peeks out of the cling wrap on the leftover pizza, soliciting. I pull it off and put the artichoke in my mouth. Tennyson wags his tail. 'Not for you,' I say. I peel back the cling wrap a teensy bit more. One slice. That's all. I seal the rest up tightly and close the fridge. I haven't had pizza in five years. Especially cold pizza. Travis always had warm hands. He'd start in the small of my back and wrap them around my front, cupping my breasts. He'd lift my hair and sort of suck my neck as I fed him cold pizza over my shoulder after hours of lovemaking. Pepperoni supreme. Mexicana with chilli. Hawaiian with jalapeños. A pizza menu is my porn.

Tennyson's thumping tail on the wooden floor brings me back to the present. He's looking at me so plaintively, I can't bear it.

'Okay, okay,' I say. Can't I even have a weekend of reprieve from personal sacrifice? I open my precious tin of tuna in spring water, the only buffer between me and a million-calorie lunch. I watch Tennyson finish the whole lot. If you do lunges at the same time as you eat cold pizza, you can probably work off the calories as you're taking them in. He slurps up the spring water too. I swear, he thinks it's Christmas.

'Now that is the last thing I am doing for you, you understand?' I lick my fingers.

That dog turd again. Suddenly I think of Maeve, whose sister, *silly goose*, had a cerebral aneurism and dropped dead. Maybe she was making a cup of coffee, just like this. Or thinking about what she needed from the supermarket or if it was time to renew her parking permit. Maeve took that soiled and hungry baby into her arms like he was hers. She cleaned him and fed him and loved him. I bend down and pat Tennyson. His owner is dying.

'You do know your future is fucked?'

He wags his tail.

Maybe he will never know this in the way that humans know these things and grieve for what is irretrievable.

'And I wouldn't rely on Virginia. She's just not that into you, buddy.'

He pants, which is probably how dogs sigh.

I'm not saying I'm a good person. But I grab some paper towel and pick that dog turd up, choking back my gag reflex. I run to the toilet under the stairs, throw it in and pull the chain.

I don't hear her come into the kitchen. As a result, I spill my coffee on my brand-new jumper when I turn around and there is Ereka.

'Enough for another cup?'

'Please, have mine.' I hand her my coffee, privately mortified about the stain on my jumper and hoping I don't smell of pizza.

'Don't be silly, I'll make some more. Here, wipe that.' She gives me a tea towel. I take it from her and dab at the stain.

'Did you get some sleep?' I ask.

'A bit. Summer kept me up till very late. She's quite incredible.'

I can tell Ereka is not being ironic.

'There I was, sipping on my rescue remedy, when Summer gave me some ecstasy,' Ereka whispers. 'My god, it was awesome!'

I avoid approving of such things, but from the look on Ereka's face ecstasy is just what she needed.

'Jesus, Ereka, I'm so sorry about last night.' I watch as she fiddles with the Bodum.

'You gave me a lot to think about,' she says.

'Yeah, but still . . .'

'If my friends can't say what I need to hear, then who will?'

'Why don't you go sit on the veranda and I'll bring you a coffee?' I say.

'Don't mollycoddle me.'

'I think some mollycoddling is in order after I clubbed you like a baby seal last night.'

She puts her hands on her hips in exaggerated exasperation. But she lets me.

I cut them just in case—two huge slices of her ginger cake. When I arrive with a tray bearing the cake and coffee Ereka is swinging back and forth in the suspended wicker chair. Tennyson is lying in a patch of sun, his head on his paws.

She takes her coffee but does the stop sign at the cake. 'No thanks. See? You taught me how to say no.'

Ereka studies me as I break a piece off with the side of my fork.

'You don't have to do that, you know.'

'I know . . . but sometimes saying no is overrated.'

I am being sincere. I'm sure I am. It can be hard to tell. I can't tell whether Ereka likes me. Whether I am likeable. Whether she will let me mop up the mess I made last night.

Ereka sips her coffee and watches the mist peeling itself off the landscape like lifting a bridal veil. *Goodness me, is that really you under there?*

When she turns to face me something has unsettled in her eyes.

'Tell me, Jo, do you and Frank . . . are you . . . is there still *passion*?' she asks, the word almost a wish.

Do I know where she is going with this? I would be lying if I said I did. But I need to be as generous as I can with her after last night.

It's just that I don't know how to answer her neatly, conversationally. In the six years since I last really hung out with Ereka, Frank and I have been through several incarnations in which passion, like an itinerant passenger, has come and gone. There was that patch of two years where I dreaded him coming to bed and having to make yet another excuse about why I didn't feel like sex—again. I watched how my rejection took its toll on him. How he went from angry to sad to uninterested. He even stopped waking up with erections. And that scared me. Frank without his morning glory was like Frank without his zany humour, his cat-hair-induced hay fever, the deformed butterfly birthmark on his shoulder. I felt like a serial hard-on killer, really. Without my desire to mirror his own, to offer it a homecoming, his just perished in lonely exile. That's what pining is. I wasn't prepared for how much I missed his sexual overtures. Even all the ones I rejected.

I tried to be interested. I wanted to be interested. But I just didn't feel 'it' anymore. And when I did, I had a quiet quickie on my own. I knew that would upset him more than anything. That I'd 'wasted' an orgasm on myself. But I've never seen it that way. When I lived alone, I could merrily spend hours preparing a complicated Thai meal with ingredients I'd have to pre-order at the deli just for myself. This bewildered Frank in much the way he is puzzled when I buy myself flowers. (If I don't, Frank, who will?) When he lived alone he considered opening a can of baked beans 'going to trouble'. When you do kind things for yourself, you never feel taken for granted.

Frank, let me say, considers masturbation a concession of personal failure. For him, it's as tragic as being homeless or friendless. It's for losers and people who can't 'get any'. I can only guess it reminds him of being a pimply teenager when there were no other options for relief. Whatever his feelings about self-gratification, I don't share them. To my mind, masturbation is like a drive-thru—speedier and more convenient. It has an unequalled efficiency because the person doing the pleasuring knows exactly how to please the person being pleasured. Second, there's no risk of falling asleep mid-action, which is a danger when one is very tired and the other person is taking too long. Finally—and this really clinches the case for masturbation—you don't have to beat yourself up that you've let anyone down or, God forbid, are no longer turned on by the other person if an orgasm happens to slip through your fingers just when you thought you'd nailed it. And you never ever have to fake it—not that I ever have with Frank, but I'm just saying.

During this quiet season between me and Frank, there was that little flirt on Facebook with an ex-boyfriend who privately messaged me: *You still have 'it'*. And just knowing another man desired me made me want Frank again. The mind's a floozy that way, it really is. Frank asked no questions. I think he was just grateful I still had a working vagina. He then got a bee in his bonnet about a vasectomy, after which we took to sex like newlyweds again. The sensation of a naked penis after eight years of condoms was, come to think of it, like cold pizza after months of celery and cottage cheese.

But then the fibroids grew, squashing my insides. I became like overstuffed luggage that might burst if anything else tried to squeeze itself in there. My libido faded again. And thus began a new dry season. Poor Frank. He took to late-night television and Scrabble on Aaron's DS.

But after my fibroids came out, I took a vow: I'd work at our sex life. I read books. I made notes. I drove myself to Oxford Street and slipped into the Tool Shed, where I spent an hour in the company of Fred, who apart from being old enough to be my grandfather made rather useful recommendations about outfits and equipment which I put on Frank's credit card as an 'investment in our relationship'. I'm open to suggestions, no-one can say I'm not. The books advocated role-playing. I suggested to Frank that he just shag me like a cheap prostitute—or a more expensive one, if he preferred. I thought he might find this confronting, but it came to him like second nature. All I'm saying is that we had some pretty explosive encounters.

But once, when I offered to do the dominating, he replied, 'No, it's my turn. I want to dominate you.'

'Why don't you want me to dominate you?'

'Because you dominate me all the time.'

'Shut up. I don't.'

So that was funny. We didn't end up having sex, but we snuggled up in bed and read our books together, which you know, at our age, is a pretty underrated way to spend an evening.

History suggests we're slap-bang in the fat years. But that lean years will follow as sure as winter shadows autumn.

I haven't forgotten Ereka's question. 'It comes and goes . . . passion's unstable. But just because it's gone, that doesn't mean it's not coming back. You've got to leave the door open for it.'

She stretches her legs out on a chair. Her skin is prickled pink from where she's recently had a wax.

'Summer says everyone is unfaithful—if you don't actually have a physical affair, you have emotional affairs.'

Summer says.

She's trying to tell me something but I can't be pushy. Like a cop doing an interrogation, she's the one asking the questions here.

Ereka twirls a strand of her hair. I've never seen her do that before. It's the kind of thing a woman would do if she thought she was being observed—lusted after, I suppose.

'Perhaps Summer's not the best judge, given her track record.'

Ereka's face folds into a frown. 'Don't judge her.'

'I'm not,' I fib. 'She's right—humans are not wired for monogamy. It's a convention, not an instinct. We all consider cheating, don't we? Actually doing it is what separates the faithful from the unfaithful.'

I'm supposed to be eating this cake, that's why I brought it here. I take an amend-making bite and stifle a groan. I want to lick the plate, suck the nipples of this ginger honey cake and shag the hell out of whoever baked it. I remember once when Jamie was small and I baked her a cheesecake. She grabbed my hand and sighed. 'I love you more than cheesecake, Mum. But only a teeny bit more.'

Ereka clears her throat.

'I've been . . . I think I've cheated on Jake.'

I swallow carefully. She's confessed and I've sinned. I give Ereka what I hope is a loving and therapeutic look. One that says it's okay for her to go on. People need to know that it's okay to continue. I nod slowly as I fork another compensatory wedge of cake into my mouth.

'He's the dad of Olivia's friend—the one with Down's.'

'Have you slept with him?' There are cloves nestling deep in this dark moist cake.

Ereka shakes her head. 'We've kissed.'

I am being kissed by sweet plum. All the way down.

'I don't know how to say no. It's not just food. Grant's marriage is falling apart; his wife has never come to terms with Todd and she's seriously depressed. Been in and out of institutions. He and I spent a lot of time together at school on the parent committee . . .'

These things want to be said. They leap from her mouth.

'Okay, so it was a one-off,' I say, wiping my finger across the plate. The lemon myrtle crème fraîche is laced with another flavour too, but I can't pick it.

'Actually, we've done it a few times. I've even let him . . .' She lowers her head. '. . . touch my breasts.'

Tennyson, as if disgusted by our disclosures, gets up, shakes himself off and trundles down the veranda stairs towards the dam.

'Does Jake know?' The husband. Yes. I wonder how he feels about all this.

'God, no. He'd be shattered.'

'Would he?'

'Of course he would. He'd never do this to me.'

'You sure?'

'We're talking about Jake, remember?' She seems a little annoyed that I've forgotten Jake is the man he is—the one we all agreed we'd love to clone for our single girlfriends for Valentine's Day. I do remember now. That no-one would hurt Jake on purpose. Unless it was a matter of life and death.

'But if I'm honest—' and for a moment, I detect something in her soar, a hot-air balloon freed from its sandbags '—it was the highlight of the last five or six years of my life. I feel so . . . naughty . . . so selfish . . . so utterly alive!' She is radiant. I can't not be glad for her. 'It slapped my joy back into me. And look at me—how much male attention am I ever going to get? It was a gift from the gods. A gift . . .'

I smile.

'He's a singer. He writes songs.' She cups each word like fine china. 'It's clean and light between us. It opens something in me I thought was caved in. Jake and I don't have that purity anymore. It's all been tainted. But, Jo, I don't want to end up like Liz. I don't want my marriage to end because of an affair. I love Jake. I love him like rain, I love him like sorrow. We are storied together forever. We still have a lot to get through and I can't do it on my own. I need him. But I've also needed this.'

She is talking in lyrics.

'Well, then you must do it—go with it, see where it takes you.' I get a small rush just saying those words, as if I'm the one kissing strangers. At this moment, I am having an affair with the cake.

She narrows her eyes at me. 'Shouldn't I have just said no? Like you said last night? Isn't it about willpower?'

That pizza incident, mark my words, is going to follow me to my grave. 'You need energy for willpower. And all yours is taken up with Olivia.'

'Why are you making excuses for me?' She is getting weirdly indignant.

If a disabled child doesn't come with a licence to cheat, what does? 'I don't know—we all do what we have to do to survive. Stop seeing Grant if it's not good for you. But whatever you do, forgive yourself.'

'Forgiveness is just a licence to repeat your mistakes.'

'It's also a radical act of self-love.' I read that somewhere. Honestly, I can't take credit for it.

She snorts as if I've just suggested she get herself a facial tattoo.

'Do you want to be my friend?' Her eyes are ice-pick sober. It's not a Facebook request.

'I do, Ereka.'

'Then tell me what I need to hear.'

Why she thinks I have the answer is unclear to me. As if I've made such a success of my life. She should hear Jamie have a go at me. I fumble as much as anyone else, really I do. Even if I did manage to lose sixteen kilos. And right now, I can't understand why anyone would say no to this cake. You'd have to be dead not to want it. I wonder if Grant lifts her hair and sucks on her neck, biting her earlobe gently. Husbands never do that.

I grab hold of her hand. I squeeze it. I look around me for inspiration. Empty birdcage. Coloured bottles playing hide and seek with the morning sun. I could do with a line from a poem. Where is Maeve when you need her? Somewhere in my mouth, I taste the throb of ginger rubbing itself up against Manuka honey. In the distance, Tennyson barks.

For ere she reach'd upon the tide
The first house by the water-side,

The Reunion

Singing in her song she died,
The Lady of Shalott.

Some things, once in you, are never lost. Forgetting isn't the same as losing.

I gaze at Ereka. Something in her has fallen. I can see the space left behind. There's a small scab in the fold of her elbow. A spot she has scratched unawares, that has bled unnoticed. I witness the fine hairs above her lip. A faint red capillary in her left nostril. The vein above her eye, pulsing. The weight of her leaf-shaped earring, pulling the lobe.

'Remember holding Olivia for the first time?'

She nods sadly.

'Remember how we looked at our babies in our arms? How we had to attend to them with a vigilance we never knew we had in us? An attention that had lain dormant inside us until we were needed in that way?'

'I remember,' she whispers.

'Give yourself *that* attention.'

Ereka's hand goes slack in mine. She drops her head.

'You need you. You need yourself.'

'When?' she barely says. 'I don't have the time . . .'

'Make time, Ereka. Have an affair—with yourself.'

She smiles.

'Tell me one thing you do for yourself.'

She thinks. 'My toenails.' Her laughter is as soft as Persian feta. She points her toes.

'And when did you last paint? Properly. On a canvas?'

A tear gathers, teeters on the rim of her eyelid and then drops, trailing a clear path down her cheek and then clinging to the ledge of her double chin. Twice in twenty-four hours I've made her cry.

'I haven't been into the studio for ages. Jake keeps on at me to just go down and sit there,' she sniffs. 'But it feels like sitting vigil next to a coffin. It's like when that spark goes out in a relationship. What do you do? You can't force it to reappear. It's like chasing toothpaste back into the tube. But I just want to feel it once more, to fall in love—with anything—again. To know that thrill once more before I die.'

'I hear you.' I'm not in love with Tuscany. You can't love something you've never known. For all I know it's touristy, expensive and the coffee is shit.

'You know, when Jake and I were married in those early years before Olivia was born, I'd be down there all night. Time would pass and the next thing I'd hear Jake's footsteps on the wooden stairs and there he'd be in his boxers with his morning erection holding a hot cup of coffee with condensed milk for me and only then would I know I'd been at it all night. I had so much passion I could've expressed it and passed it on, like mothers with too much breast milk. Pity I didn't think to save some for a rainy day. Now it's gone. Missing in action.'

'Ereka, you know it comes and goes. All artists know that.'

'What if it's died and it's never coming back?'

It can, she's right. But what sort of a friend would it make me if I agreed with her? Right now I'd lie till my last breath to keep her from going under.

Singing in her song she died,
The Lady of Shalott.

'Don't write it off just yet.'

We sit there like that on the edge of the morning. The mist is crawling its way up the hills, divulging its landscape. Dawn is sweet and agile and we are partners with this day. Ereka lifts her head and there is hospitality in her eyes. Not an open door, but a crack. Which we all know, because of Leonard Cohen, is how the light gets in.

12

Not a Trick of the Light

'Worth the calories?' Ereka asks.

I seem to have finished my piece of cake. Inside I'm warm as caramel.

'Actually, it is.'

Ereka pinches off a tiny corner of the piece I cut for her and tastes it. 'Olivia would love that. She's like Winnie the Pooh. You can get her to do anything with honey.'

'Jamie's like that with cheesecake.'

'How is your Jamie?'

'She can't wait to run away from home.'

Ereka chuckles. 'I was like that as a teenager.'

'She's been nagging me to let her go to Borneo for three weeks—bloody Borneo!'

Ereka blows her nose on a serviette.

'I mean, seriously—I don't even know where it is.'

'It's in Malaysia somewhere. I've heard it's beautiful.'

I grunt. Beautiful shmeautiful.

Ereka sips her coffee noisily. She looks like she's preparing to say something.

'The morning Olivia was born was one of those perfect spring mornings. The sky was clear, the air smelled of blossoms. Our peach tree was full of them, these little nests of colour. And I remember thinking to myself, 'What a good omen.' It was only hours later when I was looking at the terror in my midwife's eyes. You know they're trained not to panic, but I guess she couldn't hide it. And I had this weird sense like I was watching from afar and could see the whole thing play out. Not just that moment, but my whole life, everything, every sound, every colour, including those lusty pale-pink blossoms. And I had . . . maybe this will sound kooky to you, a sense of déjà vu.'

'You didn't see it coming, Ereka.'

'No, not like that. Just, I wondered if I didn't somehow bring it on myself.'

She exhales deeply.

'C'mon Ereka, how can you blame yourself? You did everything right.'

She shuts her eyes and shakes her head. 'As a teenager, I used to like the whole "suffering artist" thing. I was always in black, mascara, clothes, stockings, like I was a widow in mourning. My mum used to say to me, why do you have to dress like someone on her way to a funeral?'

'You can never go wrong with black,' I say, and realise I am sounding like Summer. Seriously? Did I just offer Ereka *fashion* advice? I can't be trusted to open my mouth.

Ereka continues. 'You should hear how I yell at Kylie. And over the smallest, most irrelevant things. Her incomplete homework. Her dirty clothes on the floor. Her lost jumper. She's become so resentful and jealous of Olivia because I never shout at her. How could I? So in our house, there are always two different standards. Kylie's constant refrain is "It's not fair", and she's right, of course. But that doesn't mean I'm going to stop shouting at her for the things she does that make me mad.'

'It's never fair,' I say. 'Younger kids get treated differently from the older ones, the boys get treated differently from the girls. We're the Unfair Standards Bureau.'

'Yes, but what I'm saying is: don't feel bad about my life. Don't compare yours with mine.'

She's cornered me. Slick move.

'You can talk to me about your problems.'

'They seem so petty.'

'They're just different. Don't protect me. It makes me feel so . . . lonely.'

'Okay.'

We sit there quietly as the coffee cools and the mist lifts. I hear someone in the shower upstairs. The old pipes of the house convulse. It's almost human in its sadness, this old house.

'I'm bitter about Olivia,' Ereka says.

She is bewildered by herself, almost weepy.

'Sometimes I wonder what my life would have been like if she'd died in childbirth, instead of being revived. You know, I could have mourned her. That would have been easier than this. There are worse things than death. But what kind of person could even think such a terrible thing about their own child? And what do I do? I waddle off to the fridge to stuff my face.'

'I'm sure I'd do the same, Ereka.' Of course, I have no idea what I would do. She is tethered to a lifelong commitment of servitude to her daughter. What will happen when she dies?

'I'm just so tired, Jo. Tired of it all. The whole package.'

I reach out and rub her shoulder. She slumps under my hand.

'I'm sorry I've been so slack about keeping up with you.' Belated commiseration. What a poor effort.

'It's okay. When you have a kid like Olivia, you lose your friends. Your only friends become other people with disabled kids. And we're all just fighting to get through our own particular hell. People eventually give up on you. They stop inviting you over. I don't blame them. If I didn't have Olivia, I'd also want to complain about school camp fees and girls binge-drinking and having sex. I wouldn't want to listen to some mother talk about wrestling with her daughter to take her medication and clean herself and not play with her privates in public.'

I do not know the days she lives. I have never even visited those hours. If I ever complain about my kids again, I will recommend a public flogging for myself, truly.

'Is it getting harder as she gets older?'

She nods. 'People have always stared at her, now even more. But no-one ever really sees what's behind her, the effort it's taken for her to do the things everyone else takes for granted. Tie a shoelace. Wash a cup. No-one thinks about what drugs she needs, what drugs I'm on, just to get through the day.'

'And all that adds up financially,' I say, remembering our conversation of yesterday, hoping I don't come across as patronising. I'm just trying to be a friend.

'The other day I was standing in line at the supermarket and there was a pregnant woman in front of me. I don't know why I asked, because I didn't care, but I inquired if she was having a boy or a girl and she said, "I don't mind as long as it's healthy." So I asked, "And what will you do if it's not?" She gave me a death stare. So I said, "I'm just saying that not all babies are born healthy," and an old lady behind me tapped me on the shoulder and said, "That's quite enough."' Ereka laughs.

'Troublemaker.'

'I sometimes think I'm doing it for revenge. Because when I'm dealing with Olivia in public places, even public toilets, people stop and abuse me. They say, "Do you have to do that here?" As if I'm urinating or streaking. As if my child is offensive because people have to see her.'

'Idiots.'

'I'm so jealous of all of you. I'm jealous of the freedom someone like Maeve has.'

I let her be jealous, not saying, 'If you knew what road Maeve has had to walk to her freedom . . .' She has every right to be jealous. I'd be jealous of me if I were her.

'What's it like, Jo?'

'What?'

'To have a life without *Why?* knocking on your door every day?'

I flounder, trying to find something wise and true to offer her. But I fail. I am guilty of all these silent judgements and stupidities, of harbouring the smugness of a life unblemished. I am a disappointment, really.

I put my hand on hers and we sit there, holding hands like little girls. Suddenly she releases my hand and says, 'I've been having . . . symptoms.'

'Such as?'

'Terrible thirst, tingling in my hands and feet, needing to wee all the time.'

'You should get it checked out.'

'I'm scared.'

'I'll come with you to the doctor.'

'I'm a big girl, I don't need to have my hand held.'

'Even big girls need a mother.'

Ereka rests her head on the side of the chair and tilts her face to the sun. 'I could do with my mother right about now. She was my best friend.'

I remember Ereka telling me years ago that her mum had a stroke just before Olivia was born, and that she lost her speech and her mobility. She now lives in a home.

'When did you last see her?' I ask.

Ereka shrugs. 'I can't remember. Visiting her makes me too sad. She was such a fiery capable woman. She was a magpie, she never threw anything away—broken crockery, old newspapers. She always mended things, reused them and found ways of making things last. I sometimes think she would have known what to do about Olivia.'

'I miss my mum too,' I say. 'She's another one who always knows what to do, even though she lives in another country.'

'Seems silly to be so far away from her,' Ereka says.

I nod. Something coarse lodges in my throat.

'Whatever you do, don't feel bad about last night,' Ereka says.

She must know it's too late for that.

Ereka takes hold of my wrist. 'You know why my mum had a stroke? She was massively overweight and smoked forty cigarettes a day. She didn't take care of herself, but she was fastidious about taking care of us. What is it with mothers and their double standards, huh? If she could speak, I know she'd be saying to me, "Do you really need that piece of cake, Ereka Lucy Fleur? Do you want to end up a vegetative elephant like me, not even being able to wipe your own enormous arse?"'

'After being stuck mute in a stroke for fourteen years I'll bet your poor mum is thinking, "Get me a stiff gin and tonic and why do they keep me in this silly nightgown all day?"'

Ereka laughs wildly.

'Look,' I say, opening and shutting the gate to the birdcage. 'Maeve fixed it.'

Ereka reaches out and moves the gate, which squeaks, on its new paperclip hinges. She opens and closes and opens and closes it with an ineffable smile on her lips, as if the morning mist had stolen all heartache as it slipped away.

Tennyson trudges up the pathway and bounds up the stairs carrying something in his mouth.

It is a half-dead mouse. He drops the small squeaky thing with its innards oozing out at my feet.

'That is truly disgusting,' I say. 'You are a horrible creature. That poor innocent mouse.'

Ereka laughs. 'It's a gift, silly.'

She carefully picks the mouse up in her hands. She goes down the stairs onto the grass. The dog follows her. She walks all the way to the dam in her bare feet. I watch her cup the mouse gently in her hands and throw it into the water. Tennyson barks at the splash. Ereka then bends down and washes her hands in the dam. I watch as she pats the dog on the head and walks back up, her arms swinging by her side. I think, *I want to do something nice for Ereka.*

When she gets to the veranda, she says, all out of breath, 'Let her go.'

'Who?'

'Jamie. To Borneo.'

'Ereka, I . . . it's not so simple.'

But I struggle to look her in the eye. Ereka would give just about anything to have a daughter she could send to Borneo.

'Okay, forget I said anything,' she says. 'It's none of my business. Come help me with breakfast. I was going to make ricotta honey pancakes with cream and berries. Is there any way of salvaging that so my mum would approve?'

Back in the kitchen, we survey the options. Cream is out. Butter and honey too. I open the fridge and look at what else we have at our disposal. And just as I'm bringing my creative culinary skills to bear, Summer bounds into the kitchen with a breathless, 'Good morning. Isn't it a lovely day?' She's sweaty from what looks like a morning run in the countryside, but is still glamorously made-up with foundation, blusher, eye shadow, the works. She throws her arms around Ereka and gives her a hug which would have overwhelmed me with inadequacy as a friend, reminding me that Ereka gave her—not me—access to her room last night . . . if my attention was not drawn magnetically to her feet, on which—can this be a trick of the light?—are my new trainers.

When she finally sees me looking at her feet, Summer says, 'Oh, you don't mind, do you? I forgot to bring my running shoes, and I saw these at the door, and thought, "Oh my utter god, they look just like my size." And they're so freakishly comfortable.'

'Um, actually,' I start, 'I'm not great on sharing shoes . . .'

'Oh, silly me, I should've waited and asked.'

'Yeah but I would've still said no.'

She giggles, thinking I am joking.

'Summer!' Ereka chastises soothingly. 'You don't borrow someone else's shoes . . . silly.'

'Yikes, really?' She looks so surprised, as if I'd just this minute made up this social convention.

'It's like borrowing someone's undies, or toothbrush.'

'My bad, sorry,' she says brightly. She takes them off immediately, dusts the toes, and asks, 'Where shall I put them?'

'Just where you found them,' I mumble, turning back to the breakfast, fuming silently and wondering how you get someone else's feet sweat out of your new shoes. These are conversations I have with Jamie. Jamie, who grew inside me and to whose DNA I personally contributed. *Ask before you take my things. Please don't wear my jewellery without permission. If you use my makeup, put it back where you found it. Are those my stockings? Why is my stapler under your bed?* These are the small acts of partition that buttress selfhood. I can't help wondering what qualifies as 'being brought up' in some households.

As Summer dashes upstairs for a quick bath before breakfast, Ereka says softly, 'She means well.' Yes, well, I'm sure puffer fish have no malevolent intentions when they poison you to die your slow and painful death. Really, they probably have no feelings about it at all.

Maeve and Virginia wander into the kitchen, Maeve in lively Nepalese cotton pants and shirt and a sun-hat, and Virginia, bleary-eyed, in a maroon velvet tracksuit that is probably by some fancy designer but is definitely not the kind of thing you actually exercise in. She flexes and straightens the fingers of her left hand in patent agony, her iPhone in her right hand.

'Where've you two come from?' Ereka asks.

Maeve explains that she was up at dawn, found an elevated spot in which to do tai chi and on her way back bumped into Virginia, who was wandering around trying to find a mobile phone signal or Callum, whichever came first. Without Tennyson? Even I know that you don't go for a walk on your own if you have a dog.

'Thanks to whoever let Tennyson out,' Virginia says.

'He left a little present on the floor for you. I had the thrill of disposing of it.' I'm not complaining, just reporting.

'I'm so sorry,' she says, laughing. 'Dogs are not my forte. Or pets of any kind. Guess I'm going to have to find him a new home. Put him on the market.' She pockets her iPhone, unstraps her wrist guard and redoes it.

'It's not so easy to find homes for old animals,' Ereka whispers. 'You may have to . . .'

'Yeah, I know,' Virginia says, casual.

The dog is right here. Hovering at my feet looking up at me with unfounded adoration. I've no idea whether dogs can understand, but why take a chance?

I try to catch Maeve's eye. She's been out at dawn. She's done tai chi. Her night-light is packed away. She doesn't even look my way. As I grind black pepper over the eggs, I suppose I'm hoping for something different from the morning-after of some of the sexual encounters of my youth, where the intimacy of the night didn't survive the awkwardness of breakfast. I'm not holding out for any grand gestures. She's not that kind of person. Still, it would help me, really, if there were some small acknowledgement that we shared something: *Rich Man, Poor Man*, Solange, Jonah. She doesn't want me to treat her differently, but after last night our relationship *is* different. But her eyes are empty of our midnight stories. Instead, she pours herself a coffee, smiles at Ereka and wanders out to the veranda.

'Found Callum. Lucky him, he's so cute. He didn't know anything about the landline being cut off,' Virginia tells me as if I too have been anxiously awaiting news of the telephone situation. I try to look interested. 'And he has a key somewhere for the upstairs room. He was apologetic and says he'll come around a little later and take us on a guided tour around the property and into the memorial garden.'

'So what's in the locked room?' I ask.

Virginia shrugs. 'We'll know when it's unlocked.'

'And what's the memorial garden for?'

'The couple who owned this place lost a son in his twenties. He was a brilliant concert pianist. His mother planted a rose garden in his memory. A thousand rosebushes.'

Ereka and I turn instinctively to look at each other. She has tears in her eyes, grief never far from the surface.

Virginia offers to wake Helen, and a few minutes later leads her down the stairs in her daggy pyjamas, her once-were porno tits dangling like potato sacks beneath her top. As I watch her descend, I vow I'm going to buy her some new sleeping gear. Something cotton and without plastic cartoon characters on the front.

I am paying attention to my friends and their needs.

13

What Was Never Cherished

'Do you really have to leave after lunch?' Summer asks Ereka, as if she's her new BFF. Summer is sitting opposite me chatting as if it is perfectly normal to have just 'borrowed' someone else's shoes. She is unfazed, really. Before breakfast, I'd retrieved my trainers at the French doors, and put them back on my own feet. I should probably do an audit on my undies too.

The table on the veranda is covered with a hand-embroidered tablecloth Ereka found in a drawer in the kitchen, as if breakfast deserved its very own beauty. As Ereka serves up helpings of our herb omelettes with smoked salmon and ricotta, Virginia's phone rings. I find even I am relieved.

'Hallelujah,' she exhales, excusing herself to take the call.

'I've got to get back to give Jake a break. It's a parenting relay,' Ereka says.

Summer makes a pretend sad face as she sips on her Diet Coke. 'I'm gonna miss you,' she says.

When Virginia returns, she's holding the bottle of Moët. It would be hard not to notice that her face is troubled.

'Everything okay?' Helen asks.

'Update from the ICU nurse.'

'How's your mum?' I ask.

'Dying.'

'Is she . . . is she in pain?' Dying people are generally in pain. It's a fair question.

'She's on a lot of pain control medication, and in a coma, so it's hard to know.'

'What did the nurse say?' Helen asks.

Virginia shrugs. 'Same old story: bad night, not long to go . . .'

'It must be really tough for you.' I am generally not this lame.

'Yes and no. She and I haven't exactly had what you'd call an ideal mother–daughter relationship.'

'Now you're being kind,' Helen says.

'True. And she's almost gone.'

'Do you want to go back to be with her?' Helen asks.

'I doubt anything's going to happen in the next twenty-four hours. She's been like this for nearly two weeks. Besides, she wouldn't know whether I was there or not.'

Ereka opens her mouth, as if she might contradict Virginia, but closes it.

'Was she really that terrible?' I ask, straining to imagine the sorts of sensational perversions of affection that might result in someone being this casual about their own mother's demise. Daily beatings? Starvation? Being locked in a cupboard for years? You read about such mothers in cheap magazines. They pop up on *Jerry Springer*. And it does, you'll agree, raise questions about whether one oughtn't to have to earn the right to reproduce, or at the very least have to pass a non-invasive multiple-choice exam, just to weed out the complete psychopaths.

Helen and Virginia look at each other. It's a gaze packed with a history I will never know.

Helen answers. 'Let's just say that Celia wanted a son. So Virginia really screwed things up, being a girl and all. Why do you think she called her Virginia? Scramble the vowels and you've got "vagina".'

'That can't be true,' I say, aghast, suddenly wondering about the silent thwarted hopes of the mother of a boy I was at school with called Dick Cockburn.

'I nearly called Jemima "Virginia",' Summer declares. 'She's a Virgo, so we thought about Virginia, but then we chose Jemima, because it's got "gem" in it, and she is such a darling. Jemima sounds like Virginia—just with J and M instead of V and G. I *adore* the name. It so doesn't sound like vagina to me.'

We all blink. Listening to Summer's stream of consciousness is like being on hallucinogens. Or being caught in an episode of *Teletubbies*. There's something very relaxing about it, as long as you don't fight it.

'It's just a family joke,' Virginia says. 'I'm actually named after Virginia Woolf, whom Celia did love, given that zero actual affection is required for a deceased author. But luckily for her, Conrad came along eighteen months later. Conrad who is perfect and beautiful in every way that counts, and very much a boy.' She squeezes out a metallic smile.

'Tell us where Perfect Conrad is now that his mother is dying,' Helen prompts, eating the last of her omelette.

'He's on Very Important Business in Jakarta. Lucky boy, he's missed the whole cancer saga—which, let's face it, is a bit of an inconvenience when you're trying to close deals.' There is horseradish in her words, I can just about taste it. Walking in on someone's lifetime of emotional neglect is tricky, like stumbling across a stranger's adultery. It's hard to care either way without sounding forced or phony. I swallow. Where am I when my parents need me? Halfway across the world. It's my sisters who have to take care of them when my dad needs a hip replacement and my mum puts her back out. I am, quite possibly, a terrible daughter.

'But, please, don't let's bad-mouth Conrad. He spends a fortune on flowers from Interflora. Except that Celia's allergic to pollen. I end up throwing them out or palming them off on other patients. I frigging despise arrangements, especially those in little green blocks of sponge. I mean, what's with that sponge?' Virginia is irked by the sponge. I guess enough sponge *could* push you over the edge.

'It keeps the flowers in place,' Summer explains. 'We use them all the time when we put houses on show.'

'I guess it does.'

'Well, we can't all be perfect,' Helen says. 'Somebody's gotta be the BSF.'

'BSF?' CJ asks.

'Black Sheep of the Family,' Helen and Virginia say in unison. 'Snap!' And it's giggles all round.

'Black sheep are so special.' Summer tries. 'Like there's a little Ethiopian girl in Jemima's class. She's an albino. We invited her to our place for a play date. And I swear, not a word of a lie, the poor thing had never seen a Wii before. Like, never.'

It's impossible, really, to know how to respond to her insights.

'Being an albino, wouldn't that make her more of a *white* sheep?' Helen suggests.

Summer thinks and nods. 'I . . . I guess . . .'

Suddenly Virginia giggles, followed by Helen. CJ joins in and even Ereka is unable to resist. Summer, hating to be left out, chortles along. Maeve remains impassive.

But all this banter is funded by genuine suffering. Summer's big-hearted invitation of the albino child is a fleeting diversion from what this is really about: a child who was unloved, unmothered. My children know how to wring me to the ends of patience and my own human decency. I don't always like them. They sometimes make it impossible. But I cannot—simply cannot—imagine not loving them. Even if I wished for it. It would be like instructing my body to stop digesting food. I can't even feel neutral, as I do when I see strangers arguing with a person in a uniform and think mildly, *That's a silly thing to do*, instead of rushing over to intervene, explain and help fix the problem. My love for my kids is like my heartbeat, my breathing: biological. But this is clearly not the case for all mothers.

'I give you the true-blue white sheep of her family.' Virginia does a drum roll, gesturing towards Helen like a ringmaster presenting a new act. 'Mothers do love their daughters. Helen's living proof. Tell us, Helen, how does that feel?'

Helen grunts. 'There's a downside—and I'm just warning you all—when my mum dies, I'm gonna be a wreck. For a long time.'

'How is Roz?' Virginia asks.

'Probably sipping on some expensive cocktail on the upper deck. She and Dad are on a cruise to the Bahamas.'

'Remind me I've got something for her for Mother's Day—I picked up a clay-bead necklace for her while I was in Ghana. She admired mine last time.'

'For Mother's Day?' CJ asks.

'She was my surrogate mum. Thanks to her, I actually know what real mothers do.'

'Thanks to her you didn't become a teenage mother at sixteen. Where would you be if she hadn't put you on the pill when that boyfriend of yours—What was his name? With the Adam Ant haircut?—insisted that his balls would fall off if you didn't have sex with him?'

'Cute little Barry Wendall. But he lied about his balls.'

'I told you boys' balls don't fall off if they don't have sex.'

'I'll tell you what was one of the highlights of my pitiful childhood—that chicken soup Roz made when I came back from our camping trip with pneumonia.'

'You did insist on skinny-dipping at three am in that lake . . .'

They are overcome with hilarity. Which is how people react to an in-joke or a memory only they share. You can't feel too left out. But Virginia must be envious of Helen. I mean that would only be natural.

'Being sick was the best fun. When Celia threw me out of the house if I came home with a forty-degree temperature or coughing up phlegm, I'd have an excuse to run off to your house and stay there till I was better.'

'That's awful,' Ereka says, reminding us of what's really being told here.

Virginia quietens.

'Yeah. I've bungy-jumped, I've parasailed, I've been in an open field during a lightning storm—and none of them has anything on the terror I felt telling my mother I was sick. Seeing the hippo chomping off the guide's foot was probably the only thing worse. If I coughed, Celia would fly into a blind rage. Like I was intentionally ruining her life, disrupting the order, keeping her from her bridge, her tennis, her charity baking . . .'

'She baked the best bread you've ever tasted. Let's give her that,' Helen reminds her friend.

'Yeah, she knew what to do with flour and water.'

'You reckon we could get her to bake one more caramel custard pie before she buggers off?'

'The smell of those makes me sick now.' Virginia wilts.

Virginia has perfected this telling, the way people eventually come to talk about a tragedy without cracking. The surfaces have been wiped clean, no traces of pain or self-pity in her voice. It's a sterile environment. But there must be grief here. Maybe not for a dying mother, but for what was never cherished. I hate waste. The squandering of a child. What was the point of going through it all and not revelling in it? Like Amy Winehouse. Poor silly girl.

My own mother, who was not a fusser generally, fretted over me only when I was ill. I remember her soft, warm hand on my forehead checking for fever. The worry in her eyes I knew as love. How she'd sit and colour in with me when I was home sick from school. She had such an even stroke, the way she handled crayons. She could have been an artist, I suppose. I never really asked her about that. But what is true is that I never felt as adored as when I was projectile vomiting or had burning tonsillitis. There was a certain attentiveness she could only give me when my health was threatened. I cherished those times with her. It's probably the source of my rampant hypochondria.

'We loved it when you were sick,' Helen tells Virginia. 'It was like having an extra sister. My mum always wanted more kids.'

'More than four?' I ask, shocked.

'I reckon Mum could've easily had six.'

'Some people are just wired for the job,' Virginia offers.

I wanted four kids, you know, when I imagined being a mother someday. But Frank and I stopped at two. There is space in my heart for more kids, just perhaps not in our budget. After Frank's vas deferens was pulled out and severed during his vasectomy, I found myself sobbing in the waiting room. Frank didn't get it. It was the finality, I suppose; the ultimate surrender of the fantasy of a big rambling family, lots of back-up, busy corridors. Frank tells me not to romanticise it and to think of the laundry. But there's something to be said for dilution. Small efficient families breed possessiveness and privacy: *How dare you come into my room/borrow my things/walk in while I'm in the shower.* Big families are communities where people share rooms, sometimes beds, undies, showers and take turns on the computer. I'm not saying I would have been a less controlling mother. For all I know, it might very well have doubled my anxiety.

'My bloody mother seems like she's going to live as long as she can so she can annoy me for as long as is humanly possible,' CJ says.

'Why don't you get on with her?' Virginia asks, buttering toast, corner to careful corner.

'How long do you have?'

'Summarise.'

'Here's what an honest dating profile might have looked like: *Pathetic and passive Catholic, afraid of driving, seeks co-dependent alcoholic to father two unwanted daughters. Can quote extensively from the Bible. Comes with exceptional house-cleaning skills.*'

'Why's she afraid of driving?' Summer asks, curious about the transport.

'Look, I'm sorry her brother died in a car accident when she was small, but that's what therapy is for, right? My sister Gail and I had to walk everywhere, like we were poor white trash. My overwhelming memory from childhood is humiliation.'

'Walking is good exercise,' I say.

'Gail once cut the tendons in her hand on a broken glass, and my mother couldn't drive her to the hospital. Gail fucking nearly bled to death waiting for an ambulance. When it rained and one of us had a science project, we'd arrive at school with gloop, everything ruined. My mother knew that bloody Bible cover to cover and cleaned that house like she was preparing to perform open-heart surgery on our kitchen floor. Why? *Because cleanliness is next to godliness*. Gail and I used to cut pictures of cars out of magazines and newspapers and keep them in a scrapbook. And of course we learned to hitchhike.'

'Dangerous,' I say.

'I sometimes used to offer boys blowjobs for a ride.'

'What?' Helen, Virginia and I all chime in unison. Even Maeve has blinked.

CJ laughs. 'I *offered* blowjobs, didn't say I gave any. It takes a minute to unzip. I got good at jumping out of the car as soon as we got to our destination. Only ever had to dish out a couple.'

'That is seriously disturbing stuff, CJ,' Ereka says.

'Well, it did me no harm, look at me now. Ta-da!' As if she's a poster girl for Normal and Well-adjusted.

'Your dad was an alcoholic?' Maeve asks.

'Yeah, but my mother could have driven the Pope into rehab. He was defenceless against her. But when my dad died ten years ago, she just went off the rails. Like a switch had been flicked. She stopped going to church. Threw away all her crosses, including that huge wooden one in the kitchen with Jesus draped all over it. Next thing, she's internet dating, going to the races in red stilettos and betting, using up what little inheritance I might have had. The other day—get a load of this—she tells me she's got a "fuck-buddy". Please—at her age, how does she even know the term fuck-buddy?'

'She sounds awesome,' I say.

'Points for going down fighting,' Helen cheers.

'That is, like, so sick, CJ,' says Summer and laughs.

Even Maeve chuckles.

'And how old is she?' Virginia asks.

'Seventy-five. And her little fuck-buddy is *fifty-two*. I pointed out to her that she's old enough to be his mother, and she winked and said, "Exactly."' CJ shudders.

'She and I need to go out for a drink. Maybe I can pick up some tips on how to land a fuck-buddy,' Virginia says.

'And of course, given her hectic lifestyle, she's never ever available to babysit for me,' CJ complains.

'She's a reborn person,' I say. I'm thinking that CJ's mother would have probably made it to Tuscany if it were on her bucket list.

'She was a crap mother, the least she could be is a half-decent grandmother.'

'My mum is, like, so mega-helpful,' Summer says. 'She picks the girls up from school every day. She does homework with them and makes them dinner.' Then, sensing it's not the popular thing to have a cool mum, she adds, 'But she gets so frigging depressed, since Dad left . . .'

I wonder what exactly it is Summer does as a mother; she seems to have outsourced just about all of it.

'When did your dad leave?' Maeve asks.

'Two days before my fifth birthday. Like, super uncool, right? My mum said it was vile, what was two extra days? She had to cross out "Dad" on my birthday card, because she'd already written "Love Mum and Dad". So we went to live with Uncle Bernie, my mum's brother. Otherwise it was community housing for us.'

I find that I am rethinking things. Summer hasn't had the ideal upbringing. There'd have been clothes-sharing. Shoe-sharing. I get where it all went wrong for her.

'I can't remember a day when I haven't spoken to my mum,' Helen says. 'I run *everything* by her. And I swear, no matter what it's about, she's always right. I don't know what I'd do without her.'

Virginia smiles into Helen's happiness. But you can see where she went without. The holes are there. The unevenness of someone who had to stretch awkwardly to get from girlhood to womanhood. I glance at Ercka. Her mothering stories got frozen when her mum had a stroke, locked away inside a semi-person. And Maeve. She's built a fortress around her losses and just doesn't go there anymore.

Before bed each night, I email my mum. She wants to know what the dentist said and how much the car service cost, how Jamie's geography test went and whether Aaron scored any baskets in his match. If I miss a day, she's on the phone the next day asking if everything's alright. She is invested in my daily happiness in a way I couldn't pay anyone else to be. You get things for free in families.

'When did you last speak to your mum?' I ask CJ.

CJ shrugs. 'Can't remember.'

'Mother's Day, surely?' Helen says.

'Puh-leez,' CJ says dismissively. 'She was a fucking useless mother. I'm not wasting twenty-five cents calling her on Mother's Day.'

'You don't mean that,' I say, hoping she doesn't.

'I most certainly do.'

'If you've been unmet and unseen your whole life, it's hard to muster enthusiasm for a little chat on a commercially designated Love Your Mum day,' says Virginia, siding with CJ.

'I don't have anything to say to her. She was never on my side, never took care of us. Even when I left home, I never felt I could introduce her to any of the men I was dating, because the only thing she wanted to know was: "Is he a Christian?" Not is he a decent man? Does he take care of you? Does he bring you chamomile tea in the morning and rub your tired feet at night? None of that counted for anything,' CJ elaborates.

'Sounds like yours and mine read the same mothering manual,' Virginia says.

'But surely now . . .' I start.

'What, that she's dying?'

Virginia looks like she doesn't have the energy for this conversation, but I see her dig deep. She owes me nothing, really. 'Up until a few weeks ago, I always hoped someday we'd reconcile—before it was too late. But I've expended so much energy in my life over her, and it's got me nowhere. You see these?' She gestures to her orthodontics. 'Conrad got braces for his cross bite when he was thirteen. But me? I had to wait to be forty-eight and get my own. So I could be ridiculous. At my age. As if being a fat teenager wasn't enough. The only thing she has a perfect record in is disappointing me.'

'You were never that fat,' Helen says. 'Chubby, maybe.'

Summer puts her hand on Virginia's arm. It is a sweet gesture, you can see why she's doing it, even though Summer hardly knows Virginia. Virginia doesn't quite know what to make of it.

'Aw, fuck her, you can go it alone,' CJ says.

Virginia makes to high-five her. They miss, they try again. It is a gesture of camaraderie, of mutual acknowledgement. I have no idea why it makes me so sad.

Maeve, I'm noticing, hasn't said much at all through this conversation. I wonder if she's thinking what spoiled brats we all are, whingeing about our mums. At least we have mums to whinge about.

'Do you think our kids will say these things about us one day?' I ask. I'd want Jamie and Aaron to speak about me the way Helen speaks of Roz. But I guess for that to happen I'm going to have to rely on their forgiveness and amnesia.

'Count on it,' Helen says.

'It's in the small print,' CJ says, 'under Liabilities—that no matter what we do, we will always disappoint our children. So we're off the hook. We can just drop the whole business of trying so hard to be perfect, and just be ourselves.'

Tennyson comes over and sniffs my ankles. That's Summer's smell on my feet, so he's confused. He jumps up and puts his front paws on my knees. I push him down and he slinks away to a corner and sits facing the wall. I didn't mean to be cruel.

'Come here, Tennyson,' Virginia says.

The dog ignores her.

'See? Even her dog hates me.'

'He's depressed, give him a break,' Helen says.

'He's totally missing your mum,' Summer diagnoses.

'He's been lying curled into the crook of Celia's arm for weeks,' Virginia confirms.

'Animals have an uncanny sense when people are dying,' Maeve says.

'Well, good luck to him,' Virginia says. 'Apart from my brother, he's the only creature on God's earth who was somehow good enough to be loved by that cold bitch.'

14

Only the Weak Forgive

The Moët stands on the table unopened, waiting for the right moment. Maeve has not given me anything yet. A glance. A thumbs-up. I'd have been happy with a 'Please pass the salt'. The nectar of that midnight conversation could drip away, sink into the earth, as if it never was. It might already be too late. You have to catch these things early.

CJ's phone rings. She looks at it, but her face falls. She doesn't answer.

'Who is it?' Helen asks.

'Liam.'

'You're not taking calls from your kids?' Freka asks.

'I told them not to phone me. Besides, I'm not talking to him.'

'What's he done now?' Helen asks.

'Wasn't he your favourite?' I ask. He used to be.

'He's become a little shit. The apple doesn't fall far from the tree, apparently.'

'Don't say that about Liam,' Ereka chides.

'You have no idea what he's put me through in the past few years.'

'He has turned into a little prick, hasn't he, CJ?' Summer says, whispering the word 'prick'.

'He's just been suspended from school this past week for planking—the idiot child.'

'What's planking?' I ask. 'And is it different from wanking?'

'My kingdom for a wanker!' CJ huffs.

'Oh my god, Jai does this stupid planking too,' Summer exclaims.

'What is it?' Ereka asks.

'Aw, c'mon, you must have read about it in the media—it's this new craze,' CJ says.

Maeve clears her throat. 'It's a social and cultural phenomenon which began in 1997 in north-east England. Adolescent boys seek out unusual or incongruous public spaces and lie face down, arms at their sides, like a plank, and photograph it to put up on the internet. It's also called "playing dead" in South Korea, "on one's belly" in France, "extreme lying down" in Australasia or "facedowns" in the US.'

She is a font of information, really.

'Sounds pretty harmless,' Helen says.

CJ scowls. 'On the balcony of a third-floor apartment? These boys plank on moving vehicles, railroad tracks—two kids died recently, one fell off a seventh-floor balcony.'

'Adrenalin plus stupidity multiplied by testosterone. It's a toxic cocktail,' Maeve agrees. 'The frontal cortex in boys only develops when they're around twenty-four or twenty-five. Which accounts for so many deaths of young men in their late teens and early twenties. The majority of road deaths, bar brawls and suicides happen just before that frontal cortex kicks in.'

'Oh my god, that, like, explains so much,' Summer says.

'No, it doesn't explain anything, Summer. You shouldn't let Jai talk to you the way he does.' CJ addresses the rest of us. 'You should hear the way he talks to her.'

'He totally doesn't listen to me.' Summer is helpless.

'If he were my son, I'd get Kito to sort him out. If a boy calls his own mother a whore or a slut, he needs a man to knock some sense into him.'

'That's ugly,' Ereka says to me quietly.

'Well, he doesn't talk to me like that in front of Craig.' It is not clear to me in this moment why I feel oddly protective of Summer. But the years of cross-examination have made something of a bully out of CJ. Summer is her friend. What's wrong with all of us? Have we forgotten how to play nice?

'What about Jai's dad? Can't you get him to speak to Jai?' I ask.

CJ gives me a knowing look. 'Where do you think he learned to talk about his own mother like that?'

Summer sips her Diet Coke in silence, her eyes on the floor. Ereka rubs her back kindly.

I find that this conversation is not easing my anxiety about my own son. I am certain Aaron is privately tortured by having a mother to whom the delights of rugby, basketball and cricket are illegible and who cannot appreciate the joy (which apparently must be shared with others) of genital hubris. Don't get me wrong—I'm very grateful his parts all work. It's the bragging I don't get. I personally find that I'm most pleased with my vagina. But I've never felt the need to boast about its achievements, which, okay, if they must be listed, include its capacity for self-cleansing, two different kinds of orgasm and accommodating all sizes of male genitals (unlike the penis, which cannot—lamentably—expand depending on the requirements of a particular vagina). As far as genitals go, vaginas are tactful, well-mannered and unaggressive, like well-brought-up children. They ask permission for sexual contact and require the consent of an erection before pouncing. So if any bragging were warranted, you'd think it'd be done by those *without* the schmeckel. This is just an observation, you understand.

I admire male anatomy in the appropriate context, with a personal preference of circumcised over uncircumcised, a certain width over length. I can go so far as to imagine it might be fun to wield a body part over which one could hang a towel. But I have never hankered to be attached to one and wonder what Freud had in mind when he claimed women suffer from penis envy. Perhaps he meant it ironically.

CJ picks up her phone and squints at it. 'Jesus, the mobile-phone coverage here is crap the way it comes and goes. And I haven't spoken to Kito in nearly twenty-four hours.' She stands up and walks down the steps to the grass, holding her phone up to the sky. She heads around the side of the house. Eventually we hear her shriek, 'Babe, can you hear me?' Laughter follows.

'Isn't love wonderful?' Summer sighs.

Helen guffaws. 'Give it another six months.'

'Nasty,' I say.

'It's untested is all I'm saying,' Helen says.

Breakfast is over like a blind date bereft of chemistry. Omelettes, no matter how fluffy or low calorie, are no match for a young one-eighth-Asian lover who is hot for you despite the fact that you are technically perimenopausal. We all fall into a silent coven, not obviously eavesdropping. But other people's love lives are outrageously tempting. You just have to look at the wistfulness in Ereka's eyes to know that.

'Has anyone ever told you,' Summer says, leaning towards Maeve, 'that you look like Susan Boyle?'

Maeve blinks at her and smiles. 'Really? Thank you.'

'Yeah, I just had to say, because I, like, find her such an inspiration.'

'The resemblance is uncanny,' Virginia says. 'But I figured you'd probably heard it before.'

Maeve shrugs, resigned to this comparison.

After several kissy sounds into her phone, CJ bounds up the stairs like a schoolgirl who's just been asked out by the captain of the football team. She sits down and pushes her plate away, as if love has filled her up more than enough. She looks up at us. 'So, all is forgiven after last night?'

'We've patched things up, me and Ereka,' I say, shooting a hopeful glance in Ereka's direction.

'Let's hear it from Ereka,' Helen says.

Ereka nods. 'I was just having a bad moment.'

'Yes, but do you forgive Jo?' CJ drives, playing with that soft little spot at the base of her neck where sweat pools when you've had more than enough sex.

I glance at Ereka wide-eyed, momentarily panicked.

'Nothing to forgive,' Ereka shrugs with a broad smile.

'I would like your forgiveness,' I say. I mean, I'd like to actually hear her say the words. Not that I'm looking to be let off the hook for last night or anything. I was one hundred per cent wrong. I have no right to dish out tough love, which is called tough love for a reason. It's not the ambling scenic route. It's boot camp not yoga. Backbone not breast tissue. It's the mongrel bitch in us marking her territory with an 'Uh-uh, I won't take that crap'. It's always easier to soothe rather than call people on their shit. It's less strain on the nerves to make Aaron sausages rather than watch him gag on the 'mushy' biryani or go hungry. It takes no energy to ignore the slamming of a door. But to walk down the corridor and face the face on Jamie, or call her back and have the talk, exact the apology, that's hard work. You have to pick your fights and train accordingly.

Jamie, of late, has taken to doing her own version of tough love on me. 'If you keep pampering him,' she says, referring to her brother, 'the Little Prince will never learn that life isn't one long indulgence.' Getting parenting lessons from my almost-fourteen-year-old has been an unexpected delight I hadn't counted on, thank you very much. I told her the other day that I am the parent, not her, to which she replied, 'Well, you're not doing a very good job then.'

I don't say I have all the answers. Mothers have to walk a tightrope between respecting our kids' individuality without inflating their sense of entitlement and exacting discipline without crushing their spirits (though Frank's theory is that a bit of spirit-crushing is 'character-building'). I read the other day that overpraising and overprotecting our kids only breeds depressed adults, who cannot cope with the rigours of the real world where no-one gets a gold star for simply pitching up at work. Sometimes in life, there is no choice, so they might as well practise on *eat your broccoli because I said so*.

But then I read somewhere else that 'If you don't offer your kids a choice, you're just bullying them.' Yes, well. What parent hasn't bullied their child at some point? The lines between bullying and parenting are fuzzy to say the least. I've always thought of 'I'll wash your mouth out with soap', or 'give you something to cry about', as a couple of little catchphrases to help parents get by, as long as you don't carry through, and you chuck in a few treats here and there.

But right now, tough love or not, I'd like it witnessed that Ereka has let last night go.

'Of course I forgive you,' Ereka says, putting her hand on my knee. It is warm and slightly sweaty, and it feels wonderful.

'I think forgiveness is overrated,' CJ says. 'Speaking for myself, of course.'

'You haven't forgiven Tom?' Ereka asks.

'Only the weak forgive. The strong seek revenge.'

Summer titters. 'That's a good one—I need to remember that, CJ.'

'How's that working for you?' Maeve asks.

'How's what working for me?'

'Holding on to your anger.'

'Just fine, actually.'

'She loves being a sourpuss,' Helen jokes.

'I'm not sour. Fuck that! I'm not sour.' CJ pouts.

'Okay, you're bitter.'

CJ turns her chair away to face the view.

The eggs on my plate are golden and perfect, but I am drained of any appetite, shored up by cold pizza and ginger cake. Ereka has wiped her plate clean with a slice of bread. Summer has given breakfast as much attention as she'd give a fat man at a bar: enough not to be rude, but hey, don't get any ideas. Maeve has eaten half and left the rest. Helen would have more if there were seconds. Virginia has too much on her mind, leaving the omelette untouched, unloved. She moves to the hammock, kicking off her shoes and shielding her eyes. Maeve shifts her seat to catch a bit of the sun slanting onto the veranda and takes out *The Consolations of Philosophy* and her reading glasses from her bag. I've lost her to Alain de Botton.

'I'm not bitter anymore,' CJ says. 'I was. For a while I was. But you know what? You get over it. What really gets to me is how Tom treated the kids. I was just a casualty. Tom's not the only man in the world. But the kids are stuck with him as their dad. I just can't get over how he CBK-ed them. He put his Cock Before Kids.'

'Don't you reckon men always put something else before their kids? If it's not work, it's something else,' Helen says.

There are general murmurs of agreement from those of us who are still listening.

'I can't remember the last time David was home in time to say goodnight to the kids. On the weekends, when he's not working, he passes out on the couch from exhaustion. It pisses me off. The kids miss him. Especially Nathan now that he's manning-out, getting all gruff in the voice and sprouting hair.'

'That is, like, so true. And if it's not their kids, it's another woman. Sergio always put his mother first.' Summer is doing some limbering-up stretch against the veranda pillar. 'She could do no wrong. He put her on a parasol. She could cook better than me, clean better than me, was a better mother. I swear, he'd take her calls even if we were in the middle of . . . you know.'

'And he was husband number . . .?' I ask. I'm not going to correct her malapropism. She's been punched around enough this morning by CJ. But the image of Sergio's mother on an umbrella is pretty comical.

'My first.'

'No-one could blame you for chucking him out,' Helen says.

'Actually,' Virginia's voice comes from the hammock, 'I ended up breaking it off with a guy who put his kid before me.'

'Which one was he? The Spanish actor?' Helen asks.

'No, not him. You always ask about Carlos. It was Brad Bernstein, a Jewish boy from the Bronx. When I met him, I didn't mind that he was divorced with a six-year-old kid. I figured we'd add a couple to that. I actually could see us as a happy family. He was the first guy I thought, "You'll do as a dad." But it was always about Rachel, and fitting me in around his time with her. I thought it showed character. She was his priority. It was touching. At first.'

'That's dead sexy.' Ereka smiles.

'I don't know about Brad Bernstein,' Helen says. Virginia ignores her.

'But then he'd cancel our date because Rachel had a dress rehearsal for *Aladdin*, or she had a temperature, or suspected chicken pox (she didn't have them, it was just a rash). It got to be all about Rachel, and never about me.'

'She became The Other Woman,' Ereka gasps.

'Actually, *I* became the other woman. Then there was all the guilt—about the divorce, about not spending enough time with her, being a good enough father . . . It just got . . . boring.'

'At least he was grown-up enough to make it about her and not about him,' CJ says.

'When did you go out with Brad Bernstein?' Helen seems to be talking to herself.

'It's just another form of narcissism, don't you reckon?' Virginia continues. 'There was no balance. He couldn't make the shift from it being just the two of them to include me.

And isn't that the problem? That men can't adapt when things change? In my work, things never go the way you expect and you always have to adjust on your feet, at the last minute.'

Virginia kicks the veranda to get a little movement going in the hammock. She flexes the fingers in her hands. My guess is arthritis. That slow, crippling, disfiguring corruption of the joints. I hope it's not rheumatoid. Never to wear rings again. Probably not high on her list of priorities right now. Like Maeve, she doesn't wear self-pity. She's radically self-reliant, a tigress. After last night, I thought she'd be the kind of person you'd want with you if you had to face a disciplinary tribunal or make a complaint. Even with the braces she's imposing. But not now that I see it. The vulnerability, eked from the contemplation of loneliness in the long term. Without the amniotic suspension of domestic life, without a person to come home to, to whom you confess the trivialities of bizarre interactions or small injustices performed by bank clerks and parking inspectors, the accomplishments—even the extreme ones—of a 'career' must feel petty, mocking. It's not my place to wish things for her, but I do.

'You said it, sister,' CJ says. 'I am so over men who can't handle the transitions. Life changes. Two becomes three and then four and then five. You can't keep behaving like a teenager who's just discovered what his dick is for. So when your wife suddenly has a belly and isn't all glam in her bikini anymore, are you going to take that personally? Like your private fuck-object has just betrayed you? And when she's breastfeeding and exhausted and can't muster up the energy for your usual blowjob, are you going to sulk and jerk off to porn? Or tell her, "This is why men resort to prostitutes." That's what kids are for—to help men grow out of their sexual narcissism. To figure out ways of loving and being loved that does not involve their cock.'

Summer applauds.

'So, did he get all weird on you when you had kids?' Virginia asks.

'Total meltdown. Couldn't handle it. Thing is, I married Tom before I knew who I was, and I didn't ever stop to ask myself: Courtney-Jane, when you strip away the steel-blue eyes and that sandy hair, what do you actually like about this guy? He was a player, always was. Even if he had both eyes gouged out, he'd still find a way to look at other women.'

Summer laughs. 'Good one, CJ.'

'So you knew what kind of guy he was?' Virginia asks.

Maeve looks up from her book, interested in CJ's response.

'I thought I'd be enough for him. But there were signs early on . . . I just pretended not to see them.'

'Men like that should have tattoos on their forehead: NMM—Not Marriage Material,' Ereka offers.

'OMG, what a brilliant idea,' Summer says, without really considering that perhaps she's the one who could do with that tattoo.

'What were the signs?' Virginia inquires.

'Where do I start? First, he never talked about work, mine or his. I'd ask him questions about his day and he'd say, "Honey, I never mix work with pleasure." All he was interested in was how often he could fuck me. In all the years we were married, I don't think I ever said no to him sexually. I found him so goddamned sexy, and I liked that I gave him pleasure. That he found pleasure in me. But then, during my pregnancies, I sensed a dimming in him, like those switches you can use to adjust the light in fancy homes and hotels for ambience.'

'They're pretty standard these days, CJ,' Summer says. 'In modern homes.'

'I thought, just give him time. I wanted to be a good wife, not to force the issue. It started that night he lay on his right side. I was five months pregnant with Liam. Until then, he'd always sleep on his left side, facing me. So we could spoon. I asked, "Is anything wrong?" He said he was giving me *space*. But when you haven't asked for space, what he's saying is he's taking space. That was Tom to a T—he could even twist a take into a give. I spent I don't know how many years of nights looking at his back. I could tell you the location of every hair, every freckle. If I'd reach out to stroke his shoulder, he wouldn't acknowledge it, even with a grunt or by turning his head to kiss my hand.'

That memory burns in her. I can feel the heat from where I'm sitting.

'And still . . . I never put myself in that category of women whose husbands have affairs. Even as I was dealing every single day with divorces with the same stories as my own life in them. That's what was so hard to get over. What it said about me. Can you be smart in the rest of your life and a total train wreck in your relationship?'

'Oh, absolutely,' Summer says consolingly, putting her hand on CJ's. CJ rests her head on Summer's shoulder, her mood clouded.

'Well, Tom's history, so you can move on,' Ereka says quickly.

'Yeah, he's history.'

We all agree on that. That's what CJ needs to hear right now. And no-one is about to point out that if you speak so long and with that much passion about anything or anyone . . . No, forget it. Tom's history.

'So are you living with Kito now?' Helen asks.

'I moved in with him two months ago.'

'So how's it working with the kids? I mean the living arrangements?'

'He's got a stunning place in Surry Hills, a two-bedroom semi with a little garden. We've moved in with him.'

'So the girls are sharing a room?' Helen asks.

'Yeah.'

'And Liam?'

CJ pauses. She clears her throat.

'Liam's moved in with Tom.'

There is a brittle silence.

'Liam moved in with *Tom*?' Helen repeats.

'Uh-huh.'

'Why?'

'Because he wanted to.'

'Ouch,' Helen says.

'I'm so sorry,' Ereka whispers.

'That's crazy,' I add.

'It's fine, really. It's his choice. And anyway, it takes a load of financial pressure off me.'

'What were his reasons?' I ask, just out of interest.

'Number one: Dad promised me a new iPhone. Number two: Dad doesn't nag me about homework. Number three: Dad plays *Call of Duty* with me on the Xbox. Number four: Dad lets me bring girls home and smoke in the house. Number five: Dad is cool. Ergo—you, Mum, are not. There were other reasons—he gave me a list of fifty. I couldn't get past the first ten.'

There is a small prickle of moisture on CJ's upper lip.

At our last get-together, CJ spoke about Liam as her 'special boy'. How he used to crawl into bed with her when she was single to keep her company. I'm just remembering that.

'Do you think he's threatened by Kito?' I ask.

'Of course he is. But you know what, girls?' She pauses dramatically, her eyes grow wide and there is lava in her voice. 'I am *over* men who are threatened. I am over men who can't cope. I am over giving my guts and heart and soul only to have them thrown in my face. So Liam can go live with his dad and good luck to him. And they can both rot in testosterone for all I care.'

I think of Aaron right now, and in my thinking I see my failure to grasp everything that brings him alive. For now it is bewilderment that stands between us, but I suppose antipathy isn't far behind. I'm trying to work out when our babies, our little boys, cross the line and become the 'men' we have zero tolerance for. And what part of ourselves we must disown and desert when we wash our hands of them. I just, you know, hope we aren't all Susan Klebolds in the making, just waiting to say, 'I had no idea who my son was.' That would make me sadder than I can bear. There must be a way for us to hold them to the shores of their sweetness even as they hurtle like hormonal surfers into the oncoming waves of life.

'Don't give up on him,' Ereka says softly.

Maeve looks at CJ over the tops of her reading glasses and says, 'He'll grow up. He'll figure it out all by himself someday. Don't be surprised when he arrives on your doorstep with a bunch of flowers and an apology.'

'Great, if he does. And if he doesn't—too bad. I'm finished giving my life to my kids. Wasting my energy on fighting Tom for maintenance. It is time for *moi*. And Kito. Truly, I just can't wait for the girls to be old enough to move out too and get on with their lives.'

'I'll drink to that,' Summer says, clinking her tin of Diet Coke with CJ's coffee mug.

'Here's to me. One of these days, girls, I'm going to stop working and be a kept woman.'

'You don't mean that?' I say, really hoping she doesn't.

'I most certainly do,' she says. 'Newsflash, Jo—feminism is the booby prize. I don't want to be independent, or to make it in a man's world. I want to do girl things like watch daytime TV, go for manicures and not worry about how I'm going to pay for Jorja's hair extensions. Bring back the good old days when men were men and women were domestic slaves. I'd love to have nothing more to worry about than grocery shopping, separating the whites from the colours and getting the casserole ready. I'd even do the pipe and slippers if it meant I didn't have to do another day's work.'

'You go, girl,' Summer cheers.

'Love has clearly warped your brain,' I say.

'What do you mean? That's the life Helen leads. You're happy with your life choices, aren't you, Helen?'

'Ecstatic.'

'See? And after that diatribe and two coffees, it's time for the pink bathroom for me.' CJ excuses herself, leaving us all a little windswept after the hurricane of her tirade.

I'm glad for her that she has someone to love, truly I am. At least she has a hand to hold in the dead of night, someone to scratch that spot on her back she just can't reach, another person to share a bottle of wine with, to come home to at the end of a day of quarrelling clients whose own love lives have turned feral. Unlike Virginia. But she's forgotten one thing: motherhood is like the mafia—once you join, you can never leave.

'Ooh, look, a spunk,' Summer gushes, pointing.

We all look up.

And there in the sunlight is Callum. As bright and pure as a beanstalk of testosterone. An uncanny accomplishment of boyhood perfected. And this is how men mess with our brains. No wonder we forgive them their faults.

15

The Botox Bitch

Callum came, so he says, to check that we were okay and ask if we'd like some wood for a fire tonight. He makes it impossible to be neutral about him. We flock around him like grizzled seagulls at a picnic site. There is a frenzy about it. Except for Maeve, who does nothing but lift her eyes from her book to smile kindly at him for his consideration, born, no doubt, from the awareness that she's old enough to have breastfed the man as a baby. Tennyson, infected by this general concentration of our attentiveness, shuffles up to Callum and jumps up against his quadriceps. Callum ruffles his head with manly firmness, and then sinks to his haunches to give the dog a man-hug.

'Have you found a key for that upstairs room?' Virginia asks, arisen from the hammock. She is at least six inches taller than Callum. Callum shrinks under her gaze.

'I'm still looking. It's got to be somewhere.'

'I need to see that room before I leave.' In Virginia's voice is a cool authority. She's a ballbreaker, really.

Callum nods and offers to take us on a walk around the property. No-one tempers their enthusiasm. Even Maeve puts her book aside and welcomes the chance to 'stretch her legs'.

'I'm not moving,' Helen says, plonking herself into the hammock. And here's me, unable to decide what I feel like doing. Small choices in my day like this confound me. I sometimes find myself driving in circles, unable to fix on whether to drive to the gym or the uniform shop; to pick up the dry-cleaning or the books on reserve for me at the library. It's making decisions that won't affect my life in any particular way that baffle me. The ones that do are easier to wrestle with. At the very least, they press on the heart one way or the other.

'Go ahead,' I say. 'I'll wait and tell CJ, and maybe we'll catch up with you.' I watch as they troop off with Callum at the helm, Virginia swinging her enormous camera and Summer with her arm threaded through Ereka's. Maeve and Tennyson bring up the rear.

I take the breakfast plates back to the kitchen and wash up. I hear CJ's footsteps coming down the stairs. She peeks into the kitchen.

'Where've you been? The others have all gone for a walk with the groundsman.'

'Phone sex, darling, with Kito. Remember what that was like?' And she winks.

Actually, I can't. 'You can catch up with the others if you run.'

'I don't run after men anymore,' she says.

Back on the veranda we find Helen lazing in the hammock, doing—as she swore she would—*sweet bugger-all* this whole weekend. Not even a magazine or a book to distract her. I guess peace and quiet trumps celebrity gossip because, let's face it, who *really* cares whether Angelina adopts another baby or

Lindsay needs rehab again? Not me, I assure you. CJ sits on a chair, puts her feet up on the veranda wall, and starts texting on her phone. I pour them each a glass of water from the jug I prepared with wedges of lemon.

'Ooh, vodka and lemonade,' Helen says, sitting up.

'It's water.'

'You have been a disappointing disciple.'

'Yeah, your purity has become completely annoying,' CJ says. 'Were you always this virtuous or did someone give you back your virginity while I wasn't looking?'

Helen squints at CJ. 'Hey, what have you done with your wrinkles?'

'Gone, darling.'

'Are you a Botox bitch?' Helen asks.

CJ nods.

'Are you kidding?' I gasp.

'Why not?'

'What's wrong with ageing naturally?'

'Have you looked at yourself in the mirror lately?'

'It's not so terrible,' I choke.

'I would say that depends on the light,' she croons.

'You couldn't pay me to have Botox.'

'Don't tell me you haven't thought about it.'

'Never.'

'Liar,' CJ says. 'Every woman thinks about it.' As if Botox were hot sex with Callum or something.

'Not me. All this obsession with staying young, and being beautiful . . . What sort of message does that send to our girls?'

'That with the right help and enough money, you never have to be ugly?'

Helen snickers.

'That's something Liz would have said,' I say, feeling cross without quite knowing why. At our last get-together Liz carried on about how she'd rather her child broke an arm than a tooth because an arm can heal, but a tooth never looks right again. 'All this cosmetic enhancement, vaginal reconstructions, breast implants—where does it stop?' My consternation only fuels her ridicule, and why I don't just keep quiet is a mystery even to me.

'When your money runs out?' she quips.

'I don't get it with you and Summer,' I say. 'It seems excessive.'

'She's only had her boobs done. The rest is all natural.'

'Besides, what do you care if CJ has Botox?' Helen asks.

It could be that I have no friends. None at all.

'What about all the weight you've lost—isn't that the same thing? Trying to reclaim the glamour of your past? And is that a colour I see in your hair?' CJ asks. Lawyers distort things. It's best to be careful around them. I lost my weight naturally. My hair colour washes out, eventually. They're not the same at all.

'Do you have any idea how hard I've had to work to lose weight?'

'As hard as I've had to work to afford Botox? I'm saving up for a tummy tuck next.'

'You say "tummy tuck" like it's cute. It's massive, invasive, life-threatening surgery.'

'That gives you a flat stomach.'

I wonder whether falling in love has taken CJ out of reach. I think I preferred her when she was bitter and twisted.

'Summer took me to get vajazzled for Kito's birthday last week, wanna see?' CJ asks.

'Show me,' Helen says.

CJ stands up and drops her pants and then her G-string to reveal a hairless vulva bejewelled with little silver and blue dots in the shape of a heart.

'I don't get it,' Helen says, and in that moment I forgive her completely. For the pizza. For choosing Virginia. For all the unfriendliness of the weekend. She is the least vain person I know. If Helen didn't get Ereka's toes, vajazzling is one adorned body part too far.

'I found bits of your vaginal decoration all over the bathroom.' I laugh.

'It's just a bit of fun,' CJ says crossly, pulling her pants up. 'Except when these stickers get inside, you know . . .'

'Too much information,' I say, opening my bag to check my phone. There is Jamie's unanswered SMS from yesterday. No new ones.

And there it is: my anger is about Jamie. Not so long ago, kids in her class were calling her 'Jamie the fat kid'. Kids have an uncanny ability to break someone down psychologically by focusing on their weak points. Red hair. Freckles. Glasses. Height. Braces. Buck teeth. The usual unforgivable sins of appearance.

But—and here, really, was my objection—Jamie wasn't fat. Her beautiful body was negotiating the awkward divide between puppy fat and teenage hormones, straddling these two worlds, holding back on a little tummy to help plump out those nascent breasts and feed her ravenous brain.

She confessed to me, but only through the usual channels of communication—by spoiling for a fight until I erupted, blasting open a space for her to spill the terrible truth—that the boys in her year were 'rating' the girls out of ten. She told me earnestly, as if it were a *fact*, that she was somewhere on the scale between four and five. One boy—I could put a face to the name—rated her zero out of ten. A group of her peers found this funny.

I resisted verbalising that this particular boy must have had some amphibian ancestry if his physical characteristics are anything to go by, but only because I don't like to think of myself as someone cruel enough to call a child ugly. Even an ugly child. I am also in the game of teaching my daughter that we don't judge people by their looks, so it would be to give with one hand and take with the other to tell her that a boy with a face like a cane toad should hardly be the source of her own self-image. Though she understood the injustice of his observation, right then she would have been happy even for this Shrek-like bully to rate her somewhere closer to ten. That aches.

I cannot remember such naked cruelty being inflicted on me at school. It could be that I have repressed it. Jamie is—take my word for it—much prettier than I ever was. I had a large nose to deal with. And I was tall. Like Virginia, I towered over the boys. Schoolgirls like me find that we have to wait until we're adults to meet the real men who find us sexy. The ones with glasses. The ones who don't talk themselves up or laugh too loud. The ones who got ninety-five per cent for art. Who were probably themselves called 'nerds' and 'geeks' at school. But these boys—like Jamie—outgrow the barbed wire of those playground names. In the real world, where the arbitrary inhumanities of schoolyard popularity cannot take root, they become muscled with intelligence, glamorous with creativity.

I want to share this with Jamie, so she knows what is waiting for her. But I don't want to freak her out by telling her how men, sturdy with self-confidence and crisp with wit, will soon enough be thinking of her as 'Jamie the sexy brunette', and fantasising about that strong wonderful body that is taking shape before my eyes. She's only thirteen and three-quarters.

But there, in that nascent insecurity about where we rate on the scale of one to ten, is the same impulse that sees intelligent women like CJ rushing to smooth out every wrinkle. It's just a grown-up version of the he-won't-like-me-if-I'm-not-pretty anxiety. I know how that feels. But I don't want to model rampant vanity for Jamie or to be so desperate that I'll Botox myself into frozen youth.

I saw a sign in a changing cubicle while I was trying on swimming costumes the other day. I took a photo of it with my iPhone. It read: *No more than six garments permitted in changing room at a time. It is unlawful to compare your body to an airbrushed genetic freak. This dressing room is monitored regularly for happiness and wellbeing. Please purchase only those items that make you feel good.* I'd like to swamp the universe with messages like that so that no teenage girl will ever look at herself in the mirror and ask, 'Do I look fat in this?'

I steel myself for what I am about to say next. 'You know how smokers always get on their high horse about it being their choice and their body . . . well, when people smoke, I *am* affected by their passive smoke. And when you, CJ, keep going on about how women need to look young, it just reinforces all the negative media images—we're not meant to look young when we're forty-five and fifty. We're meant to look forty-five or fifty.' As I finish, I realise how badly I need to hear these words myself. Bloody Oil of Olay. It's done very little to stall the inevitable.

CJ reclines on the chair and gives me a Cheshire cat grin. 'Methinks the lady doth protest too much.'

'You were gorgeous before Botox,' I say, shaking my head.

'But I'm more gorgeous now.'

'I read something the other day that said in the long term Botox might actually make wrinkles worse,' Helen says.

'I could be dead by then,' says CJ, smiling. 'But for now, I'm the one without the wrinkles.' She puts both her feet up on the veranda wall, nudging the birdcage. Its newly fixed door swings open on Maeve's makeshift hinge. I remember Ereka's fragile happiness this morning as we sat here and she held something fixed in her hands.

I stand up. 'Some people have real issues,' I say. 'And others of us just get to frolic in self-indulgence.'

'Bitchy,' CJ sighs.

I ferret in my bag for my mobile phone. 'Excuse me,' I say, walking back into the lounge room. 'I have an important phone call to make.'

If I can only find where Helen put that card.

I am a good person, I think as I look at myself in the mirror on my way back downstairs. I mean, I can be a harridan in the days leading up to my period, but I don't consider the crazed nasty things I shriek at Frank and the kids to be a true reflection of my personality. I may be a terrible mother, but the rest of the time, I am a good person.

There is no mobile-phone reception downstairs. I try all the rooms, even the downstairs loo. Eventually, I get through by sitting on the bidet in the pink bathroom.

When I return Helen and CJ are discussing the musical instruments their children play. The others are already on their way back up from the dam, Callum chatting to Virginia and pointing to something in the distance. Tennyson is loping along at Callum's side.

Maeve and Summer bound back up the stairs, smiling from the sunshine. Ereka follows, puffing, jangling with jewellery and endorphins. Sweat has formed along her brow and upper lip. She sinks into a seat and waves her hand in front of her face.

'You should so totally have come with,' Summer says. 'You missed out big-time.'

'I'll go for a walk later by myself,' I say, miserably. As if anyone likes to feel left out.

'Let me know when you're ready and I'll come with you,' Maeve says. Just like that.

I turn and smile into her one brown and one green eye, so beautifully disconcerting.

See? She remembers last night's whispers.

16

The Lies in Our Eyes

'What are you doing?' Maeve asks.

'Responding to my daughter's contempt.'

I'm just happy we're talking again. But maybe we never weren't. Either way, I'm grateful.

I won't tolerate, I type on my iPhone. I delete it. *Don't get huffy*, I write. I delete it. I mean, it is very easy to spew out some reactive small-minded invective. That doesn't take much effort at all. But I should aim for something that models maturity, I suppose. The other day, Frank lost his temper with the kids. There was yelling, threats of lifelong electronics bans, cancellation of all social arrangements and an eternity of detested household chores. Things escalate in our house like this.

The kids looked bored, even bemused by his eruption. 'Tragic,' Jamie mumbled.

I took him aside and suggested that by shouting and carrying on perhaps we were treating them like babies, when they weren't really babies anymore. Maybe negotiating and facilitating might work better.

'But *they* shout and carry on,' he huffed.

'You're the adult.'

'Not by choice,' he muttered.

We are charting new waters with our children's burgeoning adulthood, having to forsake some of our most effective parenting techniques, such as intimidation, deprivation and manipulation, all of which have served us well in the past. But things are changing. A few weeks ago, after our first horrible fight about Borneo, there was a note on the kitchen table. *Gone for a walk*. Jamie didn't say where. She hadn't taken her phone.

You have to admire her strategy. For the next hour and a half, I contemplated my response for when she walked through the door, weighing up these options:

Shouting: 'You irresponsible, manipulative little brat; how dare you put me through such emotional trauma. It's a week-long electronics ban for you!'

Ignoring her, as if nothing had occurred worth mentioning, never letting on that I'd just spent an hour intermittently freaking out and praying for her safe return.

Inquiring calmly: 'So, how was the walk? See any dolphins? Isn't the fresh air and sea breeze lovely? A great way to clear the head after a fight, right? Oh . . . maybe next time take your mobile phone in case it rains or you get lost and need to contact me for any reason . . . my darling.'

I know the last option was the right one and trust me, I am working towards it. But I only managed a version of the first. I know she's changing. I don't say she has to be my little girl forever. She's replacing herself anew all the time. Updating her status. I'm the one who has to keep up. I guess things have been changing for a while. I remember that incident when she was eleven. Something was going on at school, but she wouldn't give me any details. Something about 'not being chosen'. Cabins at camp. Being pushed against a fence. *There, talk to your only friend*, the pusher had sneered.

I tried, I really did, not to make it about that time I wasn't chosen and how I'd ended up in a room with the new girl who had terrible skin. I found myself telling Jamie this, and how, in the end, it 'wasn't so bad' really.

Your life is bigger than the playground. You probably don't want them as your friends, anyway. You're special and they are mediocre. They're just jealous of you. Bitchy girls have bitchy mothers. Those sorts of encouragements. I caught myself wondering, as I spoke them, whether I in fact believed them, or whether they were the same lines I'd been told at some desperate friendless point in my own childhood.

'Someday,' I'd said, aiming for wise, 'you will find your friends. I only found my true friends when I was in university.' It was, if you think about it, a comfortless notion for an eleven-year-old.

'Yes, Mum,' she'd said, an enormous tear finally escaping from her big brown eyes. 'But what about *now*?'

Yes. What about now?

Now is hard, I'd heard myself say. *But it will all be okay in the end.*

She had chewed her lip.

Is there anything else you need to tell me?

And suddenly, Jamie gave me an inscrutable look. To put words to it, I'd have to say there was something faraway and terribly astute about it. And then, bang, I understood. She was assessing me, judging whether I could handle what she was about to tell me. Then she produced a small crumpled note from her bedside table. A string of Jamie-directed nastiness, as if a group of girls had gotten together to gossip in black and white.

I found it in the bin. While everyone was at recess. Last week.

Last week?

I didn't want you to get upset.

Do you see where I'm going with this? It was supposed to be *my* job to comfort and protect *her*. Given my superior vision and experience of life and, you know, being her mother and all. But there in her strong dark eyes, the clarity of who was doing what job tumbled. *She* was protecting *me*. We'd had an ordinary week together where I'd yelled at her for intermittent cheekiness, moodiness and nastiness to her brother. I thought I was doing my job. Meanwhile, she'd been holding this alone in the locked room of her heart.

At a certain point, our children gauge our strength and, if we're not up to sharing their pain with them, they will shut theirs away, learning that pain is too agonising to be shared. And what I'm telling you is that *they* decide. You don't realise you're being watched. But they're monitoring us, watching for weakness. Keeping us safe from harm.

Maeve clears her throat. I look up at her. 'Speaking for myself, I've always found *I love you* is the shortest route to reconciliation.'

'She hates me. I don't know how that happened. Why I didn't catch it sooner.'

Maeve rests on the ledge of the veranda. 'It's called *psychic differentiation*. It's how she figures out who she is separate

The Reunion

from you. And you want her to be different from you, even though you don't realise it.'

'She expects me to let her do things I would never do myself—to expose her to dangers I wouldn't risk myself.'

'It means you've done a good job.'

One should be willing to accept overtures from people who have greater experience, like Maeve does. From her vantage point, she would have a sense of 'arrival'—her kid is grown up and doesn't need her anymore, he's probably decked out with an array of helpful life skills, like how to swim, read, cross the road, drive a car. I keep feeling if I can just get my kids to X point, they will be okay, you know. But that point keeps shifting. My new X is their fortieth birthdays.

It's not that we fight all the time, don't get me wrong. The other day Jamie stayed home from school. We shared sushi and I sat through *Eat, Pray, Love* with her. I'm not being sentimental about it, but we could have been two girlfriends hanging out, painting our toenails and envying Julia Roberts. And then, sometime in the afternoon, she asked me about my first kiss. So that's when I told her about Simon Cooper, who was tall and skinny and wasn't really interested in me; trust me, girls know these things. But I was fourteen and I'd never been kissed. He was eighteen and drove a car and played Bruce Springsteen on his tapedeck. ('What's that?' Jamie asked.) I told her how he dropped me home and walked me to the front door and then swooped down on me, like a missile, sticking his tongue halfway down my throat. And I let him. Because I wanted to know how it felt to be kissed.

'Oh, Mum . . .' Jamie had sighed. 'That was your first kiss?'

I could see she felt sorry for me.

I had to give her something else, it would have been wrong to leave her with Simon Cooper. So I told Jamie, I really told her, about that kiss on the beachfront with Travis when I was eighteen. How cold my face, streaming with rain, felt against the warmth of his lips and how he put his hand on my chest (I said chest, not breast) and said, 'Your heart's beating a million miles an hour.'

'He was the first man I really wanted to kiss. And it was like . . . like nothing I can describe.'

I could tell she was glad for me, the way she smiled shyly. And let me say right now, that I want those to be the kisses that await her. Though I hope she knows there'll be plenty of Simon Coopers out there too. What I didn't know back then (and what I will never tell Jamie) is that there's a limit to the wonderful kisses that await us in our lives. What she'll slowly see is that they're endangered. You don't get people marching about it or signing petitions like they do for the ozone or the Tasmanian devil. But they're still treasures. It's a mistake to ever expect there will be more. All I'm suggesting is that we shouldn't approach them with the voraciousness of collectors, but with the reverence of archaeologists, hoping to find that one precious fossil.

Kissing, you'll come to accept, is the first casualty of marriage. The next is either the back rub or foot rub. I am quietly grateful that Frank approaches my nether anatomy as if it were a plate of stuffed zucchini blossoms. If all other reasons for staying with him deserted me, this appetite alone would probably ensure my devotion to him. I don't advertise this. Why would I? But it would be nice if Jamie found someone like her father—not in the creepy Freudian sense, but in the ways that matter. I wish all the glories of mine and Frank's sex life for her in the fullness of time and in the privacy of her connection with someone I've yet to meet. Many years down the line, just so we're clear.

The other day she asked me, 'You and Dad don't still have sex, do you?'

''Course they don't.' Aaron can talk from the back seat without taking his eyes off his iPod Touch. 'Dad's had a vatescomy.'

'God, you are so tragic and so in need of some basic sex education,' Jamie churned. 'First, it's a *vasectomy*. And second, that doesn't mean they don't have sex. Just that there's no sperm. Moron.'

'No name-calling,' I muttered feebly. I never signed up for the role of Adolescent Nomenclature Correction Officer. It's repetitive. There are no perks.

'Is that true, Mum?' Aaron asked.

'The vasectomy thing is true, and, um, most happily married people probably have sex. It's part of what married people do.'

'Just tell me you don't do it while we're in the house. You don't, do you? That is, like, so . . . so *gross*.' Jamie grimaced.

I hadn't started this conversation, but, okay, no-one wants to go there. I remember a friend at university confessing to me that all her problems—and trust me, she had a few—were because she'd found her father masturbating in front of her mother when she was twelve years old. Admittedly, not one for the old wedding speech, but great material for the therapist's couch.

'Well, no, we . . . don't really,' I said. Which is not so much a lie as a convenience. For now. Though ask Frank and he'd probably say we never have sex. Which we do, trust me, we do.

After the tooth-fairy incident, my preference is to stay away from bald-faced lies. Though, I have to say, at the time I didn't think of the tooth fairy as a lie so much as a fantasy. Had I known what the fallout would be, I might've done things a little differently. When Jamie lost her first tooth it seemed so straightforward. It was a clean exchange—the tooth for two dollars. Then rumours began to circulate and Jamie confronted me one morning. 'Isabel says it's her mum. And I want to know: is it?'

I tried not to notice her little frown, the mark of budding suspicion, taking root in logic. Lying came easily, I'll say that much.

Her shoulders dropped in relief. 'Poor Isabel, thinking it's her mum!'

But as the years passed, who knew she'd develop an elaborate ritual for the fairy? Notes. Gifts scattered around her room. Jamie is an embellisher, not a minimalist, more like me than Frank. I found it charming, but I began to dread every wobbly tooth. One night, I suppose I simply forgot. I probably fell asleep before her. The next morning, she was there, at the foot of my bed. Why had the tooth fairy *rejected* her tooth?

It was a fair question. But it was six am. And there were still three more of those baby teeth. Surely she knew? Who believes in the tooth fairy at the age of eleven?

'Jamie, there's no tooth fairy, my love. It's me.'

Her eyes filled with tears.

'Always? Has it *always* been you?' she asked with the same tone a cheated-on wife asks, 'How long has it been going on?'

The Reunion

I'd nodded. There was no turning back now.

'You're a witch,' she'd yelled, and she ran from the room. Her door slammed on its hinges, the wooden hand-painted J fell to the ground and chipped. And it was only 6.04 am.

From that day on, I've just worn the punishment, rolled with the punches: *How can I believe anything you say? You've lied to me before. I don't trust you.*

When you think about it, we are conscripted traitors. Maybe we have no choice but to betray our children. Maybe we have to be the first ones to break their hearts, so they know how to survive when they are broken again. I hope that's how it goes.

Now, I smile at Maeve.

'Our kids come back to us. They always come back,' she offers.

'She'd run a million miles away from me if I let her. But Jamie isn't anywhere near ready to sail off on her own.'

'Perhaps,' Maeve pauses, 'you're the one who's not ready.'

She means this in the nicest possible way. There is no judgement there. Lying now in the autumn sun, I inhale the soft countryside and in capital letters, I text: *I LOVE YOU MORE THAN CHEESECAKE. MUM XXX* and press send.

17

The Chosen Ones

CJ and Summer's lunch offerings are uninspired and predictable—a series of cuts of processed cold meats, cheeses, pickled cucumbers and the cheapest, highest-GI white rolls, as if linseed or sourdough hadn't yet been invented. And this, mind you, has been a team effort. Come any night of the week, and I'm serving up the lowest-common-denominator dinners of spaghetti and meatballs, chicken schnitzel and baked potatoes, sausages and mash at my dinner table, where vegetables are treated as second-class citizens, sponsored only by dessert-bribery. Unless on a 'fried' visa, and escorted by chips, fish doesn't get much of a warm welcome either. Too many years like this, and without preventative action, one's culinary standards and finer epicurean sensibilities can die—really, I'm not being melodramatic here. This is, of course, how mothers get fat. By eating off the children's menu. Anything accessorised with 'nugget' or 'finger' is designed for the metabolism of a four-year-old. Unless one intends to spend eight hours a day running around the garden and climbing monkey bars, these foods are to be avoided like syphilis.

So on the rare occasion when we get together without small people, I suppose I do hold out for a touch of style at the table. I'm not talking lobster or Wagyu beef—just a stuffed olive or a marinated eggplant that you can pick up right there at the deli along with all those cold meats. Without Kito and his stuffed zucchini blossoms, CJ is still an 'open a tin' person. Something about this thought makes me feel as if I've just unintentionally cast an evil spell over CJ and Kito's relationship. I try immediately to do a counter-spell by nibbling on a pickled cucumber and thinking how delicious it is.

No-one really has an appetite after our huge breakfast, so the salami sits in the sun, sweating, while Ereka cuts herself wedges of cheese, working her way through the brie and the roquefort.

'How hard can it be to find a key?' Virginia mutters, returning to the veranda. Her hair is slicked back from a shower.

'Lovely young man,' Ereka says, almost to herself.

'I'd like to see him do some Zumba,' Summer says, then giggles. 'Yikes, don't tell Craig I said that, right, CJ?'

She's a dangler. Between sophistication and utter girlishness, she just can't choose.

'Why don't you go into Zumba full time?' I ask. 'It's clearly what you love doing best.'

She gives me a searching gaze as if I've just seen into the recesses of her soul, though I haven't. I was just making conversation, you understand.

'You're so utterly right—it is. But, like, there's no money in it. And I make such awesome commissions selling houses. I'm saving up for plastic surgery. But maybe after that.' She gives me such a wide grin I can't help but smile back.

'How exciting,' I say, wondering what else someone might plan to add to such perfectly sculpted features. Maybe a vaginoplasty?

Seeing the look on my face she says, 'It's not for me, it's for my daughter.'

Ereka leans across the table and squeezes Summer's hand.

I'd like to think this makes it less objectionable. But handing down a perfection obsession to one's daughter is fraught with silent dangers, even if she gets a pretty nose or a bigger bra size in the deal. But, really, is this my problem? I've come here to relax.

'Hey, Virginia, what about some lunch?' Ereka asks. 'You haven't eaten a thing.'

'Maybe later. I'm feeling a bit ordinary.'

'You okay, Cati?' Helen asks.

'Bit nauseous, Zukes. Nothing a glass of red won't fix.'

'Hey, maybe you're pregnant?' Helen smiles. 'It's time for a baby, Cati. Imagine, it'd come out reciting Shakespeare and the periodic table.'

Virginia answers quickly. 'Not likely.'

'You've gotta be having more sex than me. I think even dead people are having more sex than me.'

'I'm definitely not pregnant.'

'You're not too old—yet,' Helen continues.

Virginia looks away. Nothing about her looks very well.

'I saw a YouTube thing about a woman in her sixties who had a baby,' Summer says. 'What's up with that? Creepy, much. I mean, if you know you're gonna die in the next ten or twenty years, why do that to a kid? Make it into an orphan on purpose?'

'It just depends on how badly you want children,' Ereka says. 'Some people keep trying. I think it's beautiful. The human spirit just never gives up.'

Virginia is flicking through the images on her camera.

'Aw, go on, your crusty old ovaries can still do it,' Helen says. 'Those are look-a-charging-hippo-in-the-eye ovaries.'

'Zuki,' Virginia says. 'It's. Not. Gonna. Happen.'

Nobody uses all those capital letters and full stops without it meaning *something*. I swing my gaze from Virginia to Helen. Maeve has also picked up that we seem to be shifting from the shallows of banter into serious life-ache waters here.

'Good choice,' Summer says, filing her false nails.

Now Virginia is smoothing down the crease of her maroon tracksuit pants. 'Not exactly.'

'Could you say what you're saying, for fuck's sake?' Helen asks.

'It's no big deal, okay?'

'What is?'

'I had some tests done a while back.' Virginia puts her camera on her lap. 'The arthritis is getting pretty bad, and I thought I'd just check out a few other things . . .'

We all wait for her to continue.

'And?' Helen prods.

'It's all a little medically complicated, but the bottom line is nothing's happening in here,' she says, patting her belly. 'Ovaries are completely dried up. Two little rocks. Early menopause. So that was a little tough to hear. Funny, I'd never thought about my ovaries before, but if I had, I'd have liked them to be soft and spongy, more like fruit than like stone.'

'No way,' Helen says. 'Are they sure?'

Virginia nods. 'They're three thousand, five hundred and forty-six dollars' worth of tests sure.'

'For that price you could've bought a kid on the black market,' CJ says.

'Never mind,' Summer soothes. 'You get to so totally live your *own* life.'

'Probably no space in my life for a kid anyway. Got a busy year coming up.'

My heart plops, like someone's dropped a whole pavlova. It feels messy inside me. *Don't indulge in feeling sorry for me.* Maeve was stern about that. But it's involuntary. I've always wondered how childless people fill their days—you know, after tennis lessons and concerts. How they spend their love.

'Are you *sad*?' Ereka asks softly, slipping the word into the cold waters of this banter like a warm child's hand.

'A bit numb, I think. It's all coincided with Celia dying, and so . . . I guess I'll have to wait to see how I feel. I did go through a stage about a month ago where I couldn't bear to see a mother in public with her baby. Does that count as sad?'

Ereka nods. 'I'm so sorry, Virginia.'

I do not try to say, *I'm sorry, that's terrible*, or anything like that.

Virginia stretches uncomfortably. 'Wasn't meant to be. I'll survive.'

'Kids are overrated,' CJ says, in what she must imagine is a helpful way. 'Count your lucky cards.'

Virginia doesn't look like she feels lucky.

'Jeez, Cati . . .' Helen looks troubled. It's not an expression I know on her.

Virginia rubs her puffy knuckles.

How does someone end up maternally shipwrecked? Bad luck? Crappy karma? Or . . . possibly taking too long about it? It's not like we have all the time in the world. There's a biological deadline. For me, motherhood was my destiny; like it was Harry Potter's to kill Voldemort and Sir Arthur's to remove Excalibur. I pursued motherhood like a crazed *Twilight* groupie stalking Robert Pattinson for his autograph. I'd have given up everything—travel, career, lovers, wealth—to have my own baby. Which, if you think about it, I did. I wasn't being scandalous when I announced to my mother on my twenty-ninth birthday that I was going to have a baby the following year. *With who?* I hadn't thought that far ahead. Frank and I fell into a love affair soon after. On our third date, I told him that I wanted a baby next year and that if he didn't, I'd have to move on.

It was too soon for it to count as an ultimatum. We'd barely started loving each other. And of course I gave him time to think about it, respecting, as I always have, those who choose not to have kids. I don't know what went through his mind. Really, does it matter?

So I can't help wondering how you miss that boat, presuming all the equipment could have worked had it been used before it rusted. I'm not accusing Virginia of carelessness. My heart is aching for her and I would rather stick pins in my eyes than ask, 'Why did you not reach for it with everything inside you?' I feel like a procreating snob even thinking it.

'Isn't it terrible how a woman's fertility drops dramatically after thirty?' Ereka says. 'Just when we're all emotionally ready to have kids. Before then, you're not much more than a child these days.'

'Truth is, I didn't think about it much even in my thirties,' Virginia says. 'My career was really taking off and I was having a great time. Flying all over the place, dating different men. And I'd look at all these women getting pregnant and going off to have babies and losing their jobs and career prospects and you know what? I used to feel sorry for them. But then suddenly you're forty. And there's no man on the horizon. And you know you're working against time. You're so on the wrong side of motherhood you want to weep, rewind, go back, make different choices. Maybe try to work it out with the guy you liked everything about except that he never read a newspaper or always had sex with his socks on.'

'Oh my god, I hate that too,' Summer says. 'Sex with socks. Far out.'

'You're not saying you should have settled?' Helen asks.

'I don't know what I'm saying.'

'Maybe there isn't a perfect guy out there for you—or for any of us,' Ereka says.

'Maybe . . .'

'Do you really need a man to have a baby?' I ask, knowing I would have lied, cheated or stolen semen when I was twenty-nine. I was wild once, you must believe me.

'Been down that road. Two years ago, I figured I'd do it on my own. So I approached my buddy François . . .'

'Frankie the Mankie?' Helen gasps.

'Yeah, remember him?'

'Didn't he become gay after you and he went out?'

'Yeah, I was obviously not a very inspiring advertisement for heterosexual snogging. Anyway, we once promised to be each other's relationship back-up plan. So I asked him and he agreed to donate sperm—even though he said it was a public announcement to the world that I'd officially given up on men. We tried it a couple of times. Nothing as undignified as the turkey baster. But I was desperate. Nothing. And there's a limit to how many times you can ask your friend to wank into a jar for you. So, I decided to get some tests done.'

'What about an egg donor?' Maeve asks.

Virginia sighs. 'Tried that.'

'Really?' Helen asks, shocked.

'I put an ad in a newspaper. Never heard a thing.'

Ereka wrings her hands, her bracelets clanking. She looks like she wants to say something.

'I've never really understood it, but women hang on to their eggs—even though they're just bleeding them out every month. Even if they've finished their families. I tell you, it'd be easier to get hold of the crown jewels than a donated egg.'

'Who'd have thought?' Summer asks.

'When it comes down to the wire, there's no such thing as the sisterhood. I've been stunned, appalled really, to witness how ungenerous women are in helping others become mothers. I almost get the feeling that women are thinking, "If you can't make them on your own, you don't deserve to have them." I paid for that ad for a year. Not a single bite.'

I swallow. I've seen ads like that before.

'You could have had mine,' CJ says. 'I'm sorry I just never thought about it.'

'Me too,' Summer says.

Ereka puts her hand on Virginia's. She seems tormented, more than usual, and is breathing heavily. For a moment I wonder if she's having a fit or something. 'This is such bad luck,' she says, shaking her head.

'What?'

'I tried. I tried to give mine away.'

'What do you mean?' Virginia asks.

'After Jake and I decided we weren't going to have more kids, I put an ad in the *Highland Chronicle* offering to donate my eggs. I got a few calls and did some interviews with couples. It just never worked out.'

'Why not?' Helen asks.

'It was all quite bizarre. One woman was so anxious, I broke into hives around her. I couldn't bring myself to inflict her as a mother on any child. The husband of the second couple gave me the creeps. I don't know if he thought he was going to get to have sex with me or something. Another only wanted a boy, and when I asked, "What if it's a girl?" they said that they'd been to an astrologer and they *knew* they were having a boy. So that was a psycho alert. When the last couple found out that Olivia was brain-damaged they didn't want my eggs, even though her brain damage wasn't genetic. So I just gave up. But it still upsets me.' She clutches her chest. 'It *really* upsets me that I couldn't give my eggs away.'

Virginia murmurs something. I'm not close enough to hear what.

'I'd have loved nothing more than to give my eggs to you. That would have felt like my "family" was complete. If I could have seen another beautiful child enter this world and bring happiness to another woman.' Ereka is crying freely now. It's been a sopping twenty-four hours. Summer ferrets in her bag and hands her a tissue. Virginia's head is heavy on her shoulders. It is one of those terrible, beautiful *Romeo and Juliet* moments. We have, if you think about it, all the makings here of a happy ending. Timing is a bitch from hell.

I also like to help people. I donate blood. I'm on a bone-marrow register. I don't do these things for applause, but they make me feel like I care. But I never tried to give my eggs away. It is, I suppose, a contradiction in my nature. And if pushed to defend it, I'd have to say because the eggs are *mine*. Not so much *mine* as *me*. It would feel like giving one of my children away. And yes, I know people give their children up for adoption all the time. It's not so strange. And that they probably look in the mirror and smile, knowing that the sacrifice was worth it because of the joy it gave someone else. I guess I will never know this kind of satisfaction and will have to make peace with the fact that, unlike Ereka, I am a selfish egg-hogging dog in the manger.

Helen has been quiet. 'Why did you never say anything to me?'

'Jeez, Zuki, what, like lay my sorry story on you while your ovaries are working overtime?'

'I didn't know . . . I didn't even know that you wanted kids.'

'All women want kids.'

'Until they get them,' Summer adds.

'That's not true. My sister Gail and her husband decided kids were a waste of money and they'd rather spend their lives travelling,' CJ says.

'Well, it's, like, totally different if you can but you choose not to. You want them if you can't have them, don't you think, CJ?' Summer argues.

CJ shrugs.

'Even when things go wrong?' Ereka asks. 'What if you had a kid like Olivia? Then your life becomes hell, and you're not allowed to die.'

'I didn't think about having a disabled child,' Virginia says. 'Sorry.'

'It's okay. No-one does.'

'You know, I've been thinking,' Virginia says. 'About Olivia. I've got a friend who runs a safe house for adults who are mentally challenged. She started it to help her brother who was left brain-damaged in a car accident. She bought the property with the settlement.'

'Really? Where is it?'

'In northern Queensland, on a beautiful piece of land, run mostly by volunteers. People who care about the land, about living ethically and inclusively. They offer work, they help organise fun days. It's small, it only houses eight, but maybe you'd like to talk to her? Go and see the place? Think about it for the future. I'd love to take you.'

Ereka nods. 'Thanks. Gee, it sounds . . . good.'

We are all quiet for a moment, buoyed by this hopeful prospect.

'And let's chat about drawing up some kind of will to make provisions for Olivia,' CJ says. 'I'd do anything to help.'

'You know, I'm going to do Zumba with Olivia and her friends.' Summer smiles.

Ereka sniffs, overcome with the generosity on offer. 'You're all very kind.'

I have nothing to give, really. Except my offer to go with her to the doctor. This is not a friendship competition, but maybe I'll take her for a degustation lunch afterwards.

Helen puts her hand on Ereka's shoulder. Ereka wipes her eyes.

'Virginia, what about adopting?' Maeve asks. 'There are so many unwanted children in the world and so few adults to care for them.'

'I don't want to adopt on my own. I could think of nothing worse than being a single mother.'

Maeve nods, as if she totally understands. The whole story of her life contracts into what seems like a concession to Virginia, if you didn't know better. But she looks at me. And we smile. Like, you know, at the same time.

'You can always be a spare grown-up. A really great godmother,' I say.

Virginia pshaws. 'You know when you're in deep shit? When people start making you godmother. I'm godmother to four kids—and I've been asked nine times by friends and cousins! Everyone's thinking, "Poor Virginia, she's never going to have her own, let's assign her with a fancy title and give her a special role in the christening or naming ceremony and maybe she'll forget that she's a barren spinster."'

'Hey, that's not what Dave and I thought,' Helen protests.

'Yeah, okay, I'm being unfair. You guys were the first to make me a godmother—before it was clear to me and the rest of the world that I was never going to be a mother myself.'

'But you see what hell I go through,' Helen says. 'How I never have time for myself, how Cameron drives me crazy with his vegetarianism, and Sarah with her foul mouth, and Nathan with his know-all attitude, and Levi in his bloody dresses. Their noise and dentist appointments and swimming lessons. You don't really want to trade your exciting life for that?'

We have reached the peak of this conversation, it sweeps through me as Helen's words are cast forth like some twister.

This is the crux of it. Who would switch roles? Knowing what we know about each other's lives?

'It may feel like hell to you, but from where I am—' her words come out barely whispered, '—it's pretty spectacular.'

Spectacular. She used the word *spectacular*. We mothers have lives brimming with chaos. We are enslaved. Encumbered. Driven to drink. Sick with worry. Overburdened and underappreciated. We are saturated with significance. Not a moment to ourselves. We are, if you think about it, the Chosen Ones.

Ereka shakes her head. 'Don't envy *me*, Virginia.'

Virginia smiles. 'I tell you what I do envy, Ereka.' She pauses. 'I have no-one in this world who needs me. If I dropped dead tomorrow, Channel A would find someone to replace me. My affairs would get tied up. My brother would have to cut short his business trip to bury Celia. My plants would die of thirst. But no-one will be standing someday at the altar, or their graduation, or holding their newborn and thinking, "I wish my mum was here." I don't matter in that way to anyone. You all just take that for granted. Ereka, when you say, "I can't die," you mean that in a way that feels hard for you. You have to be here. I don't feel that way at all. I could just slide off the planet, melt away into the ocean, and nothing would change. It would be easy for me to die. I have to work really hard to figure out sometimes what makes me get up in the morning. Especially when things are going crap at work. Just once, I'd love to know how that feels. To matter in that way.'

We've come to the end. I feel it in Virginia's words. If this was a parachute debate, Virginia would have won it, no doubt about it. The irony is, she's saying she's the last person in the world worth saving. Give the parachute to the mother.

18

Skin to Skin

The front doorbell goes.

I'm grateful to escape the veranda where we have crossed a jungle of pain since breakfast. I race through the living room to the front door, Virginia's sadness heavy in my heels.

I open the door and there is . . . Gary, I take it, since he is carrying a large fold-up massage table slung over his shoulder. He is not young and muscled-up as I'd anticipated. Why should he be? He is pitilessly middle-aged, wearing a big grin, pin-striped trousers, a T-shirt declaring PARANOID PEOPLE ARE FOLLOWING ME and a pink bowtie, which is probably some brand of masseur-humour. Perhaps he does massage-o-grams in his spare time.

'Are you Gary?'

'I am. That's me. But call me Ga for short.'

'Gary is already short.'

'Yes, but it is two syllables,' he says, holding up two fingers.

Since the man has obviously spent time thinking about this, I simply invite him in. 'Hi, I'm Jo, I'm the one who called.'

'Nice to meet you,' he says with extreme cheerfulness. 'Yeah, it'd be hard to shorten Jo into a nickname or anything.'

He strides in with his fold-up table and turns around completely like a dog circling its own tail.

'This is quite a place,' he says. 'Quite a place.' He pauses. 'Not a bad place at all.'

'What's the bowtie for?' I ask.

He touches his neck protectively. 'It's my signature. It just adds a touch of class. I don't charge extra for it.'

'Would you mind waiting here a moment?' I ask.

I walk out onto the veranda. Helen and Virginia are talking, Helen's hand on Virginia's shoulder. Maeve is back to reading *The Consolations of Philosophy*, Summer and CJ are nattering together, but Ereka is nowhere to be seen.

'Where's Ereka?' I ask.

Everyone looks around. No-one's noticed she's not there.

'I think she went up to her room to finishing packing,' Virginia says.

'Right, well, Helen, I took the liberty of calling Gary. You know—sixty dollars for a full-body massage?'

'And?'

'He's here—I wanted to surprise Ereka.'

'Guilt is a fabulous thing,' Helen says.

'Shut up, I am not doing this out of guilt. She really needs it.'

'Don't we all?' she asks, pointing at herself.

'Fine, you have one too. On me.'

'Ooh, you're so much more fun when you're feeling guilty . . . So is he a spunk?' Helen asks.

'I'm sure he's perfectly harmless under the bowtie.'

Ereka is blissed out. Or she's dead. She is slumped on the massage table and hasn't moved once in the hour in which her tired, aching body has been touched and stretched and kneaded and rubbed. It's such a human ache—to be touched. We go about our business, imagining human contact is a luxury like Beluga caviar or first-class seats, but really it's a necessity, like emptying your bladder or blinking. My friend Bella once told me how she arranged for her and her mother to have a massage together and how her mum, who had been a widow for over a decade, began to sob uncontrollably as soon as the masseuse laid hands on her. I am rendered sort of weepy by that story.

I often remind Frank that I am all for a good touching, and would he mind very much limiting himself to my back and feet? *Yes, just there, thanks.* But when skin meets skin—we're talking elbows and big toes—he takes that as an invitation for all comers. He assures me it's involuntary and that he doesn't control his erections. Sometimes a back scratch is worth the risk of a gatecrasher. And as Frank says in the post-orgasmic debrief, 'So, was that so terrible?' Which, of course, it never is.

I wonder sometimes if I touch my children enough. I know the books tell you to *Stay emotionally involved and appropriately tactile with your teenage kids.* But what if they push you away? You need new strategies, ways of holding them that don't feel too much like holding. Recently Jamie's become self-conscious and private about her body, withdrawn her flesh from observation. I silently cheer each boundary she creates, for the sake of who she is, but I don't want her to forget what it's like to be touched—to have your hair stroked, back rubbed, hand held. Occasionally she lets me hug her properly, but now that she's as tall as I am the cuddling that comes naturally with someone small is lost, awkward. She's fully grown, a shy giraffe nuzzling me. It lasts only a moment before she shakes herself free and moves on. Sometimes I get away with scratching her back if I come in to kiss her goodnight and catch her in a soft moment in the pages of a book, away from her flickering computer screen, but invariably I get berated for messing up her pimple cream. Now and then I rub her feet while she's watching television. Occasionally she allows me to help her with her makeup and straighten her hair. But her body is now her own—those little limbs I used to dry, that glorious hair I used to wash and lift lice from, those cheeks I used to kiss have passed into her care in the sanctuary of her adolescence. Maybe we forget what a privilege it is for someone to allow us to touch them. But we shouldn't. The other night when I offered to rub her pre-menstrual sore tummy, she pushed me away. As a mother, you need to brace yourself for rejection. It's the sensible thing to do.

Until a year ago, Aaron still used to hop in the bath with me sometimes. Each time, I wondered, 'Will this be the last time?' I savoured the intimacies of our conversation, our feet touching beneath the warm water, his cautious eyeing of my breasts, familiar and becoming stranger. Then, one day, it stopped. As if he'd gone to sleep one night and woken up beyond it. I tried not to feel grief about it. I think I was stoic. 'You don't want your sixteen-year-old son still wanting to bathe with you,' Frank offered helpfully.

Recently, after a day of detentions and endless trouble brought him home glum and angry, I said, 'Wanna have a bath with me?'

He thought about it for a moment. 'Okay, but make the most of it, Mum.'

I ran us a big bubble bath. We made silly Santa Claus bubble faces. I was there with him, but I was also watching, silently cherishing the close-in warmth, the enclosure of our bodies, the trust it held, the perfection of a boy leaving his boyhood and the bubble of mummy-comfort behind. Part of the ache of letting go of them as they unfurl into independence is losing that skin-to-skin contact with them. There is no freedom in it, really. It's a bereavement.

Ereka moans slightly from Gary's massage table.

Gary smiles massively from across the bridge of her back, his bowtie slightly askew.

While Ereka is distracted, I find my way to the handbag she's left on a couch in the lounge room together with her basket in preparation for her departure. It's probably not friendship-protocol to rummage around in a friend's bag, but I am doing this for *her* benefit. Besides, I asked Helen if it was okay, and she said it was.

I find her iPhone easily, and race up the stairs. I grab the gift Maeve gave me out of its wrapping but struggle to get a connection no matter where I stand. The pink bathroom offers no coverage. I go into CJ and Summer's room and am surprised to see a picture next to one of the beds of Summer with her three kids draped around her neck. I examine the photo briefly. Jai is dark and has brooding angry eyes, his face a mess of acne; her teenage daughter, Airlee, has curly brown hair and a *whatevah* look on her face. But it's the little one with her straight blonde hair who most reminds me of Summer herself. Especially in the eyes. Which you'd notice first, if her lower face were not marked by the cruel distortions of a radically cleft lip. *Don't judge her*, Ereka had said. She's saving money for plastic surgery. *It's not for me, it's for my daughter.*

I leave quickly, my heart pounding. Of course Ereka trusts her. I now know what Summer has that I don't.

I try the room with the rocking horse, wondering why Summer hasn't mentioned her daughter's cleft lip, and why I thought she was frivolous just because she's got perfect tits, and why I imagine I know anything. I finally get a connection, standing in the swell of the bay window. I scroll through Ereka's phonebook until I find Jake's number.

'Hi, baby, everything okay?' he asks.

'Um, Jake, it's not Ereka, it's Jo.'

'Oh! Hi, Jo, is Ereka okay?' There's a note of alarm in his voice.

'God, yes,' I laugh. 'Right now, she's having a full-body massage and is more relaxed than a sedated rhino.' I wonder if this is offensive. I'm not comparing her to the size of a rhino, or anything.

'That's good,' he says, sounding relieved.

'She doesn't know I'm calling you, I've borrowed her phone and, well, please forgive me if this is presumptuous—we know she's got to get back this afternoon—but is there any way at all that we could keep her till tomorrow morning? I've got a special dinner planned tonight, and I'm sure the extra day will do her good . . . that's if you can manage without her, of course.'

I scrunch my eyes tight. I shouldn't be asking this. It's not my place.

There's a silence on the other end of the line. 'Well, Jo, I'm a little confused. Ereka said she was staying until tomorrow. Everything is under control here.'

Oh god.

'Ah, I see . . . so it's fine for her to stay?'

'Yeah, I mean that was the plan . . . Why? Did she say she had to get home today?'

'Um, I've probably got my wires crossed. Look, so that's all good then. She'll be home tomorrow.'

'Yeah, great. But, uh, maybe just ask her to give me a call when she's finished her massage. Don't interrupt her now.'

You know I don't find slapstick or Mr Bean funny. When I watch it, I think, 'Who could be so stupid?' But here is the answer: me.

'Jake, do you think maybe we could just keep this call between us?'

He doesn't say anything.

'I already upset her last night by saying something insensitive, and I was trying to make things better. Maybe she said she needed to get home today so she can get away from me.' I laugh. Though nothing about this situation is amusing.

'Okay,' he says. 'Yeah . . . Sure.'

'And Jake?'

'Yeah?'

'How's Olivia?'

'Absolutely fantastic. She's a special child. Ereka and I are very blessed.'

'Yeah.'

We say our goodbyes. I slump forward and let my head fall into my hands. And this would be a good time for me to reflect. To ask myself questions. Like, why I just can't learn to leave a locked door alone.

I walk downstairs and slip Ereka's phone, together with the Leonard Cohen DVD, into her bag. Then I go out to the veranda where Gary is working on Ereka's feet. Summer is sitting sipping on a Diet Coke and chatting to CJ, trilling with stories and laughter. Unlike her false nails and pert breasts, her private sorrow and anguish are not on display.

'All done.' Gary smiles and wipes his brow with the back of his hand.

Ereka doesn't move for a moment. Then she rolls over, her face indented from the pressure of the massage table, her mascara running. Was she lying there crying?

'Thanks,' Ereka says softly, touching him on his shoulder. 'That was divine.'

He grins with pride. 'Nice toenails, by the way.'

And Ereka preens, needing so little encouragement.

'Right, I'm next,' Helen yelps, hauling herself up from the wicker chair and throwing herself at Gary.

Ereka stands up, a little wobbly on her feet, destabilised by serenity.

'Jo,' she says. 'Thanks for this. You are such a true friend.'

I gulp, and nod and do something with my mouth that I hope is a smile.

'Well, girls, I think I'd better get going,' she says dreamily.

'Why don't you stay?' I ask.

She beams at me in a way that is impossible to read. 'I've got things to attend to . . .'

Looking into her eyes, you'd swear she was telling the truth.

Everyone gets up to hug her goodbye. Summer embraces her like she is her bosom buddy and walks her to her car, helping with the bags, just as Callum comes up the driveway pushing a wheelbarrow topped with chopped wood. Summer sashays up to him, touches him on the shoulder, throws her head back and laughs as if she didn't have a care in the world. Callum picks up an armload of logs to bring indoors. Summer takes two and follows him. I suppose I should go and get some too. I'm not sure why I'm hovering. I wait for Summer to come back inside. And as she passes, I say, 'You're incredible, you know.'

And she looks at me strangely, not sure whether to trust me, then she smiles and lets it be.

'How were you to know?' Helen says, shrugging. After her massage was done, I'd offered Virginia one but she'd declined, as did Maeve. I paid Gary, ushered him to the door, and told Helen I had to talk to her. I hustled her into the downstairs toilet where we are now standing.

'I wasn't.'

'She told us she had to leave.'

'She did.'

'She was lying.'

'I guess she was.'

'Where do you think she's gone?'

I bite my lip. There are privacy issues here. Friendship issues. Boundary issues. If Ereka can't say no, it is none of my business.

I am not her keeper. Nobody put me in charge. No-one has the right to question how each of us mothers. How each of us loves. I know what it feels like to be in the lowlands of the moral high ground. I've spent a lot of time down there this weekend. Judge not lest ye be judged.

    I look Helen in the eye and say, 'I have absolutely no idea.'

19

The Wall Between Them Fallen

The secret garden around the west side of the house is a kingdom of bright pockets of impatiens and shows evidence of small careful decisions about the placement of things—birdbath, fountain, angel statues, foliage and shrubs. I see a shovel and some gardening gloves Callum has left beneath the skirt of a lavender bush, promising he'll be back soon.

After Ereka's departure, I'd nudged Maeve. 'Fancy a stroll?' She'd checked her watch, disappeared indoors and returned in an enormous sun-hat, sports sandals and pouch around her waist with a water bottle attached as if we were about to head off for a three-day hike. All I meant was a little wander around the grounds, but okay.

Tennyson has tagged along with us, grateful to be included. He lifts his leg, as if there's nothing more exciting in this life than to piss against a lavender bush. He gives an almighty sneeze.

'Bless you,' I say.

Maeve leans down, pointing at a praying mantis on a branch.

'Beautiful.' I only say this because I'm sure that's what she's thinking.

'They're actually one of nature's most perfect predators. It's not unusual for the female to eat the male during sex. She chomps his head right off.'

'That's an extreme way to avoid having to sleep in the wet patch. Which you never do, right? You just send Stan home . . .'

Maeve laughs. 'He's permitted, very occasionally, to stay over. But one wouldn't want him to make a habit of it.'

'Of course not,' I say.

We skirt the circular arrangement of lemon thyme, basil, mint and rosemary. Maeve occasionally sniffs the herbs. I stash some mint leaves in the top pocket of my jumper for my dinner tonight. She chews on a basil leaf.

'Do you ever miss the companionship of a husband or live-in lover?'

'I don't think I do. I see Stan whenever I want to, which is more than most wives can say about their husbands. I suppose one becomes calcified in one's ways after living alone too long. Stan equally so, which is probably why it works.'

'Does it feel like an empty nest? With Jonah away?'

'I've always thought eventual liberation is what makes motherhood tolerable.' Perhaps considering Ereka's plight, she adds, 'For most of us fortunate ones.'

Maeve makes intimacy hard. Not on purpose, but as if things have slid from her grasp. Talking to her is like being awake at three am when I see Frank asleep and I feel barely alive all by myself and I try not to wake him. Sleep is precious,

I know that for a fact. I'm not blaming Travis, but the first time I ever had insomnia, I was nineteen and he'd left to go overseas for a year. He was the first man I loved. The longing for him would wake me. It's hard to explain why I'm thinking about that now. It has something to do with the way things slip away from us. We never got back together again.

'What's Jonah up to now?' I ask.

'If I told you, I'd be guessing. He's not famous for his correspondence or his calls to convey any information about his whereabouts or activities. Perhaps sensibly. The less I know the better.'

'Don't you worry about him if you don't know what he's doing or where he is?'

'Ha! When your son acquires a driver's licence, you officially relinquish all delusions of control, and trust me, they are delusions. All that's left are prayers and tranquillisers, and I don't pray. But it's like I tell my students who are underprepared for their exams: "You just have to trust that you've done enough to get through."'

'Any idea when he'll be back?'

'Like most men, he abhors nagging. And asking and nagging are closer relatives than we imagine. In any event, the longer the delay, the better. He's determined that when he returns, he's going into the army.'

She turns her head to appraise my reaction. I suppose I'm not doing the best job of concealing the horror on my face. I don't know Jonah but I don't want him to go into the army.

'Don't let him, Maeve.'

She gives me a look strained with the tolerance you see in adults arguing with teenagers. 'Perhaps you know a way of persuading a man of twenty-three to change his mind? He's an adult. Apparently it's what he wants to do. To fight for his country.' I might sense a tremor in her voice, but I can't vouch for it.

'But, Maeve . . .'

She interrupts me. 'If fighting in Afghanistan is what will give his life meaning—well . . .' She sighs. 'At a certain point, one has no purchase nor influence. One has to sign off on the job sheet and accept that one's work is done.'

'Does he know how you feel?'

'I've expressed my opinion.'

'I won't even let Aaron play computerised war games.'

'Boys are adept at manoeuvring around rules they don't like. And those that don't are dull. They turn out to be accountants who do other people's tax returns. We always imagine we want children who will listen to what we say. They become compliant adults. Despite our shaky start, Jonah's a marvellous person. I look forward to his company over a glass of wine.'

Maeve removes the dead leaves from the dry bowl of the fountain. I also want to look forward to Aaron's company over a glass of wine. I want that almost impatiently. But in the meantime—he's lying to my face. Children know how to have their secrets, this I understand. Aaron is playing these games behind my back. I know what he's up to. The first time I recognised guile in him, I was genuinely shocked, almost betrayed. Like when I first smelled bad breath in my kids—and understood their sweet morning breath was only a commercial, actual product to follow. Our children won't let us hang on to our image of their perfection.

'I won't allow those games into my house, Maeve,' I say. I don't mean to sound strict with her. She's not the one playing them. She's not the child I'm trying to raise.

'I know too much about taboos. I teach a whole course on them. They invest the forbidden with disproportionate excitement. Perhaps a mild indifference is more effective than an outright ban if you really want him to stay away from them.'

I kick a shrivelled lemon that's fallen to the ground, something hot and fretful churns in my belly. I find that I am cross. With Maeve who isn't stopping Jonah. With Jonah for going into the army. With Aaron for wanting to play violent games. With Jamie for wanting to go to Borneo and making me say no.

'So did you let Jonah play violent games?' He would have acquired an appetite for war by playing cops and robbers, isn't that how boys get it?

'We negotiated all the time. He got away with some. Not all.'

'And what was he like as a child?'

'He made a valiant and rather relentless effort to alienate people around him. At school, he seemed to get into a fight every week. He exhausted the forbearance and kindness of his teachers and headmasters.'

Aha. See, he was an angry child. Who can blame him? You have to make allowances for people's back stories, their uneven beginnings.

'Well, Aaron's just had a month of detention for telling a teacher that he's sick of worksheets and that "this school is crap". He spends a lot of time in time-out.'

I'm not expecting Maeve to chuckle, but she does. I don't take detentions lightly.

Tennyson is digging up some loose soil in the herb garden. Maeve shoos him away and tries to restore the evenness of the dirt with her hands. 'Can't forbid dogs from doing what comes instinctively,' she mutters. Tennyson thinks it's a game, and starts digging a little further along. Maeve sits on her haunches, watching him. And then she says, 'When Jonah was twelve, he threatened a girl in his class with the compass from his geometry set. So, of course, he was expelled.'

'Poor kid,' I mumble. Aaron wouldn't dare.

Maeve gets to her feet with her hands on her hips. 'I sometimes fantasised about putting him into foster care and doing another PhD somewhere in the darkest heart of Africa.'

'Really?'

'That boy took me on a guided tour through the nine circles of hell. By the time he was fifteen, as Summer might say, I was *totally over it*.'

Maybe boys are designed to forge their path through hell dragging their screaming mothers behind them. I have no idea what it takes to become a man. It could be that pent-up aggression, investigation of the ways you can throw and catch something, and experiments with just how much rank stupidity can spill out of your mouth are part of the unfolding of masculinity. It sometimes seems this way.

Does a mother really need in her inventory of memories a call to the principal's office because her son informed a girl in his class that he is 'sleeping with her mother'? As his headmistress reminded Aaron with stern but patient kindness, 'Not every silly thing you think has to be expressed; I know boys like to show off and say stuff that makes them feel big, but sometimes you just have to learn to keep your mouth shut,' I imagined the million ways in which I was going to kill him. As I left her office, she touched me gently on my arm and whispered, 'Don't be too hard on him.'

So I let Frank deal with it. First, I didn't trust that I could be fair. I have enough self-insight to know my fuse is short when it comes to stupid things boys say and that perhaps I might crush when a mere wallop would do. Second, Frank 'gets' Aaron in a way I've come to accept I cannot, due perhaps to the absence of a Y chromosome and a penis. Believe me, I know my limits. Having a son has taught me everything I don't know about men. For example, how they care—they truly deeply care—about which country wins the soccer world cup and how many centuries Sachin Tendulkar has made. They care in the way one might care about AIDS orphans and world poverty. They will, I've observed, risk nose-flattening and head injury to nudge a ball across a line. They are drawn to things that go *boom* and *crash*. They are, in all fairness, alien.

Frank had recently spent a small fortune on two tickets to the Ashes, a cricket tournament the two of them were counting days towards. All Frank said about the incident in the playground was, 'I don't want to know why you said what you said, but if you ever speak like that again to a girl, losing the Ashes tickets will be the fun part of what will happen to you.' That was it.

I wondered, but only for a moment, whether Aaron had accidentally come across the joke door sign I'd bought as an anniversary present for Frank which said, 'Please do not disturb: I'm fucking your mother.' We have, I assure you, been very discreet about that door sign.

But my mortification aside, I did not feel responsible. Not the way I used to when I was peeling grapes for his lunch and

Dr Seussing him to sleep, and his tantrums, fussiness and bad language felt like *my* personal failings.

Right now, he is being colonised by the hooliganism of boyhood, his humanity more influenced by MTV, gangsta fashion and boys with older brothers than by anything I have to offer. The ugly world is entering him and I have no way of sealing him off.

'How did you deal with Jonah?'

'Poorly at first. But eventually I came clean with the story of how Solange had died, that she was his biological mother and had been for the first eighteen months of his life. How he'd been there when it happened. There've always been photos of Solange around our house, but after that conversation he expressed the desire to have his own picture, which I had enlarged and put in a special frame. Sometimes I'd eavesdrop on him whispering about this and that, details of his day, under his bedclothes, to the picture.'

Something in my heart stirs for this boy, now man.

'It's silly how . . . jealous I was.'

I catch this offering. She is letting me in.

'He then developed this habit of talking about having two mums, Mum One and I was Mum Two. That became shortened to Mutu—he still calls me that.' She pauses and takes her water bottle out of her holster and has a long drink from it. 'I suspect we inadvertently twist our children into our unfinished stories: they know when something's not right, and without an explanation, they assume it's them. I've found that we need to speak the things that need to be spoken. There really is no other way.'

We are holding a thread together spun in last night's darkness.

I sit down on the edge of the fountain. The stone has absorbed the heat of the sun and warms my butt. I've always protected my kids from painful information. I'm just remembering that when Jamie and Aaron were ten and eight, a friend invited us to join her and her kids at a Holocaust memorial function. I declined simply because I hadn't told my kids about the Holocaust. I hadn't yet worked out how to explain it. It's easier to pretend some things are not there.

But then Jamie found out about the Holocaust soon after—by watching *Raiders of the Lost Ark*. How can I describe it? I watched the childhood drain from her eyes as I answered her questions, handing over awareness like a poisoned apple. I probably should have intervened before Steven Spielberg got there.

'Shall we take a stroll to the memorial garden?' Maeve says, leading the way in large strides for someone so small. I run to catch up with her down the slope of the garden towards the rosebushes in the formation of an S. Together they create yin-and-yang enclosures, in which stand two single rocks. The bushes are thirsty, tired with the effort of their recent summer blooming without sufficient rain. Maeve and I do not sit. One seldom wants to rest in other people's grief.

'What happened after you told him the truth?'

'I took him to India.'

'India?'

'Then Egypt, then West Africa. I wanted him to stand on the banks of the Ganges and see children poking dead bodies floating in the water with sticks. I wanted him to look up at the Great Sphinx looming above him, an astounding accomplishment of human effort. I wanted him to watch the life bleed out of an ox being slaughtered by the Mursi tribe in South Ethiopia desperate for rain on their lands. Between the ages of twelve and fourteen, he came up so close to poverty and death and everything in between, he could describe them in smells. He glimpsed the kind of heartache you need to know exists in the world so you can measure yourself against it.'

'Wasn't that . . . dangerous?'

'Oh yes,' she says, her eyes glinting. 'By giving him danger, I knew he would shape himself boldly. And when we came back, I went into therapy.'

'Why you?'

'It took two years of itinerant existence for a crucial understanding to crystallise. Jonah's anger had little to do with school, or even his early trauma—it had to do with *me*.'

'You? How?' She is letting me in so close, the fragility of this conversation is like gossamer. It could snap at any time.

Maeve leans against the rock, arching her back. Tennyson licks her toes, which she tolerates with a forbearance I could never muster. She removes her glasses and looks me full in the eyes as if she's about to impart something sacred. 'I had to learn to trust him.'

'Trust him?'

She doesn't answer immediately, as if she wants me to think a bit more, to work it out. I'm not being intentionally lazy. I'm waiting to know.

'Consider the manner in which he came to be my son. My sister had to die so I could become his mother. It was a contaminated transaction. But see, if you do not trust your child, he can never trust himself.'

I turn away and look out beyond the memorial garden to where the grounds slope and then rise again to the forested boundary. I'm not saying I don't trust Aaron. But he confuses me with his volatility, the way in which small things can cause him to spiral into self-destruction. He is a testosterone riddle, a male conundrum, vulnerability and rage all rolled together, a prickly and fuzzy creature, growling and changeable. He is my snarling darling. My vicious angel. He moves from sunshine to tempest in a heartbeat. Mostly he makes me feel ridiculous— I embarrass him, I say the wrong things, I don't understand him, he wants to be left alone, I annoy him. But in the next moment he wants to tell me every single detail about LeBron James's latest three-point shooting average or the funniest jockstrap wrestling YouTube clip that's just got twenty million views. He flips from rage to euphoria in a nanosecond. Is he bipolar? Does he have ADHD? ADD? Is this a testosterone surge? A sugar high? I am alarmed and charmed by him. But mostly, I am afraid for him. I'm terrified of the day all this energy finds itself in an eighteen-year-old body, behind the wheel of a car, after six beers, at a footy game where his team has just lost.

Maeve said it herself—he's walking around with half a brain at the moment. And it's only going to grow into a full brain in another fourteen years' time. What? Am I supposed to be his frontal cortex until he grows his own?

'I need an instruction manual, Maeve. I have no idea how to do this.'

Maeve laughs. 'Western culture is the only one that has turned motherhood into a commercially exploited science. This proliferation of parenting books destroys the only reliable tool you have when it comes to parenting: your intuition. Benjamin Spock was right—mothers know more than they think they know.'

'My intuition when it comes to Aaron is wrong. I've read every manual. I've followed all the advice.'

'My suggestion would be to forget the books.'

'I've learned everything about motherhood from books.'

'Not from your children? Perhaps you're not a big fan of their methods. Possibly you're not so different from Aaron, who vocalises—what was it?—"This school is crap."'

How could anyone like Aaron's teaching methods? No-one volunteers to feel stupid and inadequate. I used to get As for everything and he makes me feel like a D-grade mother.

I need more from Maeve, but I don't really know what I'm asking. I take in the rosebushes which surround us in a whorl of bright sorrow. We are standing on sacred ground.

'Most importantly, what you need to know about yourself will show up in your child.'

I am trying to understand.

'Jonah's anger, which terrified me, unlocked the unbearable truth . . .'

I don't stir.

'. . . that I was so fucking angry—at my mother, at Solange, even at Jonah, for needing me so voraciously, for being the only person in the world I had.'

She said 'fucking'.

'What did you do?' I whisper.

'I stayed close to Jonah throughout his rages instead of banishing him. To allow the pain to flare and to be its witness. No more time-outs, which the books are so fond of. At first I thought I'd never survive the hideousness, or endure the onslaught of invective. "I hate you. I wish I was dead. I wish you were dead." You know, the sort of sweet nothings mothers long to hear.' She laughs. 'But then, astonishingly, one day he said, "I need a hug."' Maeve puts her sunglasses back on.

And that's it. Maeve has come to the end of her story. I want her to say more. To fill in the blanks. But there is no more. I can

The Reunion

make of it what I will. I know I will return to this conversation in my head at a later stage and grasp the treasure of it. She stands up, dusts off her pants and walks ahead, sun-hat flapping, leaving me with the image of a boy on the threshold of manhood, folded in his mother's arms, the wall between them fallen.

20

Leaving Our Mothers

'What the hell is that?' Helen asks, sticky-beaking over my shoulder.

The kitchen counter is busy with my dinner preparations.

'It's a quinoa and beet salad.'

'What's the first one?'

'Quinoa. A healthy grain. It's actually a protein.'

'Only you could find something obscure and healthy to serve for dinner,' Helen chuckles.

'Have you tasted it?' I ask sternly.

'Not sure I want to,' she says. 'Is that all you're serving?'

'I have a soup.'

'You're planning to make us all go hungry tonight? Tell me you've made duck breasts.'

'Duck is full of fat.' I know she knows this.

She spoons some quinoa salad into her mouth and chews.

She looks unsure for a moment. Then her head bobs. Her eyes smile. The ginger, the garlic, the chives.

'When are you going to give me the recipe for your dressing?'

'I don't have a recipe. I make it up as I go along.'

'You're going to die without ever sharing it?'

'I guess,' I sniff.

'What a waste.'

'Classy,' CJ says. I've opted for the dining room, a space we've ignored completely while we've been here. I understand the appeal of the veranda, halfway between the inside and the outside. But the dining-room chairs with their maroon velvet seats match the sari I'd brought with me to cover the table. And finding the huge silver candelabra in the sideboard to hold my white candles was just a gift.

Maeve arrives for dinner wearing a smart red Chinese jacket as if she was off to the opera. She embellishes. When Jamie was little she used to dress up, just for the love of a silver glove or the swirl of satin on the skin. These are not affectations. They are proclamations about beauty. I get why Levi loves dresses, more than I get *Call of Duty*. But seeing Helen still in her daggy pyjamas, I understand why she struggles with it.

I serve the soup in shallow bowls sprinkled with spring onion and chives and a dollop of Greek yoghurt.

And then I wait. It is different entirely from hovering.

'Ooh.'

'Aah.'

'Yum.'

'What's in it?'

'Guess.' I suppose I've picked up a few conversational tips from Summer. She beams at me.

Helen is wrong about potato.

When Summer's guess of leeks is right, you'd think she'd won a prize.

Maeve picks out the cauliflower.

Virginia covers her bases with onion and celery, the golden couple without whom there is no soup.

'Cream,' CJ offers.

'Are you not keeping up with me? Cream and I are divorced.'

'Coconut cream?' she tries.

Wrong.

'But it tastes radically like coconut,' Summer says.

'Desiccated coconut. So you get the flavour without the calories.'

I then bring out my quinoa salad, with apple-infused beetroots, coriander, roasted hazelnuts, orange zest, chopped mint from the garden, thinly sliced red cabbage, shaved fennel and slices of persimmon.

'This looks way too healthy for me,' CJ mutters.

'What a bouquet of colours!' Maeve exclaims.

'Is this the main course?' Virginia asks.

Helen is the first to ask for seconds, followed by Virginia and even Maeve.

Finally I present my fruit towers—slices of ruby grapefruit, nectarine and mango, drizzled with champagne and pomegranate seeds, and topped with a strawberry dipped in dark chocolate.

'Okay, you win,' Helen says.

Virginia looks at hers for a long time before she says, 'It's too beautiful to eat.'

It makes me wish Ereka was here.

As the girls help me clear away the dishes, Virginia comes up to me, takes my hand in her good hand. 'Thanks,' she says. 'That meal made me feel worthy. You put a lot of thought into that.'

'A for effort,' Helen says, patting me patronisingly on the back. 'And, surprisingly, I'm not hungry.'

'Doesn't effort start with an E?' Summer asks, confused.

When the dishes have been cleared and washed, Helen says, 'Flashlights and schnapps down at the pergola?'

She is so full of terrible suggestions.

Everyone else thinks this is a great idea.

'What about Matilda?' I ask.

'She's sleeping,' Helen says, as if she personally tucked the snake in and said, 'Sweet dreams.'

I'm less fun in the flesh than I'd like to be, I'll concede that. In theory I'm the first to enthuse about how much fun it might be to take a night-time stroll and look up at the stars. Turns out that in reality, sitting in the dark at the mercy of wildlife I can't see is the opposite of my idea of fun.

But I'm here. Against my will and better judgement, rugged up in a jumper and scarf and my longest socks when there was a perfectly good ready-to-light fire that Callum had prepared for us in the fireplace in the lounge room. Maeve excused herself, saying she wanted a long bath and would get the fire going for us. Even Tennyson had the good sense to decline. He watched us all walk off into the dark, then turned and shuffled back indoors.

The Reunion

The night air is crisp and bites my cheeks. I lie back and put my head in Helen's lap. I look up at the moon. It is almost full. It beams across the water in silver ripples.

'Hey, Helen, it's a full moon,' Virginia prods.

'I wonder where Butterscotch Fred is now,' Helen says.

Virginia cackles.

'Who's Butterscotch Fred?' I ask.

'He liked you, not me,' Helen says.

'I wasn't going anywhere near those lizard lips.'

'So you sent me into the backyard with him,' Helen says. 'Thanks a lot.'

'Well, if you were going to be so gullible . . .'

'He said he had something to show me outside. What else is there to look at outside at night but the moon?'

Virginia giggles.

'So there I am, looking up at the sky, and when I look down Fred's got his dick flapping out.'

'Can I tell them?' Virginia asks.

'Be my guest.'

'He told her semen tastes like . . . butterscotch!'

'And who doesn't love butterscotch?' Summer says.

'And right there was born one of the biggest disappointments of my life.' Helen shakes her head.

'Even without tasting it, I knew semen didn't taste like butterscotch,' Virginia says.

'One mouthful was all it took—and I've never been the same again,' Helen mourns.

'Freak out!' Summer laughs.

'You reckon our girls are giving blowjobs?' Helen asks suddenly.

'Not mine,' I say.

'Who cares?' CJ says. 'As long as they don't get pregnant.'

'Jorja's only thirteen,' I say.

'They start young these days. Jorja's already been to rainbow parties.'

'Airlee too,' Summer says.

''Scuse my ignorance, but what's a rainbow party?' Virginia asks. Of course, she has no reference for these things.

'It's where girls put on different-coloured lipsticks and give boys blowjobs. They leave a ring of rainbow colours up his dick,' CJ explains casually.

'That is the most disturbing thing I've heard in a while,' Virginia confirms.

'It's just harmless experimentation,' CJ says. 'Remember what we all got up to?'

'I'll kill Sarah if she starts that shit,' Helen says.

'Jai goes through a box of tissues every two days when he's home. Boys wank non-stop once they start,' Summer says. 'Don't they, CJ?'

The rest of us shriek. I find it hard enough to engage in certain conversations with my kids. Like last year before Aaron's school had done their compulsory sex education and Aaron asked me, 'What's Viagra?'

Choosing my words carefully, I informed him that 'It's a medicine that helps a man's penis to get hard so he can have sex.'

His brow furrowed in confusion. 'It has to be hard for sex?'

'Sure, otherwise how would it go inside the woman's vagina?'

His confusion turned to alarm. 'It goes *in*?'

I don't know why he didn't remember this from when I told him the facts of life when he was six. Perhaps he'd repressed it.

'Um, yeah. What did you think?'

'I thought maybe next to it . . . yuck. I don't want to put it *in*.'

'It's up to you, but generally, people want to, so they do.'

'I don't want to.'

'Perfectly fine. But feel free to change your mind.'

'I won't.'

I understand his bewilderment.

Sometimes I watch Frank drying himself after a shower, observing this man with whom I share my life, my body, my bed. I stare at the shape of him, the hair on his body, and the way the weight of his balls causes them to swing without underpants. I examine his penis, that obstinate, ever-curious creature who has inside knowledge of me. The banality of nakedness, the folding-down of sheets and the arguing about what to watch on television, lives alongside the bluntly ludicrous notion that *he* puts that penis *in me*. All of a sudden, it seems absurd, hilarious.

Yet I find that few things are as reliable or as clear in their purpose. When life is such a muddle of contradictions and ambivalences, an erect penis is unequivocal, happy to have what it had yesterday and the day before and the day before that. Like a little old man who orders the same hot beef on rye with pickles and mustard at the same deli every day for fifty years. Satisfied.

Though clumsy with his hands, Frank is deft with his mouth (he'd have been a better saxophonist than a tailor). We seldom stray from what works. As he says, 'Never send a finger in to do a tongue's work.' If he tries some new twirl or a little more pressure than usual, I might tap him on the top of his head and say, 'Don't get fancy. No chandeliers.' And now that I've spent nearly thirty-six hours with chandeliers, I have to say they're no great shakes. Fancy is overrated. I wonder if he knows just how much I cherish the ordinariness, the unfanciness of everything we have together. I really should give him more blowjobs.

'How old were you when you gave your first blowjob?' I ask Helen.

'Around sixteen. What about you?'

'Fourteen.'

'And you reckon Jamie hasn't?'

'She's much more innocent than I was.'

'Bet she's had her first kiss.'

'She has not. She would have told me.'

'Did you tell your mum when you had yours?' CJ asks.

'No.'

I'd like to say that I am certain Jamie has not had her first kiss. But I find I don't know. She's receding from me. I used to have veto power over what was in her cupboard, how she dressed, who she socialised with, what time she went to bed ... nowadays, she asks me to please knock before I come into her room, rejects all the clothes I either hand down to her or buy for her without her consent, and often forgets to come and kiss me goodnight before she goes to bed at God knows what hour.

I'm needed less. It frees me up more. To live my own life. That's a good thing, right? But within that freedom comes a challenge. It's harder to love someone who exposes your inconsistencies, who rejects the things you've saved for them, who gives back the precious items you buy specially for them. The trick is not to take it personally, really.

Just last week I noticed that a bag I ordered specially for her off the internet with 'BIG: Beautiful Intelligent Girl' on it was crumpled at the bottom of her cupboard, unused. When I asked her if she wanted it, she rolled her eyes at me and said, 'Do you really think I'd walk around with a bag that says I'm BIG?' As if BIG was a swearword, not a synonym for tall. And when she started menstruating, I bought her a pink singlet with *If you can dream it, you can achieve it* on the front. I had to hold back my tears when I found that singlet in a pile of clothes she wanted to get rid of, still with the price tag on it.

The other day, Helen dropped off some of Nathan's old clothes for Aaron. As she walked past Jamie's dishevelled room she said, 'That's a disgrace.' I told Jamie what Helen had said, hoping it might shame her into tidying it. Instead she said, 'You've taught me not to care what other people think.'

'But it also drives *me* mad.'

'Yes, Mum, but you are "other people" too. You are not me.'

I am Not Her. She is Not Me. Her job right now is not to be me. Everything she says and does is about recruiting the woman she is who is different from me. I still love it when people comment on how she looks like me, with her thick dark hair and her eager brown eyes. When she was little, she loved it too. *I look like you, Mum.* Now when people say it, she sighs and rolls her eyes. It's not quite contempt. But she is leaving me. In every way.

It's good. It hurts in a way that makes it hard for me to breathe, but it is good. Olivia cannot leave Ereka. That is worse. Not to be left. I left my mum. When I moved out of home in my early twenties. When Frank and I moved cities. And then when we emigrated. We're always leaving our mothers.

The sky is so clear here.

The moon is almost full tonight. I've caught it on a full night, but tomorrow it will change, shrink again to nothing, only to start all over again, swelling, ever-hopeful.

I arch my head to look at all these women, hugging our knees, buffed by moonshine. Our daughters and sons are finding their hearts and making their own footprints in this sweet damaged world. We are doing the hard work. Imperfectly. But someone's got to do it.

Something tugs inside me. A loosening, like rock crumbling, giving way to water. I don't see them coming, but I feel them. Baby tears. Right now, the certainty powers through me: daughters and mothers are not meant to be so far away from each other, whole continents, almost worlds apart. Something primal and pulsing, like a heartbeat, holds me close to her, even as I cannot reach her. But I feel her in every cell of my body which grew inside hers. My DNA sings of her. My blood whistles her name. I want my mummy. A grown woman like me. Silly goose. What will happen to me when she dies? What will happen to the song in my veins? A torrent of anguish gushes through me: I miss my mother. I *miss* her. Her beautiful green eyes, and her funny little fingernails on her thumbs in the shape of an upside-down heart. She isn't dead like Maeve's mum but she is far away and sometimes that feels like death because absence of touch is a bereavement. When she's close by, I know it. I know it in a way that is impossible to explain or describe. It's a knowing in my plasma. I am grateful for the darkness which honours my privacy. The way my mother always did.

The Reunion

We fought too. We had our words. I also wanted to run away. She didn't always understand me.

But look, *look* how I love her.

Mothers never forget the babies they breastfed even as they change into strangers.

Remembering is how we stay close to what we love.

I hope Maeve remembers that she and I have remembered things together.

Under the moon, I suddenly remember a woman on talk radio the other day who'd 'gone to Asia' to pick the gender of her child through a medical procedure which is illegal in Australia. Callers said she was 'evil and disgusting'. But I loved that she had wanted a girl. *A girl.* In Asia, people pick their child's gender to make sure it's a boy.

'Hey Virginia,' I say.

'Mm?'

'Would it . . . would it be okay if we said a prayer—for your mum?'

There is a long silence that grows longer.

I am astonishingly slow in learning to keep my mouth shut.

But then she speaks. And it is not the voice of a grown woman who has travelled to eighty countries and can flirt in a hundred languages and has seen a man's foot bitten off by a hippo. It is the voice of a little girl, troubled by her imperfect girlhood. It is the voice of every little girl who cannot reach her mother, cannot be loved, cannot be enough.

'Sure. That would be . . . Why not?'

I sit up and reach out to hold Helen's hand.

In the dark, she lets me.

In the dark, I see her reach for Virginia's hand.

Summer puts her hand on CJ's shoulder.

And CJ puts her hand on my shoulder.

'Bless the mother who lies dying. May she rest from her suffering. Forgive her for all her failings of affection and handicaps of kindness, for she did the only things she knew born from her own pain. Bless her daughter. Release them from the pain of their bond. As the one dies in peace, so may the other live in peace. Amen.'

'Amen,' whispers the night.

'Amen,' smiles the moon.

'Amen.'

21

The Spoiler

I am dreaming of bells. A chorus of glass raindrops. When I open my eyes the melody doesn't die away. I glance over at Maeve's bed. It has been stripped. Her bag is packed and is sitting neatly on top. And I think two things—I slept through the night. I *slept*. And, then, how come usually everything from the cat's snoring to the drip of an outdoor tap wakes me? How come I'm awoken by Frank, checking the time on his digital watch, turning over in the bed or just breathing in the wrong way (which can be quite selfish at times)—and yet Maeve can host a party in the next-door bed and I sleep through it? I'm not deeply troubled by these thoughts, you understand, just curious.

The tinkling is coming from somewhere in the house.

As I splash water on my face in the pink bathroom, I remember the hot chocolate Maeve made last night with dark chocolate and marshmallows. We sat around the fire blazing in the grate and drank it and, for reasons only she understood, it reminded Summer of her post-natal depression after Jemima was born, and how she'd called her mum to tell her she was depressed. She made us guess what her mum had said. No-one guessed right. The answer was: 'Motherhood is depressing.' She had laughed as she told us, no recrimination there, just bewilderment, the way anyone might feel in a moment of abandonment. But then, in a flash, she'd jumped to her feet, set her iPhone playing some tinny music and got us all—even Maeve—to do some Zumba moves until we were all silly with sweat in front of the fire.

I throw on last night's clothes that are smoky from sitting around the fire. As I pad my way down the stairs, the aroma of baking greets me like open arms. The smell of something exquisite and warm, like buttermilk, fills the house. Here is another thing I never knew about Maeve—that she plays the piano. It is Bach or Mozart or something else classical and classy.

I see her in the mirror before I see her at the piano. It's not Maeve. It's Summer in a striped sundress.

She stops playing. 'Oh, sorry, did I wake you?' she asks.

'No, I don't think so.' I remember Helen's warning that no-one is to touch the piano and I'm about to share this with Summer, but something stops me. 'But please, don't stop. It's lovely.'

'You think you've forgotten, but your fingers don't forget.'

Summer plays classical music.

I can't even play the triangle.

'Where'd you learn that?' I ask, sitting down in a huge chair.

'Uncle Bernie. He said I had the talent to be a concert pianist. But he always said things like that. To build self-esteem.'

Tennyson runs in from outside with festive fury in his tail. He has leaves stuck to his matted fur and is delighted. I reach down to pat him. His time is running out. What will become of this dog?

'OMFG, he made me practise every day, like those Chinese mothers do. I used to spend hours every day at the piano . . .'

The history of those hours shows in her pencil-straight back on the piano stool.

'But when I fell pregnant with Jai . . .' I watch her fingers moving lithely over the keys, her false nails clacking. 'That,' she says, '. . . was that.'

There are many stories wrapped around that story. As my gaze wanders to the bookshelf, I wonder if Delia, the jolly good wife and mother, ever got to feel like she'd done something of value beyond her crocheting, the tending of her secret garden, and the sweeping of the floors of Blind Rise Ridge. I wonder if Ereka will ever go back to her painting. And whether I will ever make it to Tuscany.

I inhale the soft smell that has butter in its heart.

She laughs. 'It's good, huh? Virginia's baking fresh bread!'

Virginia, I'm thinking, is baking a prayer.

'Couldn't you have done both?' I ask. 'Gone back to your music after Jai?'

'No frigging way! Then I would have sucked at two things. At least I only stuffed up being a mum.'

Who talks about themselves this way without it being a shield against some deeper pain? Perhaps it is a smokescreen. I find I can't tell whether she is fishing for compliments, the way you hear skinny girls sighing, 'I'm so fat,' desperate for denials from their peers. I suppose I would like to know if Summer really is a bad mother.

'We're all messing up at more or less the same rate,' I offer.

'True—nobody's perfect. Uncle Bernie always used to say that. "*Everyone* makes mistakes". Still, you can understand having one kid by accident, but three?' She lets out a small puff of irritation. 'Like . . . hello!'

'Were they *all* accidents?'

'Pretty much.'

'So how did that happen?'

Her fingers trail along the keys. 'I, like, so suck at saying no . . . Sometimes I'm not sure what I think. I'm so blonde. Someone says "let's do this" or "let's do that" and I get, like, all "yeah, let's do it" and the next thing you know . . .' She shuffles on the piano stool.

Even Jamie knows how to resist peer pressure. Summer's missed out on some of the basics.

'And then the breastfeeding. I mean, what's with that latching? It hurt like torture. I didn't wanna do it. Sergio said I was a wipeout and I'd stuffed Jai up from the word go.'

I let out a small gasp. 'C'mon, Summer, that's ridiculous—heaps of mothers can't or don't want to breastfeed and their kids are perfectly fine.' I only breastfed for a short time myself.

'I've only met, like, one other mother who couldn't breastfeed. And at least she wanted to. When I put Jai on the bottle, I crashed. Loser Mum.'

'He'll be okay for it.'

'He hates me.'

I've learned some things this weekend. I've been paying attention.

'It's called *psychic differentiation*. It's how he figures out who he is separate from you. It's good that he's different from you. It means you've helped him to be himself.'

As I speak, I realise I haven't checked my phone since yesterday when I sent my SMS to Jamie. That's progress for me.

Tennyson jumps up and puts his front paws on my thigh. His tail is like a paper windmill caught in the breeze, a churning blur of joy. This time, I don't push him away. I scratch his head and he closes his eyes, just like a real person in ecstasy.

'Know what I hate?' she asks.

'Commitment?'

'No, I *love* commitment,' she says, bemused, as if I haven't been listening properly. 'It's mess I hate. I so want things to be perfect. One hundred and twenty per cent perfect. If I can't be, like, the most perfect at something, I'm, like, I'm outta here.'

'But, Summer, no-one can be a perfect mother. Or have a perfect marriage.' I know she knows these things.

She opens her eyes wide. 'That's why I really suck at both. But,' she says, and stops playing, looking at me with childish delight, 'there *is* such thing as a perfect house. And you know what? I *see* every single problem in each house. I know just how to fix it. And as soon as it's perfect, I can move on and fix something else.'

Summer, I'm finally understanding, doesn't want to hear platitudes about being a good-enough mother. She likes being a 'bad mother'. It keeps her free. That way she doesn't have to embrace imperfection or ambivalence. As I watch her play—almost perfectly if it weren't for those nails—I can nearly see the stream of her story working through her. She is a girl, unready for life, with an unopened gift, a locked room she could never enter. It is part of the mythology of her life, the myth that both defines her and explains to her who she was meant to be.

I'm starting to need coffee, and am just about to offer to bring her a cup when she says: 'Mum shouldn't have taken us to live with Uncle Bernie.'

Something plays itself out in her face. It hovers on disgust.

'Everything went wrong after that.'

Things fall into place. I am a fool. I really don't look properly.

'I'm grateful he taught me to read and play the piano. He didn't mind that I was dyslexic. It was just . . . the other stuff . . .'

The Other Stuff.

The luggage of language to hold our pain. So banal, you'd never stop to pick the locks, to wonder, 'What's inside?' I exhale. There is no safe passage to adulthood.

'And he was right about one thing.'

I wait for her to finish.

'My mum would never have believed me if I'd told her.' Her fingers never stray off the keys nor play a false note. I'm afraid to mess up her song, to distract her, but I'm sad to know that her fun-fangled personality, like her immaculate makeup, has to be put on each day, perfected in front of the mirror. I hold back my questions. I close my eyes into her music, Tennyson too. Our wounds, like the foundations of a house, shape who we are. Around the bricks and mortar of our childhoods, between the cracks of the love we got or were denied, we build the homes of our selves.

She has been soothed by her own playing, reaching note by note back into the well of her own possibilities. To a time when she knew who she was and what made her happy, unclouded by other people's sins. I watch as she intermittently lifts her head to look at her own reflection in the mirror, as if she's glancing at a likeness from whom she's been separated forever, but remembers with unspoiled tenderness. For a moment I envy her clarity.

Just then, Virginia hobbles into the lounge room—is she hurt?—wearing an apron. There is flour on her cheeks and her iPhone is in her hand. She falls to her knees. Tennyson runs to her and she buries her face in his fur. When she looks up she says, 'The wicked witch is dead.'

And the house is filled with the smell of baking bread.

There are a gazillion calories here. But it would be rude to care. The bread is hot and the butter oozes into it. So bad for the belly. A sabotage to the thighs.

Virginia's freshly baked bread partners Maeve's Egyptian eggs—poached eggs with hummus, dukkah and feta cheese. The Moët in our glasses fizzes and sighs, enough for a toast. 'To Celia,' Helen says, holding up her glass. 'Try not to complain too much while you're in heaven or they'll downgrade you.'

'Cheers.' We all clink our glasses.

'Speech from the BSF?' Helen asks.

'No speeches,' Virginia says. 'Just that, I want to say that this was the best weekend for me, I couldn't have asked to be in a better place. I just have felt very . . .' I suspect she wants to use the word 'loved', but it's foreign to her, so she simply says, 'supported'. I guess bra terminology will do.

Maeve puts her hand on Virginia's back. Summer reaches out and touches Virginia's hand.

'We're, like, all so here for you,' Summer says. 'And if you need to cry, just cry.'

'Thanks,' Virginia says, 'but I'm good. It's a relief actually.'

'You can get on with your life now,' CJ says.

And Maeve says, 'Take time to say your goodbyes. And don't be surprised if you miss her.'

Virginia nods. 'Thanks.'

'And grow your hair,' I say.

Virginia looks at me. 'Really? You think so?'

'Definitely, let it grow.'

Tennyson sniffs at our feet to see if he might get lucky. You have to admire his hopefulness.

'What are you going to do with her dog?' I ask Virginia. He is officially an orphan now. And no-one has thought to break the news to him personally.

She shrugs. 'I can't keep him. I live in an apartment and I'm on the move all the time.'

'Hey, I've got the best idea,' Summer says.

And once again, she really does.

Virginia walks back up from the dam where Callum is still raking leaves. Tennyson stays down there with him where the views are better.

'Okay, fill me up with some more champagne,' Virginia says, holding out her glass. 'I am so relieved that is sorted out.'

Helen tops her up. 'Just before we all leave, I have . . . news.'

'You're pregnant again?' CJ asks.

'You will never hear that I am pregnant again,' Helen says.

'If you have another one, I'm taking it,' Virginia says.

'Have any one of mine—take your pick,' Helen says. 'In fact, I'll pay you to take the vegetarian off my hands.'

'Take Jai,' Summer says.

'Any one of mine,' CJ offers.

'So ungrateful, the lot of you,' Virginia says.

'What's your news?' Maeve asks.

'So I don't want this to be a big deal or anything . . .' Helen says.

'Have you got cancer?' I ask, afraid.

'You're getting a divorce?' CJ says. 'Welcome to the club.'

'No and no—Jesus, you lot, shut up for one minute, will you? We're going to live in California.'

Virginia yelps in excitement. 'Where? When?'

'Somewhere in the Bay Area. David's business has been sold, and he's been made an offer to start up a similar one there. We've got to be there within the next three months.'

Helen looks glowingly from one face to the other.

'OMG, I *love* California—it has the best beaches,' Summer says.

'I'll give you my friend Paulina's details, you'll get on so well with her,' CJ says.

'So, is that exciting or what?' Helen says. I feel her eyes on me.

'It's . . . far away . . .' I mumble.

'We'll be back for holidays. And you'll come visit. We'll probably only go for a few years. You know, just to give the kids a bit of a different life experience.'

I nod. 'When did you find out?' I ask.

Helen pauses. 'A few weeks ago.'

I turn and look out at the view. I have Egyptian eggs in my throat, something harder. It won't go down.

'Aw, Jo's crying,' CJ says.

'I'm fine,' I say. 'It's fantastic news. Maybe it could have been delivered a little earlier, so that some of us could have had a chance to emotionally prepare for it, but that doesn't detract from the excitement.'

'I didn't want to spoil the weekend,' Helen says.

'That was very considerate of you.'

'You know me. I don't like goodbyes.'

Suddenly everyone is silent and it's as if it is only me and her in this conversation.

'Yes, who does?' I say.

'You would have been morose the whole weekend if I'd told you when we arrived.'

'You don't know how I would have been. You are not me. And anyway, if I had been, that would have been my choice.'

'You would have been a wet blanket. You know you would have.'

'Well, I managed to ruin it anyway.'

'You would have wanted to talk and talk and talk about it.'

'Maybe, maybe not. Of course, *lying* to your friends is far preferable to emotional honesty.'

'I didn't lie.'

'You didn't tell the truth.'

'And what good would the truth have done?'

I turn to face Helen now and I can't help the tears, they seem to be doing their own thing, running down my face. 'Well, for starters, maybe some of us would have liked to have served your favourite food instead of all that healthy shit. Maybe some of us would have gone to the effort of making duck breast with apple sauce and cherries and cheese soufflé with cranberry jam. Did you ever think that maybe just letting us know that this was going to be the last time we'd have a girls' weekend away would have given us a chance to make it super fun? Because maybe your friends would have wanted to make it special.'

'It *was* special. We sat in the moonlight. I had a massage. We did Zumba. We got to perv at Callum.'

'No it wasn't. It was a disaster. I didn't eat the pizza you made. I insulted Ereka. I kept Maeve awake with my snoring. I phoned Jake and practically told him his wife is having an affair. I served quinoa, for heaven's sake!' I realise I am shouting.

'Ereka's having an affair?' CJ asks eagerly.

'Is she?' Helen demands.

'Well, she didn't want to go home, and she didn't want to stay here either,' I say. 'You work it out.'

And Summer, like a mother bear, rises up, her perfect breasts leading the way, and with no syrup in her voice states, 'She went to visit her mother.'

I blink at Summer.

'Didn't she?'

'Sorry,' I mumble. 'My mistake.'

And then, turning back to Helen, I say, 'I even accused Ereka of having an affair. Besides, I don't need you to protect me. I'm an adult. I can cope. And if I'd known . . . I would have done lots of things differently this weekend.'

Virginia puts her hand on my arm. 'Don't have regrets.'

I shake my head. I rewind the weekend in my head and wonder how I would have lived it had I known that Helen was saying goodbye. In the past few years we haven't spent much time together, only snatches here and there. But she's always been there, at the end of a telephone line, her laugh and her steadiness an invisible force that held me sturdy. I look over at Maeve. I don't know how she held it together after Solange died.

'It was a perfect weekend,' Helen says. 'I had no chores. No-one nagged me. I was with some of the people I love best in the world. And no-one was sad.' As she says this, I see a tiny chink in her unsentimental bulletproof vest. What she means is that no-one but her was sad. She kept her sadness to herself. She held it together for us. She didn't pass her suffering on to us.

'Why should anyone be sad?' Virginia says. 'We're happy for you. Your life is a big adventure about to happen.'

'California rocks,' Summer says.

'Exposing children to a new culture and way of life is a gift. They'll be citizens of the world,' Maeve says.

'Just make sure you get a big enough house so we can come and stay with you,' CJ says.

I reach out and grab Helen in my arms.

'Oh god, she's about to start,' Helen says, but she enfolds me in her arms and I feel her heart beating in her chest. My face is against her face and the wetness on my cheeks is not only from my own tears.

'You won't even notice I'm gone,' she says, burying her face in my hair.

'You're right,' I say. 'It'll be a relief not to have you carrying on and trying to force-feed me and boss me around.'

'I don't want you to make a fuss,' she says, untangling herself from me.

'I'm going to be in California in May next year for a whole month,' Virginia says. 'We're shooting a couple of scenes there. We'll hang out. When will you know where you're based?'

They start chatting about their plans for California. I stand and look out at the morning mist rising from Blind Rise Ridge. Everything changes so quickly. Morning becomes afternoon before you know it. You arrive in the country with a weekend ahead of you and suddenly it's time to pack up and go home to your family. I don't know how to hold on to things, or how to let them go.

'Hey,' Maeve says, putting her hand on my arm. 'Let's go for one more walk before we leave, what do you say?'

22

On the Market

'It's a black-throated finch,' Maeve whispers, pointing at some trees up ahead. She has led me past the memorial garden, around the dam, down towards where the forest begins.

'Where are we going?' I am struggling to keep up with her.

She strides ahead, watching that bird like it was her north star.

The only thing I know about birds is that no sooner do you progress towards them than they fly away. Maeve moves swiftly, as if she's tracked birds before. We skirt the edge of the forest. How can she even tell what it is when it's so far away? After a while, I can't see the house anymore; we've come down at least a kilometre past the far end of the dam. Maeve slips between the trees into the forested area and this is where I draw the line.

'Maeve, we should be careful, we could get lost in there.'

I see her snaking through the trees fifty metres ahead of me. She then stops, looking up. I wave at her. She indicates with her finger on her lips that I must be quiet. I creep in among the trees and finally I am standing beside her.

'I wish I'd brought my binoculars with me,' she whispers.

Up ahead is a small bird with an orange belly and a black chest perched on a branch. For this we are risking our lives?

'Black-throated finches are an endangered species. Do you have any idea how lucky we are to see one?'

I clearly do not. I shrug and whisper a meek 'Wow.'

She looks at me with wide eyes. 'They are almost extinct.'

I can see that this information pains her in a way I don't fully appreciate. She is telling me something that matters deeply to her and I am being flippant.

'That's . . . terrible,' I manage.

'Yes, and when they're gone, they're gone. *Forever*.'

She looks up at the finch and sighs deeply, holding on to the trunk of the tree. And in that look, I see a sort of love I recognise. To Maeve, the whole world is her responsibility. There is no exclusivity to her consternation. No selfishness or ownership to her wards. When she stepped into her sister's shoes, she understood that she would be responsible for all that needed tending. Unlike me, who cared less about the world as soon as I became a mother. When Jamie was handed to me straight from my womb, the world and all its agonies, fights, grievances and struggles dropped to second tier.

At times it is hard to tell whether motherhood has made me wholly selfish or entirely unselfish. My children have become the meaning I attach to everything: the threat of nuclear disaster, environmental decline, increased costs of living, who I vote for, what I buy at the supermarket, my boycott of all products with MSG, the amount of radiation and bad language I will allow in my home all derive from my love for them and them alone. If the world had to be sacrificed so they could live, it is a deal I would make in a heartbeat. It is both an astonishing and horrifying thought.

Jamie and Aaron are the two stars in my galaxy between which I chart my existence, from which I determine the coordinates of meaning and significance. I am the bouncer between them and the wicked, wicked world. If the world wants to get to them, it has to go through me first. And as I think this, I know that all I want is simply to be with my children when they suffer. I cannot divert their suffering, nor take it on as my own. Everything is shifting as my children take themselves from me, bit by bit, giving me back to myself. Though I haven't really figured out what I'm going to do with me when I'm all put back together.

I feel rushed. As if it's all coming to a close. And I must get back to them before things change again.

'Come, Maeve, let's go back,' I say, turning to leave. Maeve follows me grudgingly.

We exit the forest and start walking back up the hill towards the house. Alongside us runs a boundary fence between Blind Rise Ridge and the next property, with narrow wooden rails and barbed wire. Maeve grabs my arm.

'C'mon,' she says.

'What?'

She doesn't wait for me to answer her. She runs ahead of me, her scarf flapping behind her. I do not recognise this person as I watch Professor Foster step onto the lowest strand of the barbed wire and hoist herself up onto the narrow top rail of the fence in a kind of fit of glorious madness.

'Be careful,' I shout.

She slowly straightens her body along the rail, toes pointed, head down, arms by her side.

'Don't fall,' I say, running up to her.

'Where's your phone?' she asks, her chin tucked into her chest. Her body trembles with the effort of keeping itself balanced.

'I left it at the house.'

'Bugger,' she says, gripping the rail with her hands and carefully swinging her legs down. 'For it to count as an official planking, one has to have photographic evidence.' She jumps off, breathless. Her cheeks are flushed pink. There is a jet stream in her eyes. 'Go ahead,' she says. 'It's your turn.'

'Isn't it dangerous?'

She narrows her eyes at me. 'Most accidents happen . . .'

'. . . in your own home,' I finish.

'Precisely.'

I know. I've read Aaron's *Deadly Peril* and I know you can electrocute yourself, break a limb getting dressed, fall off a balcony, sleepwalk down the stairs or eat a tin of beans infected with botulism, and that these are as likely to happen as being eaten by a lion or swept away in a tsunami.

I approach the fence. The knots of that wire appear especially unfriendly. I hope my kids have the sense never to do anything this stupid. I pray I have done a good enough job of scaring them shitless from jumping off rocks into water, accepting rides from strangers and dashing across busy roads. Because accidents happen. And I don't want my kids to be there when they do. I take a deep breath and I hold on to the rail. I balance my feet on the wire and slowly raise one leg up, straighten it, then bring my body weight up to the rail, and gradually lift my other leg. My body wobbles as it finds its centre on the rail. My heart is thrashing around in my chest like a caged finch.

'Bring your hands to your side when you're balanced,' Maeve says, placing her hand in the small of my back.

I let go of the rail and bring my hands to my side.

Maeve's hand leaves my back.

'You're planking,' she says.

'Oh my god, I'm planking,' I say.

And as the words leave my mouth, my body, shocked into recognition of what I'm doing, loses faith and I tumble off the fence, snaring my new jumper and catching my necklace on the barbed wire. I land on the grass with a thump.

'Ouch,' I groan.

I look up and Maeve is laughing. Not quietly to herself as you might when someone has just done something stupid and you don't want them to feel any worse about it. I believe what she is doing is called cackling.

'Cow dung,' she wheezes, pointing to a large wet pat of dung hidden by the tall grass beneath the fence.

As I lie on the grass, in my torn body-hugging jumper, my jeans covered in cow shit, and blood seeping from the gash I got as I fell, I feel a small chuckle punch its way out of my belly.

'You're a terrible influence, Maeve. I don't know why I hang out with you.'

'Didn't your parents warn you about girls like me?'

'Planking is dangerous.'

'We can safely say we know now how dangerous it is.' She gives me her hand and helps me up. She dusts me down. I hobble a little. I have planking injuries.

I feel around my neck. My necklace with my silver circles!

Maeve helps me scratch around in the grass until we find them both. I carry them back in my closed fist along with the broken silver chain.

The house comes into view as we climb the hill. I hear Helen's laughter spilling from the veranda. I see Virginia standing with her camera facing the day, all alone inside herself at last. Summer and CJ are chatting, seated on the ledge.

And what I know as Maeve and I walk towards Blind Rise Ridge is that though it's probably not possible to survive a charging hippo, it is possible to survive the death of a mother at fifteen. The death of an only sister. You can survive your children's suffering even when it has no expiry date. There are ways of living even after you've been brought to your knees. I know that it takes a thousand rosebushes to mark the earth with the loss of a child. People carry on after infertility and loneliness and infidelity.

Motherhood blasts open your shadows and magnifies your faults. Along the way, you'll probably realise you are not the half-decent sort of person you imagined and you'll think more often than is probably healthy how grateful you are that you're not your own mother. You'll be astonished at the pitch of your voice and rise of your fury. You'll be certain you do not deserve children and suspect that under the right circumstances, you'd be capable of crushing puppies with your bare hands. You will then come to see that you are just an ordinary, good-enough mother doing her best.

I am starting to know that what we don't come clean with, in ourselves, we hand on as dirty laundry to our children. They will carry our stories and cry our tears for us, until we take back our pain. The only way to do this is by untorturing our own narratives, sealing the foundations, fixing the leaks and treating the damp of where-it-all-went-wrong. And in this transaction, the mother is the person we become to someone who is becoming themselves. Each moment is an opportunity to meet them, so that we can meet ourselves, eye to eye, like a charging hippo.

Down at the dam, Callum is throwing pine cones and Tennyson is doing his best to run on those fat little legs to fetch them and bring them back. He is jumping and barking at something only he can see. It could be Matilda. It could be a dragonfly. It could be the sunlight on the water. I'm not a dog so I don't know what makes dogs bark. But it's not heartache, of that I feel pretty sure.

Helen and I are the last two to leave. Virginia was packed and gone within twenty minutes of Maeve and I returning from our walk, with hardly a backward glance at Tennyson. Shortly after that, Maeve excused herself to get home to prepare some notes for her eight-fifteen lecture on Rituals and Taboos as a Form of Social Compliance. CJ and Summer stacked the dirty breakfast dishes, gave hugs all round, and CJ accelerated down the driveway to (giggle) 'get back to her lover'. Women of our age who refer to their partners as *lovers* generally need a good slap, but I let it go.

Callum lopes up to the house, the dog at his heels.

'I take it you've acquired a dependant,' Helen laughs.

'Be good to have some company around here. Sorry to hear about his owner.'

'Yeah, well, everyone's gotta die sometime,' Helen says.

'I found the key. But I guess I'm too late.'

'Yeah, Virginia's long gone.'

'Sorry. I know my dad had kept the key for the old lady, I just couldn't find where he'd stashed it.'

'Why was your dad keeping the key?' I ask.

'He was the groundsman here for thirty years. The emphysema forced him into early retirement. But he was a stickler for his word. And he promised the old lady. She didn't want anyone going into that room after what happened.'

'What happened?'

'Didn't Virginia tell you? He took himself out. The son, Steven. With one of his dad's hunting guns. It was messy, so I heard.'

I turn to Helen and before I can slap her with a recrimination, she says, 'You wouldn't have come if you'd known.' I can't believe she knew and didn't tell me.

'It just about finished the old lady, Mrs Wiltshire. He was her only one. She was down on her hands and knees every day with Dad the spring after, planting the rosebushes.'

'But he was a great musician, wasn't he?'

'They say he could play the piano all right. Sure would've gone places. No-one knows why he lost it. They reckon it was because he was queer. I don't mean anything by it. The blokes around here didn't make life easy for him. And his old man, he was old school. Typical war vet, loved to hunt. Men should be men kinda thing. Mrs Wiltshire, she didn't mind. Guess he was her boy, right or wrong. Anyway, she asked Dad to keep the room locked until after she died. That room hasn't been opened since 1976.'

'So when did she die?' Helen asks.

'Last month. Ninety-three. Sad for most of it. But she still went up and down these stairs every day. We had to get a live-in nurse for the last of it.'

'What's in the room?' I venture, not sure if I really want to know.

'The old man's workroom. He stuffed the animals himself. I sometimes imagine I can still smell it, now and then. Here's the key if you want to look.'

'Got everything?' Helen asks.

We're standing in the entrance hall of Blind Rise Ridge, our bags packed, the rubbish tied in garbage bags left outside the kitchen door for Callum, the beds stripped. The few remaining minutes of our time together are being chewed up like coins on an international call. It's come and gone all too quickly. Everything is hurtling to a close.

I grab Helen's hand and pull her back into the house one last time. And there we are, Helen and I, reflected in the monstrous mirror.

'Look at us,' I say, slinging my arm over her shoulder.

'Yeah, look at us,' she says, looking.

'Not too bad for two old birds . . .'

'Speak for yourself,' she says, mock-punching me on the shoulder.

'I don't want you to go,' I say.

'You're not allowed to talk about it.' And what she really means is that I cannot live in the goodbye. That there will be time enough for us to say our farewells; though we cannot see our way through to that separation, it will come, and when it does we will know how to do it. But we can't know now. Because we're not there yet.

'Your last chance to look in the locked room,' Helen says, waving the keys at me.

'Nah, I'm good.'

And with that, she turns and leaves.

I grab the handle of my bag and follow her, down the hallway and across the threshold of the front door, shutting it gently behind me. As I do, I sense that motherhood, like the last day of a holiday, has peaked in just this way. Sometimes when I see a pregnant woman in the supermarket struggling to reach a tin of creamed corn, or taking a stroll along the beachfront, her belly ripe and glorious, the memory of my own expectant motherhood, all hope and hubris and name-searching, trips me up and I find myself thinking, yes that, *that* must have been the peak. Then I think, no, it was when I clutched them, newborn, to my startled breast, having finally met the stranger I grew inside me. But what about those times they lay beside me, tangled in my hair and singing me their private songs, before lies or 'I hate you's ever passed between us? A time when squirrels had heads.

Perhaps it's coming across *'me 2.Sorry mum 4beingabrat.xj'* on your iPhone after a fight. That could very well be the peak.

I'm not sure of anything anymore. All I know is that our children do not stay in one place, and neither can we. We just have to keep moving towards the blind rise ahead.

Motherhood is like a home rented for a brief time. We may take charge, fill it with our ideas, voices and laughter, but just as soon as we get to know its nooks and crannies, it's time to pack up and leave. It is only a timeshare we inhabit. We never get the title deeds. My children, parented by the walls, lit by the windows, boundaried by the doors of my heart, are on the market. They are leaving me, outgrowing me with every breath, shedding me with each exhalation. Whoever they are is already

The Reunion

locked in to the sinew of their beings. If I have been remiss in teaching them to honour the earth, or love their bodies, or to value people over money, I cannot undo or fix that. I can no longer tell them how to make themselves. I can only meet them, as I would a stranger, and ask, 'Who are you?' and 'What will you make of your lone and lustrous life?' I feel the rush of it all, the hurriedness with which their futures are claiming them. I am at the border of motherhood, without a visa to pass through customs into the land into which they are crossing. They must go from me. So I can remember how I dreamed them first and gave them to the world.

But right now I want to wrap Aaron in my arms and tell him that I trust him to make good choices in his life. Even those that turn out to be colossal fuck-ups. I'll say 'mistakes', so as not to model bad language. At least they'll be *his* mistakes.

This week, I'll make time. I'll knock on Jamie's door, and go in holding a slice of homemade cheesecake. I'll tell her, 'I'm not saying I'm going to let you go. That's not what I'm saying. But let's talk about Borneo.' And together we'll go through the materials on vaccinations, gear and safety hazards. I don't know if I'm ready to have no contact with her for twenty-one days, no way of making sure she is fed, warm, safe, getting enough sleep, wearing sunblock, taking her malaria tablets, not drinking the water, riding in roadworthy vehicles . . . If I think about it too much, I'll get a migraine.

I'm not saying I'm going to let her go. But if she's ready, I'm going to have to try.

Then I'll close her door and leave her to herself. I'll go for a long walk along the beach where the water meets the sand. And I'll shout into the wind: *If she goes, who will I be meeting when she steps off that plane three weeks later? And how will I know her?*

She'll be someone else, sprouted from the girl I helped make, but new in beauties I've had no hand in shaping. And there is no tragedy in that. Only mystery.

And who will I be?

I'll be the mother who entrusted the basket carrying her child to the river, joined to the chorus of maternal voices chanting prayers into the night's quiet ear, to parent in our absence. I'll be a mother who taught my child that it is safe to run away. And who welcomed her, with open arms, back home.

And one of these days, while I'm straightening Jamie's hair or fixing her mascara for a night out with her girlfriends, I'll talk to her about the sanctuary of women's friendships. I'll describe to her how to plank, toes straight. I'll tell her to kiss the girls with cherry chapstick if that's what she wants and to eat the ginger honey cake because, God help her, what sort of a person would she be, what sort of a life would she be living if she said no to that cake? And I'll tell her all about Tuscany. How one day, after a weekend with my girlfriends, I decided just to take myself off on my own adventure, and how it felt to claim a secret wellspring of selfhood to return to someday.

And how much better I slept at night after that.

'Hey, Helen,' I call out.

She turns, and as she does, I stuff a crumpled piece of paper into her hand. She opens it and smiles.

'I knew I'd get that damn recipe out of you one day.'

The Menu

The guilty menu
Salt and pepper deep-fried soft shell crab (Thai takeaway)
Ginger honey cake with lemon myrtle crème fraîche bought by Ereka
Cheezels, Lindt chocolate and various other 'couldn't-care-less-about-the-bikini' contraband
Deep-fried zucchini blossoms filled with Persian feta (made by Kito, CJ's new man)
Pizza with olives, gorgonzola, artichokes, salami, porcini mushrooms and roasted pine nuts
Dark hot chocolate with marshmallows
Egyptian poached eggs with hummus, dukkah and feta cheese
Virginia's mum's recipe for freshly baked bread with butter

The I-couldn't-be-bothered menu
Cold meats, cheese, pickles and white bread rolls

The guilt-free menu
Prawn and papaya salad—without the peanuts (Thai take-away)
Tuna salad of spring water tuna, rocket, fresh tomatoes, cucumber and snow peas
Omelettes with smoked salmon, ricotta and herbs
Cauliflower, leek and coconut soup served with chopped chives and a dollop of Greek yoghurt
Quinoa salad with apple-infused beetroots, coriander, roasted hazelnuts, orange zest, chopped mint, thinly sliced red cabbage, shaved fennel and slices of persimmon
Fruit towers of sliced ruby grapefruit, nectarine and mango drizzled with champagne and topped with a strawberry dipped in dark chocolate

Acknowledgements

Bless the mothers and the fathers. All of them. The ones who gave me life—Mum and Dad—and all those who do a hard day's work in the factories of families.

Bless the daughters and the sons, for as they are fucked up, so they will fuck up in turn. Not on purpose. Just because that's how it goes.

Bless my sisters and girlfriends far and wide—too many to be named. Bless too, for their company, great food and patience with all my questions, Tracey, Michelle, Deb Z, Jeannine and Katrina, who joined me for a weekend of planking in Kangaroo Valley.

Bless Alan and Eva Gold, who gave me sanctuary in their beautiful home in Leura to write parts of this book.

Bless Lisa and Angela for sharing the stories of what it means to mother a child whose path is beset with obstacles. Bless Kaitlyn and Stephanie for teaching us how to live.

Bless Catherine Milne, Louise Thurtell, Jo Lyons, Ali Lavau and the team at Allen & Unwin, for they are the ones who still breathe life into books in a world in which books are changing.

Bless Jesse and Aidan and Zed. They put up with me through my disappearances, sleeping habits and personality changes during the writing of this book.

I'm back, that's all I'm saying.

www.ingramcontent.com/pod-product-compliance
Lightning Source LLC
Chambersburg PA
CBHW031057080526
44587CB00011B/719